P9-DXT-698

My Greatest Day in Baseball

1946–1997

as told to

Bob McCullough

Foreword by

Ted Williams

TAYLOR PUBLISHING COMPANY

Dallas, Texas

Copyright © 1998 by Bob McCullough

All rights reserved.

No part of this book may be reproduced in any form or by any
means—including photocopying and electronic reproduction—without
written permission from the publisher.

All photos by the Baseball Hall of Fame Library, Cooperstown, N.Y., unless
otherwise noted.

Published by Taylor Publishing Company
1550 West Mockingbird Lane
Dallas, Texas 75235
www.taylorpub.com

Library of Congress Cataloging-in-Publication Data

 My greatest day in baseball, 1946–1997 / as told to Bob McCullough.
     p.   cm.
    Follow-up volume to: My greatest day in baseball. c1945.
    ISBN 0-87833-989-2
    1. Baseball players—United States—Anecdotes. 2. Baseball
players—United States—Biography. I. McCullough, Bob.
II. My greatest day in baseball.
GV865.A1M9 1998
796.357'092'273—dc21
[B]   98-10673
                           CIP

Printed in the United States of America
10 9 8 7 6 5 4 3 2 1

This book has been printed on acid-free recycled paper.

This book is dedicated to my father, Eugene McCullough,
who taught me the game of baseball, and my mother,
Sophie McCullough, who provided love and support while
we pursued our love of the game.

CONTENTS

Foreword	*ix*	Tom Glavine	*73*
Introduction	*1*	Jim "Mudcat" Grant	*80*
Hank Aaron	*5*	Ken Griffey, Jr.	*82*
Rick Aguilera	*7*	Ken Griffey, Sr.	*83*
Roberto Alomar	*11*	Tony Gwynn	*86*
George "Sparky" Anderson	*13*	Ken "Hawk" Harrelson	*90*
Richie Ashburn	*17*	Rickey Henderson	*92*
Jeff Bagwell	*21*	Orel Hershiser	*96*
Ernie Banks	*22*	Randy Hundley	*101*
Vida Blue	*25*	Todd Hundley	*104*
Bert Blyleven	*26*	Jim "Catfish" Hunter	*106*
Wade Boggs	*28*	Reggie Jackson	*110*
Bob Boone	*31*	Fergie Jenkins	*112*
George Brett	*34*	Derek Jeter	*115*
Jack Buck	*37*	Randy Johnson	*116*
Bert Campaneris	*39*	Jim Kaat	*119*
Harry Caray	*41*	Al Kaline	*126*
Steve Carlton	*43*	Tom Kelly	*129*
Joe Carter	*47*	Harmon Killebrew	*132*
Will Clark	*56*	Chuck Knoblauch	*136*
Roger Clemens	*57*	Jerry Koosman	*139*
David Cone	*63*	Barry Larkin	*142*
Ryne Duren	*65*	Tony LaRussa	*149*
Cecil Fielder	*67*	Tommy Lasorda	*153*
Rollie Fingers	*69*	Vern Law	*154*
Whitey Ford	*72*	Kenny Lofton	*156*

Greg Maddux	*157*	Alex Rodriguez	*238*
Dennis Martinez	*161*	Pete Rose	*240*
Tim McCarver	*163*	Ryne Sandberg	*244*
Mark McGwire	*167*	Red Schoendienst	*247*
Jack Morris	*170*	Ozzie Smith	*249*
Don Newcombe	*176*	John Smoltz	*254*
Hal Newhouser	*182*	Terry Steinbach	*257*
Tony Oliva	*188*	Darryl Strawberry	*261*
Steve Palermo	*190*	Frank Thomas	*262*
Jim Palmer	*199*	Luis Tiant	*265*
Dave Parker	*204*	Joe Torre	*269*
Mike Piazza	*206*	Mo Vaughn	*271*
Kirby Puckett	*209*	Earl Weaver	*275*
Jim Rice	*216*	Bernie Williams	*277*
Cal Ripken, Jr.	*219*	Billy Williams	*279*
Robin Roberts	*222*	Dick Williams	*282*
Brooks Robinson	*227*	Dave Winfield	*286*
Frank Robinson	*231*	Jim Wynn	*290*

FOREWORD
by Ted Williams

Many people say that baseball has changed, and it is true that many things surrounding the game are different. The amount of travel has changed since I played the game (and so has the *way* the players travel), as well as the amount of money players make and, in some cases, even the cities and stadiums in which the game is played.

But baseball itself is a truly timeless sport, and that timelessness is a big part of why it remains the greatest game we have. To step up to the plate in a clutch situation, to deliver a big hit or a game-winning home run, to make a great catch or come through with an outstanding pitching performance—these things in baseball remain the same, regardless of the era, and it is in these moments that the greatness of the game is captured.

Many books have been written about baseball, but the truest representation of the game in print is when the stories of the players themselves are presented. Like its predecessor, this book, *My Greatest Day in Baseball, 1946–1997*, offers the words of the players without frills or interpretations. It represents a piece of baseball history, for it tells the stories of both great players and players who had great moments, and it includes those who played with me as well as those who followed in my footsteps.

These players' achievements are at the heart of baseball history, and telling their stories is important so that people know that baseball can continue to be as great in the future as it has been in the past. I applaud the effort that went into collecting these stories for this volume—I hope they will be enjoyed by baseball fans everywhere.

My Greatest Day in Baseball

1946–1997

INTRODUCTION

When I was first approached by Taylor Publishing with the idea of doing a follow-up volume to the original version of *My Greatest Day in Baseball*, I realized the wisdom of the old adage that you do indeed learn something new every day. Despite what I had thought to be a pretty good working knowledge of historical baseball books, I was unaware of the earlier volume, which was first published in 1945 by A. S. Barnes & Company (later versions were published by Grossett & Dunlap) and contained forty-seven interviews with the likes of Babe Ruth, Walter Johnson, Ty Cobb, Cy Young, and Satchel Paige.

I very quickly became aware that I had taken on a project with an enormous legacy. The original volume, "as told to" John P. Carmichael, Sports Editor of the *Chicago Times*, featured first-person interviews done by no less than a dozen other "noted sports writers" of the era, including the likes of Gabe Paul, Bob Broeg, and Hal Totten. To be given the opportunity to follow in the footsteps of such men was both a great honor and a formidable challenge.

When I started the book, my doubts about its potential viability were fueled by a variety of factors, the foremost being the access issue with regard to modern players. The original volume was compiled during a slower-paced era when teams traveled by train and writers often functioned as confidants as well as reporters. Would I be able to get sufficient time with the players? Would they open up to me in describing their greatest day? Or would the prevalence of today's "sound bite" journalism result in a completely different and perhaps diluted version of the earlier book?

My questions were answered with resounding depth and authority during my first interview, which took place at Fenway Park on August 18, 1996, when the Toronto Blue Jays were in town to visit the Red Sox. My first subject was Joe Carter, who proceeded to chat with me for almost half an hour about his game-winning, three-run home run in the 1993 World Series against the Philadelphia Phillies. The interview took place in the Jays clubhouse and extended through the Toronto team stretch, so that it was well into batting practice when Carter emerged from the dugout onto the field.

When Carter finished describing the dream he had the night before Game 7—that something great having to do with the number "3" would happen the next day—chills ran up and down my spine, and I knew that I had embarked on a very special experience, one that would allow me to regain some of the innocence that came with becoming a fan again. (During the interviews, different versions of that sensation would be duplicated again and again in a variety of locales and situations.) A few days later in the Red Sox clubhouse, Roger Clemens recounted the traffic jam that almost kept him from striking out twenty Seattle Mariners, as well as the game that started his Cy Young/MVP journey in 1986.

I will forever remember sitting with Jim Palmer in the Yankee Stadium dugout during a September rain delay in the midst of the 1996 pennant race as he described striking out Mickey Mantle, Roger Maris, and Elston Howard back in his rookie year of 1965, just as I will always recall Barry Larkin quietly talking about his admiration for and his friendship with Ozzie Smith during the final weekend of the '96 season in St. Louis, which was Ozzie Smith Weekend.

Other memorable moments come quickly to mind—George Brett recounting with explicit precision the Kansas City Royals' 1985 ALCS victory over the Toronto Blue Jays during spring training of 1997; Reggie Jackson on the practice field at Legends Stadium in Tampa, briefly but succinctly replaying each of his three home runs against the Dodgers in the 1977 World Series; and Al Kaline's steely blue eyes as he gazed out on the Tiger infield in Lakeland and recalled donning the batboy's uniform for his major league debut.

When I started the book, I put together a running "wish list" that consisted of between three and six major stars from each team, dating from the post-war era. At first my intention was to duplicate the final count of forty-seven from the original volume, but after several months of interviewing it became clear that I was obligated to go the extra mile and would exceed the number of interviews in the original volume. To some extent, I tried to avoid some of the events that have been described almost ad nauseum in a wide variety of mainstream media outlets—Bobby Thomson's Shot Heard Round the World, Don Larsen's perfect game, Kirk Gibson's 1988 World Series home run, etc.

There was a certain randomness to the selection process as well. I have to confess that I didn't originally intend to interview Vern Law. Yet Law's account of his most memorable pitching performance is a funny, touching account of an heroic, Herculean effort. There were numerous other chance "encounters" with players who were not on the original list that produced interviews which touched me in a variety of ways and hopefully add both depth and color to the collection.

Every effort was made to talk to the likes of Willie Mays, Mike Schmidt, Johnny Bench, Nolan Ryan, Tom Seaver, et al. Fans of virtually every team will no doubt note the absence of some favorite player or other, and I apologize for my part in these omissions and gaps. Mea culpa, I tried.

In keeping with the tone and spirit of the interviews in the earlier book, the intent was to let each player tell his story. The idea throughout was to follow Carmichael's lead in allowing the player's story to take precedence over either my perspective or any questions that might have seemed relevant or necessary in the context of a normal magazine or newspaper interview.

In some instances I prepped extensively for interviews, while in other cases I decided to follow the model of *cinema verite* and merely turned the tape recorder on and just let the interview happen. Regardless of the approach, the results seemed to uniformly depend far more on the individual chemistry than on the degree of preparation. The one surprise to me was the consistent success of the interviews done by phone, which I thought might be problematic—but in many instances the "phoners" produced longer interviews that were in some ways more intimate than many of the in-person encounters.

I cannot sufficiently convey my gratitude to all of those who made this book possible by helping me set up the interviews. My heartfelt thanks go out to all the media relations departments of the major league teams that provided credentials, contacts, and even boxscores—especially those representing the Boston Red Sox (Dick Bresciani, Kevin Shea, Kate Gordon), the Philadelphia Phillies (Larry Shenk, Gene Dias, Karen Nocella), the New York Yankees (Rick Cerone, John Thursby), the New York Mets (Jay Horwitz), the St. Louis Cardinals (Brian Bartow, Shawn Bertani), the Minnesota Twins (Dave St. Peter, Wendie Erickson), the Oakland A's (Debbie

Kenney), the Chicago White Sox (Scott Reifert, Bob Beghtol), the Cleveland Indians (Bart Swain, Sue Gharrity, Joel Gunderson), and the Los Angeles Dodgers (Derek Hall, Dave Tuttle).

In addition, I am extremely grateful to Robert Stirewalt and the folks at Major League Baseball Alumni, who gave me the opportunity to consolidate much of the interviewing process via access to their well-run All-Star games that took place in St. Petersburg and Ft. Myers, Florida, during the spring of 1997. And while agent-bashing has become something of a cottage industry in American sports, for the most part I received extensive help from those who represent many of the players I interviewed.

I would also like to thank those who became a part of the writing of this book. As I traveled from park to park and game to game, I made many new friends, got some great advice, and shared a variety of wonderful experiences and conversations with fellow writers and media colleagues, players, and the fans who love this great game. These things are the hidden benefits and joys that come with getting to write a book like this, and in ways that are both tangible and ephemeral they are as significant to me as the finished product.

Finally, I would like to thank the players themselves for their generosity with their time, their forthrightness in their accounts of their experiences, and their openness in sharing the emotions connected with those experiences. I hope I have done justice to their finest moments. I myself have learned much about both the history of the game and what goes through the hearts and minds of great players and managers as they display their estimable skills—I count myself richer for the experience, as well as for the chance to listen. I would hope that in some small way I can provide some similar level of enrichment and enjoyment to those who take the time to read this book.

Robert McCullough
September 1997

HANK AARON

By all rights, Hank Aaron's greatest day in baseball probably should have been the day he hit his 715th home run to break Babe Ruth's all-time home run record. But the run for the record by "Hammerin' Hank" came with a heavy price—death threats, racial epithets, and an almost unfathomable level of pressure and publicity. Those factors led Aaron to recall two different days from early in his career with the Milwaukee Braves.

Well, of course my greatest day in baseball was in 1954. Let me start by saying that I would put two days in there, one would be equally great as the other one. One . . . was my first day in the major leagues, of course. I never thought, nor did I ever dream that I would get to the major leagues. When I put on the major league uniform that was the greatest thrill that I have ever had in my life.

The other great thrill that I had . . . was the night that I hit the home run that clinched the pennant for the Milwaukee Braves—that was in 1957. That was even a greater thrill than winning the World Series, because we first had to get there.

That night was a great thrill because I never dreamt . . . You know, I had read about, and had almost remembered verbatim, what had happened to the Brooklyn Dodgers when they played against the New York Giants and Bobby Thomson when he hit his dramatic home run. . . . I had always put myself in that same position, you know, "What if I ever get the chance—will this kind of dramatics ever happen to me?"

And then lo and behold, it comes to me in 1957 when I hit the home run to beat the St. Louis Cardinals and brought the first championship to Milwaukee. That . . . was a tremendous thrill—not only for me, but it was a great thrill for my teammates and a great thrill for the state of Wisconsin and the city of Milwaukee. . . . I'd have to put those two right at the top. . . .

The day I first put on the major league uniform, I had already phoned my mother, my parents, and my wife and all the rest of 'em and told them that I didn't think that I had a chance of being in the big leagues. Coming from A ball, you just didn't drop in to the major leagues back in those days.

So when I made the major leagues (and I didn't know whether that was the greatest thing in the world for the first couple of months) . . . I kept my bags packed. Every time I walked in the office I thought somebody was gonna call and tell me that I'd been sent down. So it was a scary moment for me. But I never did get the call. I guess they saw something in me—they kept me on the roster for the whole year.

After that first year, of course, I kind of felt a sense of belonging. . . . And that was it—that was the beginning of a long career for me. . . .

At the beginning of [that first] season, everybody was trying on uniforms. So you stand around, and you stand around, and you try on different uniforms, and guys are going up to the seamstress and telling him that this arm is too big or too little or they need alterations.

I didn't care what size mine was. I think it was too big, but it didn't really make any difference. I wasn't going up to any seamstress and telling him I needed any new anything, because I wasn't about to give him that uniform back.

That was probably the happiest moment in my life. The fact was you had a day or two before you opened the season up. . . . They bring out all the new uniforms, they hang 'em right up in your locker. . . . There wasn't even a game that day. We were working out, I believe, just getting everything right, getting the uniform straightened out and all those other little bitty things.

I really can't tell you anything about conversations I might have had because . . . you didn't talk to people. . . . For me to walk up to a guy like Warren Spahn or Eddie Mathews . . . and most of those guys were my age—maybe a little older, a year or two older—but they were already in the same group. But you just didn't talk. . . . You were always scared, and I'm sure they felt the same way I did.

The year I hit the home run . . . that was a year in which everything kind of fell in place for me. I was voted the league's Most Valuable Player that year, but the thing that I remember most . . . was that the year before we had lost out to the Dodgers by one game. And the same team that we were playing against, the St. Louis Cardinals, was the team that knocked us out of the [1956] pennant. The Cardinals were in second place at that time.

We were playing them in a three-game series, and the team had not been doing well. . . . It just seemed like everybody was beginning to say, "Well, the Braves are getting ready to choke up again."

So we played the Cardinals twelve innings that night, and I hit the home run in the bottom of the twelfth inning with Johnny Logan on base to bring us the pennant. I hit it off Billy Muffett. I don't know what he threw me; he threw pretty hard. He had a sinker ball—I don't know whether that pitch was a sinker, or what it was.

I didn't even think that I hit the ball hard enough, but I had the good Lord helping me, blowing the wind out. I don't even remember anything about the previous at-bats, I think I went 0 for 4 and that was the only hit I got.

The home run, breaking the Babe Ruth record, was a matter of leading up to a lot of things after having great years for twenty-some-odd years. . . . I went through an awful lot breaking the Babe's record, all this racist stuff, so I really didn't enjoy it as much as I did those other two events that I mentioned, not as much as I should have.

It was a happy moment for me, and it was a happy moment for my family, but still . . . it depleted me of a lot of things. I wasn't able to do a lot of things that I wanted to do; I wasn't able to enjoy myself as much as I should have.

The home run I hit for Milwaukee was something that came— it hit right there, and it helped not only me, but my teammates. I played with a bunch of great guys when I played with Milwaukee— we won a championship. I won a championship and I hit a home run. I played with [Spahn and Mathews], who are in the Hall of Fame, and I'm hopeful that one day [Lew] Burdette will probably be there as well. . . .

You talk about the MVP and the Hall of Fame—if I hadn't had a great career I wouldn't have been inducted into the Hall of Fame. The moment that I was inducted into the Hall of Fame . . . I'd had great years in order to accomplish that. But if you talk about one moment and one particular game, those two that I just mentioned outweigh all of 'em.

RICK AGUILERA

In addition to being one of the premier closers of the late '80s and early '90s, Rick Aguilera was also the pitcher of record in one of baseball's most tumultuous games, and he played a pivotal role in the championship success of the Minnesota Twins in the early '90s. In

*choosing his greatest day in baseball, Aguilera contrasted those expe-
riences with his major league debut.*

PF SPORTS IMAGES

I don't really have one particular
day, but three days come to mind. . . . A
very fond memory is my very first appearance in the big leagues. It came in relief in
Philadelphia for the New York Mets—this
was '85. I believe it was the ninth inning,
tie ball game; it was the ninth or tenth
inning. I was called up—I had started my
whole minor league career with the Mets,
and somebody was hurt. My time to start
wasn't for a few more days. I was in the
bullpen . . . in case I was needed.

It turns out, I believe I pitched the
tenth, a scoreless inning, and then we scored four runs in the top half
of the eleventh. I stayed and pitched the bottom of the eleventh and
got my first major league appearance and win all in one, in extra
innings. Obviously it was a very exciting moment in my life, just the
joy of pitching on top of getting a win out of it, it was certainly a day
I'll always remember.

I remember my very first batter I faced was Garry Maddox—
he popped up to the catcher—and I remember the very last out—I
struck out Von Hayes to win it. It was sometime in May or June, I
believe, but that would have to be one of my fondest memories in
my career.

The other two would, without question, have to be winning
World Championships—in '86 with the Mets and in '91 with the
Twins. I would have to say that just the experience of playing in postseason for the first time in '86 was a thrill. We had arguably one of
the greatest playoff series with Houston that baseball's ever had, and
then arguably one of the greatest World Series ever played in '86.

Not that I take credit for getting the victory in Game Six of the
'86 World Series, but it certainly was a memorable day in my career
as well. Everybody's familiar with Game 6 if you're a baseball fan,
what happened that night . . . What stands out the most in that game
was just the pain I was feeling emotionally after being in that dugout
after giving up two runs. You feel as if you've lost the World Series
for this organization.

We were clearly the best team in baseball that year—we'd won the most games. I remember going out pitching in the ninth inning, it was extra-inning affair, and I threw a scoreless inning. We didn't score in the bottom half, so I went out and pitched the next inning, I believe the first batter I faced I gave up a home run, and then I gave up another run as well, so we're down two runs.

I remember sitting in that dugout just feeling like I had really blown this thing for our club. And then the biggest emotional swing in my career, obviously, to sit there and watch us come back—with two outs, an 0–2 count on a batter, nobody on base. To come back and win that ball game, obviously the emotional swing was incredi-

October 25, 1986

BOSTON	AB	R	H	RBI	NEW YORK (N).	AB	R	H	RBI
Boggs, 3b	5	2	3	0	Dykstra, cf	4	0	0	0
Barrett, 2b	4	1	3	2	Backman, 2b	4	0	1	0
Buckner, 1b	5	0	0	0	Hernandez, 1b	4	0	1	0
Rice, lf	5	0	0	0	Carter, c	4	1	1	1
Evans, rf	4	0	1	2	Strawberry, rf	2	1	0	0
Gedman, c	5	0	1	0	Aguilera, p	0	0	0	0
Henderson, cf	5	1	2	1	Mitchell, ph	1	1	1	0
Owen, ss	4	1	3	0	Knight, 3b	4	2	2	2
Clemens, p	3	0	0	0	Wilson, lf	5	0	1	0
Greenwell, ph	1	0	0	0	Santana, ss	1	0	0	0
Schiraldi, p	1	0	0	0	Heep, ph	1	0	0	0
Stanley, p	0	0	0	0	Elster, ss	1	0	0	0
					Johnson, ph–ss	1	0	0	0
					Ojeda, p	2	0	0	0
					McDowell, p	0	0	0	0
					Orosco, p	0	0	0	0
					Mazzilli, ph–rf	2	1	1	0
Totals	42	5	13	5	Totals	36	6	8	3

Boston	110	000	100	2 — 5
New York	000	020	010	3 — 6

BOSTON	IP	H	R	ER	BB	SO
Clemens	7	4	2	1	2	8
Schiraldi, L	2.2	4	4	3	2	1
Stanley	0	0	0	0	0	0
NEW YORK	IP	H	R	ER	BB	SO
Ojeda	6	8	2	2	2	3
McDowell	1.2	2	1	0	3	1
Orosco	0.1	0	0	0	0	0
Aguilera, W	2	3	2	2	0	3

ble, to say the least. In World Series play, it's hard to argue that there was a more incredible game.

So that obviously stands out, it will always be . . . I guess I wouldn't call it a fond memory. I remember the pain that I was feeling then; the emotion I was feeling then wasn't very enjoyable. I wasn't in the mood to really speak with anybody. I was angry about giving up the runs, angry that I didn't get the job done.

I gave up two runs; I wasn't pleased with my performance. I wasn't talking with anybody. I was just basically sitting there kind of numb, watching things transpire, and then the next thing I knew, we're jumping all over each other on the field.

Still to this day—an incredible moment for our club, for the fans of New York, to win Game 7 of the World Series the next night—it's one of the most memorable days in my career.

And then again, the third one would be winning the World Series again with the Twins in '91. The thing I remember most about that ball club was just the camaraderie and the friendship that we had. We truly got along with one another. We enjoyed being around each other, and it showed in our performance and in the way we played.

Again, it was another terrific World Series. I've been very fortunate to play in two World Series and for both of them to go to Game 7 . . . the Twins winning the first two at home, losing the next three in Atlanta, then winning the next two at home. The fashion that we won in—the dramatics of Kirby Puckett's home run in Game 6 to win it to Jack Morris's performance in Game 7 throwing 10 shutout innings.

Again, they were arguably some of the greatest games in World Series history—and to be able to witness a performance like Morris's in Game 7. Obviously I had nothing to do with it, but just to be able to experience that game and watch somebody give that kind of performance in the magnitude of Game 7 and the pressures of the last game of the season—that's a very fond memory.

It's hard to choose one in terms of my own performance. If I was to choose one day . . . I remember closing Game 2 of the '91 World Series and striking out three batters. I don't recall the batters, but to do that was an enjoyable and gratifying moment in my career.

There's days where I struck out a lot of batters, or I threw a three-hitter . . . but the most meaningful game to me besides winning the World Series would be my very first appearance—just the joy I felt in my heart that I'd come to the big leagues now. I was fortunate to win my very first appearance . . . the reception that I felt from veteran players in that clubhouse congratulating me, saying, "Great job!" that kind of thing. Putting it above an outstanding performance, it was the one day that I'll always remember as just a great feeling that day in baseball—it was a tremendous feeling that I had.

Maybe when I'm a grandfather and I can show my grandchildren . . . "Here's a picture of me . . . in the All-Star game, this World Series game, this playoff game." Maybe those are things that I can look back on and feel good about, but I think I've always tried to prepare myself and go about my career in terms of doing what I can to help my team win. In '86 I was not a significant part in their winning—I had a decent year—but it was just as strong because it was my very first World Series and we won.

As far as feeling like I contributed, '91 certainly outweighs '86, because I played a much more important role in that team's success. But I always just tried to stay as healthy as I could to help and be out in the field if I'm needed, these kinds of things, and I've always tried to put my team first.

ROBERTO ALOMAR

In keeping with his reputation for range and versatility and for being one of the best all-around players in the game, Roberto Alomar's list of greatest days probably encompasses the greatest variety of experiences of anyone in this collection, starting with his first big league hit. . . .

For me, there are just so many moments.

My first hit was against Nolan Ryan. He threw me a curveball—it was a 2–2 count, and I just got a hit, to the left side. Nolan Ryan, he was just one of the best pitchers in the game, and getting a hit against a guy like him, it's always going to be remembered for me. I wasn't even thinking about getting my first hit against him—my biggest thing was to go out there and play baseball, to just go out there and have some fun. It was the kind of thing where whatever happened, happened.

Another big thing for me was playing in the All-Star game with

April 22, 1988

HOUSTON	AB	R	H	RBI	SAN DIEGO	AB	R	H	RBI
G. Young, cf	4	0	0	0	Gwynn, rf	4	0	1	0
B. Hatcher, lf	4	0	3	1	R. Alomar, 2b	4	0	1	0
Doran, 2b	4	0	1	0	Ready, 3b	3	0	0	0
G. Davis, 1b	4	0	0	0	Brown, 3b	1	0	0	0
Bass, rf	4	0	1	0	Moreland, lf	3	1	2	0
Ashby, c	4	0	0	0	Abner, lf	1	0	0	0
Walling, 3b	3	0	1	0	Santiago, c	4	1	1	2
Henderson, ph	1	0	0	0	C. Martinez, 1b	3	0	2	0
Ramirez, ss	3	1	2	0	Wynne, cf	4	1	1	1
Ryan, p	1	0	0	0	Templeton, ss	3	0	0	0
Puhl, ph	1	0	0	0	Ma. Davis	0	0	0	0
Agosto, p	0	0	0	0	J. Jones, p	1	0	0	0
					Thon, ss	1	0	1	0
Totals	33	1	8	1	Totals	32	3	9	3

```
Houston     001   000   000 — 1
San Diego   000   102   00X — 3
```

all my family—my brother and my dad—being there. It was my first All-Star game, which was 1990. We were just talking a lot throughout the game about how glad we were to be there. I watched my brother play, he was in the opening line-up, I watched him play and then after that . . . I came in for Ryne Sandberg. I hit a line drive for an out . . . off of Dennis Eckersley.

One of the biggest days was in the playoffs for Toronto, hitting the home run against Eckersley. It was big—we were losing 6–1, the series was 2–1 in games in our favor. After that we scored three runs, and it was 6–4. We were playing in their stadium—man on third, 2–2 count. I hit a home run to tie the game; I hit a fastball inside. I was thinking, "Just to make contact . . ." and it just happened that he threw the pitch where I was looking for it, and I just hit it.

I remember that game the most. Bob Welch was throwing a two-hitter for them. I got two of the hits, so I guess maybe he must have been throwing a three- or a four-hitter. In the seventh inning I led off with a double, and they brought in another pitcher. Joe Carter got a hit—that brought me home. Winfield got a hit, they brought Eckersley in, and Olerud got a hit. Candy Maldonado got a hit, and we got it to the point where it was 6–4.

In this kind of a series, when it's 6–1, sometimes you kind of get a little bit down—because they've got the best reliever in baseball on the mound, and we didn't think we had a chance. But we did. In the last inning Devo [Devon White] hit a triple, and I hit a home run, and we tied the game. And after that, somebody walked and got to second, I don't remember how, and then he moved to third, and then there was a fly ball, and he scored.

I remember that game because it put us ahead in the series 3–1, instead of it being 2–2. They came in and won the next game, so it would have been 3–2 in their favor, but it was 3–2 our favor after that, and we went to our stadium. We celebrated after we won, but we knew we still had one more step to go—and that was to win the World Series.

We went to the World Series, and we won the World Series against Atlanta. It was a lot of fun, a different atmosphere—this is what it's all about. This was what I wanted to accomplish in base-ball, was to get to that level, and you don't know if you're going to be there again. It was just a different atmosphere, a different kind of joy. You really enjoy those kind of moments. You enjoy every pitch, every out, every at-bat means something, every catch—it's just real-ly, really nice to be there.

When you are a World Series winner—when you have that ring in your hand—you know what it's all about in baseball. You can win a Gold Glove, you can win a batting title, you can win an MVP, you can win anything in baseball. But if you retire and you don't know what it's like to win a World Series, I don't think you will be happy. I think winning the World Series stands out the most for my part.

If you ask me about the individual achievement that stands out the most, I would have to say maybe [winning the] Gold Glove. I'm one of those people that takes a lot of pride in my defense—and in baseball not a lot of people talk about defense, all people talk about is offense. I think I always take pride in my defense. . . . All of the Gold Gloves mean a lot to me, but the first one means the most. You always remember that first one.

GEORGE "SPARKY" ANDERSON

Players often talk about individual achievements in the context of team success (or vice versa), but for managers success is defined exclusively in the context of what the team does. Despite all the great years he had managing the "Big Red Machine" and his later success with the Detroit Tigers, Sparky Anderson's greatest day was the start of his spectacular managerial career.

My greatest day was the first game I ever managed at Crosley Field. There can't be a moment in your lifetime ever more exciting or more nerve-wracking than that day. You never forget it, it's a marvelous nerve-wracking day.

Just going to the park, you're nervous, you're wondering, "How will I handle this? This is my first time ever in the major leagues!" All of a sudden you realize you're no longer in the minor leagues, you're managing in the major leagues. You've told yourself all along that there's no difference, but now you wake up and you know there is a difference.

That's the most exciting day that I ever had, because . . . it's hard to explain the magnitude of the major leagues, and Opening Day in the major leagues. That's a very hard thing to imagine, that you are actually going to manage in the major leagues—and you're the first club to open, which Cincinnati did in those days, in a great old ball park, Crosley Field. . . .

You'll never forget it. You know, I forget everything else. If you ask me about a World Series, I swear to this day I cannot tell you anything about a World Series. They just ran into each other after a while, and you were used to everything by then. They didn't have the meaning that your first day did.

I don't remember making the line-up out, and I don't remember being at home plate. I remember being out there for the pregame ceremony, and I remember Gene Mauch of all people, and everybody said Gene was tough and this and that—he became through this day one of my dear friends. He just tugged on my pants and said, "Don't forget today, enjoy today; because you will never get this moment again for the rest of your life."

And I thought, "My God, here's a guy who's been managing in the major leagues all these years . . . Who would take the time to pay me that respect?" I never forgot that; that's something that's always stayed with me.

It was a cold day, I remember, and a drizzly day. Merritt was pitching, and they [Montreal] had Joe Sparma pitching for them—I can remember those things. I can remember Lee May hitting a three-run home run over the scoreboard against the wind blowing in. That's when I knew, I said, "We're gonna have a pretty good team."

I couldn't tell you one thing about the game, other than May hitting the home run and just being totally wrapped up in the whole thing. I don't think I've ever been wrapped up that much since. After the game it was such a relief, to win your first game. . . .

I never was a rah-rah guy. I never was one of those guys that went around and rah-rahed. I never believed in it. I always·felt that this was business, and we get down to business. All the rah-rah don't get it.

But that's my greatest moment in my twenty-six years.

I was a very naive young man of thirty-five when I took that club over, and I don't think I rightly cared what they thought of me. I was there to try for us to win, I wasn't there to try and win a popularity contest. That was those days. . . . Today if you looked at it, I would probably look at it different—I know I would. I was just a very brash young man that I can honestly say at that time had no fear.

February 6, 1970

MONTREAL	AB	R	H	RBI	CINCINNATI	AB	R	H	RBI
Sutherland, 2b	4	0	1	0	Tolan, cf	5	1	1	1
Staub, rf	4	1	1	0	Helms, 2b	4	0	0	0
Fairly, 1b	4	0	1	1	Rose, rf	2	1	2	0
Barley, lf	3	0	0	0	Perez, 3b	3	0	0	0
Laboy, 3b	3	0	0	0	Bench, c	4	1	1	0
Phillips, cf	3	0	0	0	May, 1b	3	1	1	3
Boccabella, c	3	0	0	0	Carbo, lf	3	1	2	1
Wine, ss	2	0	0	0	Concepcion, ss	4	0	0	0
Sparma, p	1	0	0	0	Merritt, p	4	0	1	0
Herrera, ph	1	0	0	0					
Morton, p	0	0	0	0					
Brand, ph	1	0	0	0					
Waslewski, p	0	0	0	0					
Totals	29	1	3	1	Totals	32	5	8	5

Montreal	000	000	100 — 1	
Cincinnati	000	410	00X — 5	

MONTREAL	IP	H	R	ER	BB	SO
Sparma, L	5	7	5	5	3	4
Morton	2	1	0	0	2	1
Waslewski	1	0	0	0	0	0
CINCINNATI	IP	H	R	ER	BB	SO
Merritt, W	9	3	1	1	2	8

They thought I was crazy in spring training. I had work ethics in the minor leagues, and I used the same ones there in the major leagues that I used in the minor leagues. And that was "kill you"—that was my theory. I believed in running you to death, and they weren't used to that. And they didn't appreciate it. No, there's no question about that. They did not appreciate what I was doing. . . .

The only thing I remember about my debut as a professional player in the major leagues is that Philly fans booed us when we took the field. And I asked Granny Hamner why they're booing, and he said, "I think they're gettin' ready for what they know is gonna come."

I did get the winning hit. We opened in Cincinnati, then we went right home to Philly and opened there. But I got the winning hit off of Newcombe to win 2–1 in Cincinnati, and that's the last time I ever seen the writers. I had my one day in the sun, the first day of the year.

I had great moments watching my players all the time. In Cincinnati you had Rose, Perez, and Morgan, and then Bench and Griffey and Foster. There were great moments, great moments . . . Detroit with Morris and Petry and Parrish and Trammell and Whitaker and Gibson.

As far as anything with the Tigers goes, '84 was a great moment with me. Because I don't care who we are, if we don't care about records and things like that, we don't belong in the game—and to be the first person ever to win in both leagues was a great thrill to me. . . . That meant a lot to me. But as far as it being a thing like Opening Day in my first year—no, not even close.

The '87 club was a club that we didn't think we were gonna do much with, and they ended up winning ninety-eight games. I thought they were probably the best club I ever managed from the standpoint of accomplishing far more than I ever thought they could accomplish. So you know, you have different thoughts—the '87 club will always be a special club, because I never dreamed . . . I had said when we left camp that we would finish fourth or fifth, and they won ninety-eight games! That's a great tribute to them.

There's just times where they had great moments—it was enjoyable to watch 'em play. They were good players, and I think when you watch good players play, and when you're involved in it, you're not so much concerned about the individual as you are about the club. . . . I really don't care what an individual does, I care what we do.

Rose's record is there for history. Bench is there for history. Gibson's will be shown throughout baseball history forever, the home run that he hit . . . the two, the one he hit against San Diego and the one he hit against the Dodgers—they will always be there for us to see. But I don't have any great feelings over them, my feeling was always for the whole club. . . . The individual will get his awards and walk away with those, but what will the club walk away with?

All of those other greatest moments, they would be a like a grain of sand if I compared them to the possibility of going into the Hall of Fame. They would be centuries ago or millions of light years away.

The Hall of Fame is something to me that has nothing to do with the individual going in. In other words, I will never get long to enjoy it if I am inducted; I will never get a long, long enjoyment from it. But eternity, until the world ends, you will be there, and I think that is something that is the greatest thing that could ever happen to an individual. . . .

I'd be lying to you if I told you that I hadn't thought about what the ceremony might be like. Until they say it, or call you, you always wonder. . . . I try to look at the other ones and what they did, but you still say you don't know. But you don't know at the time when they vote, if someone's angry with you or what's going on. You don't know.

But if I was . . . yes, I have thought many times, "Why and how did this happen?" And it only happened by the people that touch me. I had no real control over it, and I truly did not do much to make it happen. It's the people . . . my father, Rod Dado, Benny Lefebvre, Bud Drubek and George Kitzel, George Sugar—I can go right on down, bang, bang. These are the people that made it all happen.

RICHIE ASHBURN

Richie Ashburn was a Hall of Fame outfielder for the Philadelphia Phillies, a perennial .300 hitter who played center field with grace and panache. Ashburn's greatest day goes back to the heyday of the Brooklyn Dodgers, when the Phillies fought off a late-season charge by "da Bums" in 1950 to force a one-game playoff for the National League pennant. A genuine triple-threat, Ashburn later went on to have a career as a writer (as a baseball columnist for the Philadelphia Inquirer) *and then as a broadcaster, prior to being elected to the*

Hall in 1995. All of baseball mourned his death from a heart attack during the 1997 season.

The best game I ever had, in my estimation, was when we were playing the Brooklyn Dodgers in the last game of the season in 1950, because it meant so much. We had a one game lead—if we lose the game we go into a playoff—and practically our whole team was injured. We lost . . . Curt Simmons, who was probably our best pitcher that year.

I think he could have been better than Robbie [Robin Roberts] that year, but that would have been the only year. He and Robbie were right there—if we went into a three-game series with Robbie and Simmons pitching, there was a pretty good chance we were going to win two of those games.

I guess the point I was trying to make was that our team was crippled. Our catcher was hurt, we'd lost all these pitchers, so if the Dodgers had won that game, they probably would have won the division. They had a heck of a team.

Well, in the bottom of the ninth we were tied 1–1, and I threw out what would have been the winning run. . . . It was at Ebbets Field, and I've made better plays in my lifetime, but that particular play was at a very crucial time—it was the winning run that was trying to score.

Newcombe and Roberts were the pitchers, so there wasn't a whole lot of hitting. The only run they scored came on that ball Pee Wee Reese hit off the right field screen that came down and sat on the ledge. That was one in a million—there wasn't even a ground rule covering it, although the next year there was.

The ball was just sitting up there on the ledge, and we couldn't reach it, and he just circled the bases. That was the only run they scored. There was no argument, that's just the way it was. It wasn't even in the ground rules—no ball had every stayed on that ledge. It was a miracle.

Bottom of the ninth, Cal Abrams got on first—whether he walked or got a hit I don't remember. Pee Wee Reese was the next hitter, and he got a base hit, so it was first and second with nobody out. Roberts was still pitching. At that point, they weren't about to take him out of that game.

Duke Snider singled to center field, and they tried to score Abrams from second. It was kind of a routine play, but it still had to be executed. Abrams was out by about twenty feet, our catcher was standing there with the ball, and he went up the line to meet him he got the ball so quickly. That was a great contribution to that game, but after I throw Abrams out, Reese is on third and Snider's on second—they took a base on the throw.

Jackie Robinson was the next hitter, and we walked him to load the bases because he had hurt us so much. We got the next batter to pop-up to first for the second out, and then I think it was Furillo to hit a fly ball to right field. Then Dick Sisler hit a three-run home run in the top of the tenth, and we win the game 4–1.

Now, I probably played as well as you can play in the All-Star game in Detroit in 1951—that's the next game that comes to mind. I had two at-bats, I got a double and a single, I scored two runs, I took a home run away from Vic Wertz over the right-center field fence, and I threw out a guy at home plate. That's an awful lot of things for one guy to do in one day, and I wasn't even the MVP of that game. . . . I loved All-Star games, I really did.

Getting elected into the Hall of Fame was a great honor, but you've gotta remember that it was twenty-seven years after I retired before that happened. I was passed over by the writers, and for three years I was off the ballot, period—I wasn't even eligible for the

October 1, 1950

PHILA.	AB	R	H	PO	A	E	BROOKLYN	AB	R	H	PO	A	E
Waitkus, 1b	5	1	1	18	0	0	Abrams, lf	2	0	0	2	0	0
Ashburn, cf	5	1	0	2	1	0	Reese, ss	4	1	3	3	3	0
Sisler, lf	5	2	4	0	0	0	Snider, cf	4	0	1	3	0	0
Mayo, lf	0	0	0	1	0	0	Robinson, 2b	3	0	0	4	3	0
Ennis, rf	5	0	2	2	0	0	Furillo, rf	4	0	0	3	0	0
Jones, 3b	5	0	1	0	3	0	Hodges, 1b	4	0	0	9	3	0
Hammer, ss	4	0	0	1	2	0	Campanella, c	4	0	1	2	4	0
Seminick, c	3	0	1	3	1	0	Cox, 3b	3	0	0	1	2	0
Caballero, pr	0	0	0	0	0	0	Russell, ph	1	0	0	0	0	0
Loppata, c	0	0	0	1	0	0	Newcombe, p	3	0	0	3	2	0
Golist, 2b	4	0	1	1	3	0	Brown, ph	1	0	0	0	0	0
Roberts, p	2	0	1	1	6	0							
Totals	38	4	11	30	16	0	Totals	33	1	5	30	17	0

Philadelphia	000	001	000	3 — 4
Brooklyn	000	001	000	0 — 1

Veteran's Committee. First of all, you had to have gotten sixty percent of the baseball writers' vote. I never got that, I got forty-some percent, so that would take me off.

Now listen to this, because this is really strange. I was barred from eligibility for the Hall of Fame, because the day they made Pete Rose ineligible there was a little statement down at the bottom of the page that you had to have fought in World War II. Well, I wasn't old enough—my brother did, though. It's ironic that the day I was drafted into the Army, the Japanese surrendered. If they'd held out one more day, I would have gotten in.

It's also strange that these so-called new rules, the year they passed that rule to take Pete Rose off, it affected one player—and that was me. It was going to affect some pretty good ballplayers down the line—Bill Mazeroski, Harvey Kuenn. It almost looked like a conspiracy. I don't know why there would be a conspiracy against just me, but I was the only player.

The Hall of Fame committee changed that after three years, because you can't throw a blanket over thirty-five years' worth of ballplayers who were voted in under entirely different rules. That wasn't fair, and I think they realized that. I think Robin Roberts, who was on that committee, was instrumental in having that changed, and I think that Dr. Bobby Brown had something to do with it too.

The first person I called when I was elected was my mother, who was ninety-two. It made such an impact on her; she was really happy. There were some things about it that I didn't like—all of a sudden the phone never stopped ringing, I started getting bushel baskets full of mail almost every day, and I didn't particularly like that.

I know it's a great honor, but I never left baseball, that was the difference for me. I think if I had been a player and had just gotten out of baseball after playing, it would have been different. But I've been around this game, and I don't want to sound like it's no big deal, because it is a big deal. I realized how big a deal it was when I got to Cooperstown.

It was on that stage up there, and I looked out and saw all those people, and they were all Phillies people, because I was there with Schmitty [Mike Schmidt]. That really did it, it just choked me up to see that. They were just up there for the Hall of Fame ceremony. They weren't up there for the game or for Bat Day or some giveaway or for fireworks. They were up there for that ceremony, and that was pretty great. I mean, you couldn't have asked for anything better than that.

Now that's a long shot, that two players from the same team and the same city would go in the same year, it may never happen again. He went in on the first ballot, and I went in on my twenty-fifth, or whatever it was. I saw Schmidt play every game that he played here, and we're great friends, and it just happened to work out that way—that's a pot-luck thing. It's nice to have that honor and that recognition.

JEFF BAGWELL

Since being traded from the Boston Red Sox to the Houston Astros early in his career, Jeff Bagwell has become one of the game's consummate run producers, a power hitter who drives in runs and hits for average as well. Like many players in this collection, Bagwell chose his debut with the Astros as his greatest day, discussing it as Houston was about to break camp from Kissimmee for the 1997 season.

Opening Day 1991 against the Cincinnati Reds. It was my first game in the big leagues. The Reds were coming off a world championship in 1990—by far the greatest day of my life. Standing in the dugout, nervous, excited, all the kind of things that you can imagine. We were at Riverfront.

The troops had just come back from that little skirmish we had, the Gulf deal. They had troops marching in—it was a big deal, it really was. By far the greatest day.

The events leading up were that I made the club in spring training, when I didn't think I was gonna. I made it as a first baseman. In fact, Darryl Kile and myself, we were traveling on the bus going to the airport. We thought they were just going to drop us off at the Holiday or the Days Inn over here, but they kept going and we made the team.

My father was there. . . . And just getting to Riverfront, and knowing you're going to be in the Opening Day line-up. They have your name up there on the board before the game starts. All of a sudden you get introduced . . . and I remember walking on the wood floors in the dugout and the bats and everything, and my heart was pumpin' so fast and butterflies and all those kind of things.

The trade from the Red Sox obviously was a tough deal for me when it happened. But then after about a couple days of getting over the shock, you kind of look over the situation. Most of the veteran guys were being traded away—they were gonna go with the youth movement. I was a third baseman at the time, and Caminiti was coming off his worst year—he hit like .247—and I was like, "Hey, I've got a chance to make it to the big leagues now!" It was a good opportunity for me.

I came to spring training as a third baseman, played good, I hit real well—but Caminiti was like fifteen for ten. He was getting hits all over the place, and my dad said, "Well, Tuscon's not a bad place." And then with ten days left in spring training—I thought I was getting sent down—they said, "Bob Watson wants to see you."

And I went into his office. I was getting ready to sit down, and he threw me a first baseman's glove, and he said, "Well, what would you like to do—play first base in the big leagues or play third base in Triple AAA?" I'm not the smartest guy in the world, but I can make that decision. . . .

That Opening Day—that's where it all began, you know? I haven't had the playoff experience, and that obviously would be a big thing—the day that you clinch, and you're on the bottom of the pile. But I think even when that happens, I'll still think the greatest day is that Opening Day—just because that's where it all began. The culmination of twenty years of playing baseball, nineteen years playing baseball, finally you did everything a kid would like to do, and that's playing in the big leagues. . . . That's an accomplishment in itself.

ERNIE BANKS

Ernie Banks didn't really have a greatest day in baseball, even though I tried every interview trick in the book to try to pin him down and get him to pick one. As Banks reminisced about his wide variety of great days, it became clear that his "greatest day" would have to be considered in the context of his role as a lifetime ambassador for the game of baseball.

Truthfully, all of my days in baseball have been the greatest—all of 'em. I mean, there wasn't one day or night or even morning (in my days we played morning games in Pittsburgh) . . . that wasn't my greatest day.

From the beginning to the beginning—I mean, it's not an end to anything, it's the beginning of something else—I went from playing to player/coach to coach to a roving coach to marketing. It seems like most of it was going from one thing to another after two years. I spent two years coaching, two years as a roving coach, two years in marketing, and from then on it's just been a love of public relations, which expands out. That's really what I do now, for my Cubs and baseball.

It's been a real . . . joy each day, day by day. I was at the game the other day with Dan McMurtry, he's a friend. He played in the minors years ago, but he's never been to Wrigley Field, and I took him to Wrigley Field, and we were just like little boys out there. I took him onto the mound, into the batter's box—that was a great day.

I sat there in the box seat with Hillary Clinton—that was a great day. I went to the White Sox park and spent time with Jerry Reinsdorf—that was a great day. I was there with Michael Jordan at White Sox park—that was a great night—when he retired from baseball. There's no single one, they're all just wonderful—morning, noon, and night. It's always been the greatest thrill of my life. My greatest day is my whole life in baseball.

I still talk to all the players—Willie Mays had his sixty-sixth birthday the other day—you know, my contemporaries. . . . And then I'll see the young guys play over at Wrigley Field. I see a lot of McRae, Dunston, and so forth. I go over to White Sox park and see Albert Belle.

The joy of my life is that there are two teams in the city of Chicago. Most cities don't have two teams. I get a chance to see all the players. I go to White Sox park and see all the players—and being a former player I can get in the dugout, and you go see the batting practice—and then when all the teams come in with the Cubs, it's the same thing. It's a joy in my life just to be connected, to be a part, to be associated with baseball.

It's a remarkable game. I know it's been beaten around a lot in the history of it . . . the Black Sox scandal, and all the different things when players and management were suspended and all that kind of stuff. But overall it survives all that, it has a resilience to survive all of that. The strike in '94, and in '72, you've seen all that—but the resilience of this game has really stayed steadfast.

It's like America, it's true America spirit. It's a sport that gives a lot. The players gave a lot of their time when I played—autographs, different kinds of things, giving away this and that—and that's like America. America's a very philanthropical society—we give a lot. And it's strong—we withstand things, we just come back. And that's where the game is, the game to me is that.

I'm just so happy to have been a part of it, me as an American playing an American sport. Because the true fiber of this country is just to stay in there. You've gotta be at bat. And when you're at bat, you're on your own—nobody can help you. So when you go in the field, you become part of the team. You can be an individual and still be part of a team.

That's another great joy that I liked about the game. When you're at bat, you're one against nine—but when you're in the field, you're nine against one. You're part of a team, you're part of a country, you're very special, it's a very special feeling.

It's also a family situation, where a father takes a son to a game, or a daughter. . . . My friend took his wife to a game. She had never been to a baseball game, so he was explaining it to her. You know, you get three outs; this guy at bat is Sammy Sosa, he's a power hitter. It's hard to explain it. . . . Baseball is hard to explain to people who have never seen it, so you have to flow with it and enjoy it, and you don't have to know a lot about each player, or the history of the team, you just flow with it because you're part of something really positive, and it's the way the world should be.

I wish all the world could be like us, like baseball, you know, where you can be an individual and still be part of a team, you don't have to be all one this, or all one that. You have freedom of expression, you see managers say things, players say things, you're an individual, but you've still got to be part of the team, and that's what I like about it.

Anyway, every day has been the greatest day of my life in the game.

It's kind of like guys like Tommy Lasorda or Sparky Anderson, my generation of baseball players—Willie, Hank, and all the guys—we're all in our sixties now. This whole game, Stan Musial and so forth, this whole game is our whole life. I mean, I dream about baseball a lot. I dream about players; I dream about events.

My dreams are about baseball, and I didn't play in a World

Series. And I think the great joy of not playing in a World Series is that you have a chance to dream about it. . . . I dream about it. I think, "Now, let me go to sleep," thinking, "Oh, geez, it's the seventh game of the World Series. . . ."—and Reggie Jackson kind of implanted that in my mind. Because he hit three home runs up there in New York against the Dodgers, and that's one thing that a hitter would like to do—that's the epitome of everything—is to hit three home runs in the final game of the World Series in New York, the Big Apple.

And lastly, the memories of the game are always there. Those of us who are fortunate enough to play the game, make the Hall of Fame, and so forth, win some awards—people still remember us, they really do.

VIDA BLUE

For a brief period in the early '70s, Vida Blue of the Oakland A's was one of the most dominant pitchers in baseball, and his rookie year in 1971 is the stuff of legends—a year in which he won twenty games so early in the season there was talk that he might win thirty. Blue talked about that season and that period in the context of his greatest day as the Opening Day starter for the A's in 1971.

I'll tell you what, maybe the greatest day of my life would be—even though I lost this game—but the greatest day, my greatest day in the game of baseball was when I was the starting pitcher in the presidential opener in 1971 in Washington, D.C. . . .

I had finally made it to the major leagues, and that solidified me being there. And the fact that my father never saw me play major league ball—that should have been the day when it all just came into perspective for me as far as the game of baseball itself goes. . . .

I remember Ted Williams was still managing the Washington Senators—they later became the Texas Rangers. I ended up being the losing pitcher. Then I ended up winning nine or ten straight games after that.

It was overwhelming, and even today . . . I still work for the Giants, and I attend Opening Day. Opening Day can be just overwhelming because of all the things, the anxiety that's inside of you—now this is for real, your stats go in the paper, and all of the pregame ceremonies that come with what Opening Day is all about. . . .

You know, you think in terms of the game that I pitched in '71 against the Chicago White Sox in August, where I became the first pitcher to win twenty games. Even though that was great, what it did was it put more added attention on me about the infamous "Can he win thirty?" Don't even talk to me about that . . . but that comes to mind, and that had to be 1971. That was my banner season.

BERT BLYLEVEN

If you hear the words "curveball" and "shutout" used close together in any discussion among knowledgeable baseball fans, you know they're probably talking about Bert Blyleven. A native of Holland, he pitched effectively for several teams during his long career, winning almost 300 games. For his greatest day he contrasted his championship experience with the Minnesota Twins with the no-hitter he pitched a decade earlier for the Texas Rangers.

PF SPORTS IMAGES

There's probably a couple of them, only because I was able to play on a couple of world championship clubs. I think the greatest day was probably in 1987, when we beat Detroit to have the Minnesota Twins go back to the World Series for the first time since 1965.

We were flying back on the airplane—back to Minnesota from Detroit after we beat them best out of seven, but in five games. We were informed on the plane that they wanted to bus the whole team to the stadium. . . . As we got off the plane we boarded two busses. The closer we got into town the more people we saw. . . .

By the time we pulled into the stadium, the domed stadium, there were 55,000 people at 11 o'clock at night—there to wish the Minnesota Twins good luck going into the World Series. That definitely for me—I think if you ask anybody on the 1987 ball club what the most memorable moment was—because it really displayed how the fans became our tenth player on the field and became the twenty-sixth man on the roster.

So I was very proud to be on that ball club, because we weren't supposed to win. Nobody picked us to go to the World Series; nobody picked us to win the World Series against the St. Louis Cardinals. But a lot of things went our way. We won the first two in Minnesota; we went back to St. Louis and lost three straight; so now we're down three games to two.

We didn't want to be another Minnesota Viking team. The '65 Twins had lost to the Dodgers. The Twins had always come so close to championships. There was a lot of pressure, but we knew when we went back, we knew that the crowd was gonna be there—55,000 people were gonna be there. It was gonna be noisier than heck. We had some great pitching, we had some timely hitting, and we ended up beating the St. Louis Cardinals in seven games. . . .

Also the no-hitter I pitched in '77 against the California Angels. As far as days, it would probably be the no-hitter. What stands out most is that I was coming off the disabled list, so I had not pitched for about two-and-a-half weeks. I had pulled a groin muscle earlier in the year, and I kept pitching on it.

I was with Texas, and we weren't really in the race, so they told me to go home and just rest it. I was [living] in Southern California, so when Texas came in to play the Angels, Billy Hunter was the manager, and I told him that it was feeling pretty good and that I'd like to pitch. He had kind of an opening, and he said I could pitch just certain nights, September 22nd. . . .

I re-pulled my groin again in the eighth inning, and I remember in the ninth inning I threw nothing but curveballs—only because to throw a curveball I didn't have to land as far, so it wasn't as hard to throw the curveball. I remember in the eighth inning Billy Hunter came out because I was in a lot of pain, and he said "How you doin'?" And I said, "Well, I've got a no-hitter going—you're not taking me out." He let me pitch the ninth inning, and I ended up getting a no-hitter. . . .

I remember leaping as high as I could when it was over. My catcher was Jim Sundberg. I really didn't care about the groin at that time. I knew I was hurt—it wasn't gonna get any worse. So I knew that once I leaped up and Jim Sundberg came out and I gave him a big hug, everything was just a celebration.

WADE BOGGS

The process of interviewing Wade Boggs for a description of his greatest day in baseball turned out to be a two-part experience. The first interview came in September of 1996 at Yankee Stadium, when the Yankees were locked-up with the Baltimore Orioles in a heated battle for the American League pennant. During that interview Boggs described his first greatest day—when he finally made it to the majors with the Boston Red Sox—and he also talked about his ultimate greatest day—winning the World Series. Thus, the 1996 postseason necessitated another interview with Boggs the following spring in Tampa, as the Yankees prepared to defend their world championship. [The beginning of the second interview is marked with an asterisk.]

My greatest day in baseball would have to be the day I found out that I made it to the big leagues, which was in 1982. I was at spring training with the Red Sox at Winter Haven, and I'd had a pretty good spring—and that was the beginning for me, the thing that got it all started.

It was my fifth year in the Red Sox organization. I'd been playing with Pawtucket, and I'd been to minor league spring training the year before, but that was my first year that I went to spring training with the big club. I think I was competing with three other players, and then there were some other decisions the Red Sox had to make regarding a roster move.

I know I hit well in spring training, but the thing I remember in particular was what Ralph Houk said near the end of the spring. He usually didn't talk about the guys who were trying to make the club that much, but he said that he didn't know I could play that well defensively—and I think that might have made him think about me differently in terms of what I could do for the club. So it was kind of ironic that it was my defense that helped me get to the big leagues.

I think it was between me and Dave Stapleton and maybe Glen Hoffman. Carney was there at the time—Carney Lansford was the third baseman—and it wasn't like I was going to beat him out. We were competing for a utility position, pinch-hitting and that kind of thing.

October 28, 1996

ATLANTA	AB	R	H	RBI	BB	SO
Grissom, cf	5	0	2	1	0	0
Lemke, 2b	5	0	0	0	0	0
C. Jones, 3b	4	0	1	0	0	0
McGriff, 1b	3	1	0	0	1	0
J. Lopez, c	3	0	1	0	1	2
A. Jones, lf–rf	3	0	1	0	1	2
Dye, rf	1	0	0	1	1	0
Klesko, ph–lf	2	1	1	0	0	0
Pendleton, dh	3	0	1	0	1	0
Belliard, pr	0	0	0	0	0	0
Blauser, ss	3	0	1	0	0	0
Polonia, ph	1	0	0	0	0	1
Totals	33	2	8	2	5	5

YANKEES	AB	R	H	RBI	BB	SO
D. Jeter, ss	4	1	1	1	0	1
Boggs, 3b	3	0	0	0	0	0
Hayes, 3b	1	0	0	0	0	0
Be. Williams, cf	4	0	2	1	0	0
Fielder, dh	4	0	1	0	0	0
T. Martinez, 1b	3	0	0	0	0	1
Strawberry, lf	2	0	0	0	1	1
O'Neill, rf	3	1	1	0	0	0
Duncan, 2b	1	0	0	0	0	0
Sojo, 2b	2	0	1	0	0	0
Girardi, c	3	1	2	1	0	0
Totals	30	3	8	3	1	3

Atlanta	000	100	001 — 2	
Yankees	003	000	00X — 3	

ATLANTA	IP	H	R	ER	BB	SO
G. Maddux, L	7.2	8	3	3	1	3
Wohlers	0.1	0	0	0	0	0

YANKEES	IP	H	R	ER	BB	SO
Key, W	5.1	5	1	1	3	1
Weathers	0.1	0	0	0	1	1
Lloyd	0.1	0	0	0	0	0
M. Rivera	2	0	0	0	1	1
Wetteland, S	1	3	1	1	0	2

So then it got down to the end of spring training, and my scout was up in the stands with my wife and my parents. It was pretty ironic—we were playing in Tampa that day, and that's where my home is. And my scout, George Digby, kind of let the cat out of the bag. He told my wife, and she comes down behind the dugout and calls me over and whispers to me that I'd made the club.

We went out after the game to celebrate, and I remember looking at her and she looked at me and said, "What do we do now?" And I said, "I don't know, but I'm gonna get packed for a road trip." We opened the season in Chicago, and then we were supposed to go to Baltimore.

I went to Chicago with the big club, and it had snowed up there for a couple of days, and basically the series got snowed out. So we turned around and got back on the bus and got back on the plane and went to Winter Haven and worked out and played for a couple of days back there. Then finally I went up to Boston with the Red Sox and opened the season there.

There wasn't any one particular point where I felt like I'd made it. When I went on that first trip I knew immediately that I was there with big league players, and you can feel the difference that makes. You have to try not to get a big head about it. I think you just have to try and enjoy it—that's the thing I learned—there are some guys that act ill at ease. It's really the best time of your life, your time in the big leagues, and it lasts a very long time for a few guys and a short time for most players.

The thing you have to do when you come up is get all your "firsts" out of the way—your first hit, your first game, your first home run. Once you do that, then the game starts to flow for you— you start to get adjusted to your surroundings and everything becomes easier. I never really thought about what would happen if I didn't make it that spring. I suppose I would have just gone back to Pawtucket and worked that much harder. I knew I had the talent, and I knew that sooner or later it would happen for me.

The reason that day stands out so much for me when I think about the batting titles and the Gold Gloves and the All-Star games and all the rest of that is that it was the first piece in the puzzle, the thing that got me started. As you go along in your career the other pieces start to fall into place, and you look back and it's all just there for you.

As far as my greatest day goes, the only thing that would top that would be winning the World Series, which I haven't done yet. . . .

*

Reflecting back on Game 6, I've had two memorable Game 6s in World Series history—one didn't come out so good, and the other one was a victory for the Yankees. It was a lot of emotion going through me, wanting to get it over with—and then I saw the pop-up go up, and the final out was made. It was like a ton of bricks lifted off my shoulders—it was finally obtainable.

And just the feeling when it was all over . . . there's nothing left—there's no more games that year—there's nothing left. The ticker-tape parade was right around the corner, just a couple days away, and you finally obtain the ring. There's just so much enjoyment and satisfaction and fulfillment. You play so hard and for so long, and the common team goal is accomplished. . . .

My perspective on it really hasn't changed. It's just a piece of the puzzle. It fit in very nicely—to obtain a ring and do the thing that I've really wanted the most . . . to finally be able to say that I'm a world champion.

You talk about individual goals, and then you talk about team goals. The team goal is to eventually win the World Series, and all your individual goals seem to fall into place after that. The team-oriented concept has been accomplished—and actually now I want to win two. So I'm selfish. I want to win two now. . . . I want to do it again. I want to go down Broadway and the Hall of Champions and watch the people throw paper again.

BOB BOONE

Bob Boone was one of the game's consummate defensive catchers, a thinking man's player who improved every pitching staff he worked with. Boone was also incredibly durable, setting a record that may never be broken for the number of games caught during his long career. Boone, who became a manager after his playing career, was also the middle link in a three-generation baseball family—his father, Ray, played in the big leagues, and two of Boone's sons, Bret and Aaron, both played in the majors as well.

I remember catching a perfect game by Mike Witt on the last day of the season, '83 I think it was, against Texas—one of the big thrills of my career being a catcher.

My greatest day was playing in the All-Star game, my first All-Star game, in '76. Just the ovation . . . not only me, but the other Philly players that were involved, Schmidt and Luzinski, we were just in a line—that was one of my greatest thrills.

The other one would probably be after clinching the World Series, the parade the next day. That was one of the greatest experiences I ever had. It was a day—and this is probably the best story. . . . We won the World Series in Philadelphia and did a lot of celebrating. I got invited that night by Bryant Gumbel to come on the show in the morning. . . .

They were asking me after the game, the champagne flowing, and I said, "Sure, yeah, yeah," and they said they'd send a limousine for me—and I lived in the woods in Medford, and I said, "Fine," not thinking about anything. They said the guy would be there about 6:30 in the morning, and I just said, "Fine," and didn't think about anything—I had driven to the stadium every day of my life. But we celebrated and got home probably about 2:00 or 3:00, and there was a bunch of people at my house then, and they kept the celebration going.

I got a couple hours sleep—got up, standing in the driveway waiting for the limo guy, and he couldn't find my house. He was late. So I get in the limo, and as I'm going into the field here's Larry Bowa and Bryant Gumbel walking out of the stadium. And they said, "Gee, Bob, it's too late. We had to go, and it's over with." So I had to . . . get in the limo, have him take me home. I had a terrible headache—we had the parade that day, which I was not looking forward to—I just felt awful. And then I was ticked that I wasn't on the show, because it's about an hour round trip.

So he takes me back, and now I call Greg Luzinski—we have to drive downtown with our families. . . . So I called Greg—I'm driving—and I said, "Are we ready? We gotta get going, because there's gonna be a madhouse downtown getting through traffic." So I get over there, they're not ready. Finally they come out, and we're heading to the place, and Greg says, "I haven't eaten." And I said, "Neither have I." I've been up, and I'm tired, and I'm cranky.

And he said, "We've gotta stop at McDonalds." And I said, "Greg, we don't have time." He said, "We're stopping at McDonalds." So we turn in and stop at McDonalds and get some-

July 13, 1976

AMERICAN LEAGUE	AB	R	H	RBI	NATIONAL LEAGUE	AB	R	H	RBI
LeFlore, lf	2	0	1	0	Rose, 3b	3	1	2	0
Yastrzemski, lf	2	0	0	0	Oliver, lf	1	0	0	0
Carew, 1b	3	0	0	0	Garvey, 1b	3	1	1	1
Brett, 3b	2	0	0	0	Cash, 2b	1	1	1	0
Money, 3b	1	0	0	0	Morgan, 2b	3	1	1	0
Munson, c	2	0	0	0	Perez, 1b	0	0	0	0
Fisk, c	1	0	0	0	Foster, rf	3	1	1	3
Chambliss, ph	1	0	0	0	Montefusco, p	0	0	0	0
Lynn, cf	3	1	1	1	Russell, ss	1	0	0	0
Otis, ph	1	0	0	0	Luzinski, lf	3	0	0	0
Harrah, ss	2	0	0	0	Griffey, rf	1	1	1	1
Belanger, ss	1	0	0	0	Bench, c	2	0	1	0
Patek, ss	0	0	0	0	Cedeno, cf	2	1	1	3
Staub, rf	2	0	2	0	Kingman, rf	2	0	0	0
Tiant, p	0	0	0	0	Boone, c	2	0	0	0
Wynegar, ph	0	0	0	0	Concepcion, ss	2	0	1	0
Tanana, p	0	0	0	0	Bowa, ss	1	0	0	0
Grich, 2b	2	0	0	0	Rhoden, p	0	0	0	0
Garner, 2b	1	0	0	0	Cey, 3b	0	0	0	0
Fidrych, p	0	0	0	0	Jones, p	1	0	0	0
McRae, ph	1	0	0	0	Seaver, p	1	0	0	0
Hunter, p	0	0	0	0	Schmidt, 3b	1	0	0	0
Rivers, rf	2	0	1	0	Forsch, p	0	0	0	0
Totals	29	1	5	1	Totals	33	7	10	7

American	000	100	000 — 1
National	202	000	03X — 7

thing. So now we get downtown and there's traffic—we got there just in time.

You know, you get the kids in these flatbed trucks with these really cushy chairs in them, and we had the whole family there. I had just been rushin' all night—I'd been drinking champagne, no sleep, and I thought, "Man, I'm gonna sit down in this chair, and I'm gonna just kick back and relax and just enjoy this thing."

We started off down Broad Street. By the time they hit the corner and turned onto Broad Street I was out of my chair, fist in the air, yelling at people—there were so many people. One of the joys of my life, of my baseball life, was that my family was there to experience that. It was the most unbelievable experience. There was a guy who ran, who followed our caravan in this parade the entire way down

Broad Street. He stood behind, you know, there were people—twenty or thirty deep—he was behind them running all the way. He just stayed right up with me the whole way into JFK Stadium. . . .

I mean, you see the fans, and you knew Phillie fans were good, because they were knowledgeable. If you were doin' bad, they were tough. If [you] were doin' good, man, it was the greatest place to play in the world—the greatest. People lived and died and you were born a Phillie fan.

That march down Broad Street was one of the most incredible things—I was on my feet the whole time. And here I was just dead tired, a little hung over, and thinkin', "I'm just gonna relax." I was more pumped during that parade than I was at any time during that World Series. It was the most incredible thing and probably the fondest memory I have of all of my playing days.

There's been some big games as a manager, but we haven't gotten to win. There are a number of games I've managed very well, and people don't know—the subtleties, where we've made all the right moves. And on the same hand, there's games when I've known—and nobody knew it—"Shit, I blew the game. I should have done this. . . ." But I don't think there's one in particular that stands out. Hopefully it's gonna be the one that wins the pennant or the playoffs.

Seeing Bret get his first hit off of Arthur Rhodes in Baltimore—I was managing at the time, I was in Tuscon, but I got to see it. They had a satellite, and I got to run in and see his first at-bat—and he got a hit off Arthur Rhodes, a line drive up the middle. I think at the time there was a lot made of the three generations. That was a special time, seeing your kid bat for the first time. That's probably as special as any of it—that's a real special feeling. I think it'll be the same when Aaron gets his first major league at-bat.

GEORGE BRETT

For twenty years George Brett was the heart and soul of the Kansas City Royals—a superb defensive third baseman who hit for both average and power on his way to a 3,000-hit career. But Brett was best known for being a great clutch hitter, and for his greatest day he chose one of the Royals' most meaningful wins, in which each hit he got was pivotal.

1985, third game of the playoffs—we lost the first two games—obviously a very important game. The series is four out of seven

instead of three out of five. I end up the day going four for four—two home runs, double, single. We win, which enables us to play Game 5—probably the best game I've ever played in my life. I made the best defensive play in my life on a ground ball by Lloyd Moseby.

He hit a ground ball behind third base. I backhanded it, threw out Damaso Garcia at the plate. It was by far, without a doubt, it was a game that was probably as important as Game 6 or 7—if you lose that one, you're not gonna come back and win four in a row. So to have a game like that, that still sticks out as my greatest day in baseball.

The first at-bat—Doyle Alexander was pitching—Willie Wilson was on first base. I don't remember the count. Willie Wilson was stealing second. I swing at a change-up in the dirt—way out in front of it—Ernie Whitt gets up and throws Willie Wilson [out] at second base. Next pitch, Doyle . . . came back with a change-up—I hit a home run into the right field seats.

Next at-bat, I get up there, he throws a slider down and in; it gets in a little bit on me. I don't get my arms as fully extended as I would have liked to—I hit a fly ball to right field. Jesse Barfield goes back to the wall, jumps up, misses—probably by about three inches. [The ball] bounces to Lloyd Moseby and—stand-up double.

Next guy up, Hal McRae—sacrifice fly to right field, which moves me up. Next guy up, Frank White—fly to right field, which scores me. Now we're winning 2–0. . . .

The Blue Jays come back and they score five runs off Saberhagen; we're losing 5–2.

Third at-bat, I get up—I think in the meantime Jim Sundberg's hit a home run off Doyle Alexander, so he's winning 5–3—sixth or seventh inning, I come up. Willie Wilson [has hit] a ground ball up the middle for a base hit. [Alexander] doesn't throw me a change-up, because I hit a change-up for a home run in the first inning; doesn't throw me a slider down-and-in, because I hit a double off the wall. He throws me a fastball up and away—I hit a home run to left-center, ties the score 5–5.

Bottom of the [eighth] inning—I'm leading off. . . . They bring

October 11, 1985

TORONTO	AB	R	H	RBI	KANSAS CITY	AB	R	H	RBI
Garcia, 2b	5	1	2	0	L. Smith, lf	4	0	1	0
Moseby, cf	4	1	1	1	L. Jones, lf	0	0	0	0
Mulliniks, 3b	4	1	1	2	Wilson, cf	4	1	2	0
Upshaw, 1b	4	0	1	0	Brett, 3b	4	4	4	3
Oliver, dh	2	0	1	0	McRae, dh	3	0	1	0
C. Johnson, dh	2	0	1	0	White, 2b	3	0	0	1
G. Bell, lf	4	0	3	0	Sheridan, rf	3	0	0	0
Whitt, c	3	1	1	0	Balboni, 1b	4	0	1	1
Barfield, rf	4	1	1	2	Sundberg, c	4	1	1	1
Fernandez, ss	4	0	1	0	Biancalana, ss	1	0	0	0
					D. Iorg, ph	1	0	0	0
					Concepcion, ss	1	0	0	0
Totals	36	5	13	5	Totals	32	6	10	6

```
Toronto        000   050   000 — 5
Kansas City    100   112   01X — 6
```

in Jim Clancy to pitch to start that inning. Jim Clancy's a guy that I hit really well over my career, and I think that the last thing he's gonna do is throw me a fastball right down the middle first pitch. He's gonna try to get ahead of me . . . he came up with a split-finger forkball recently. So I said, "I'm gonna try to get a good hitter's count, and then I'm gonna look fastball." And the first pitch is a fastball right down the middle—strike one.

The next couple of pitches are balls, away. The third pitch or the fourth pitch is a little sinker, down and away, and I tried to pull it—I hit a ground ball between first and second that Damaso Garcia dives for and misses it. The next guy up's Hal McRae—he sacrifice bunts, puts me at second. I think the next guy up was Frank White, who I think hits a ground ball to the shortstop, and I run to third.

Brings up Steve Balboni—he hits a blooper to center field. It falls, and I score the winning run, 6–5. That was the bottom of the eighth.

We go out in the top of the ninth. The first two guys make outs—I don't remember how they make outs. The third guy up is Lloyd Moseby. He hits a pop-up—I catch it in foul territory.

At the time Dick Howser, our manager, had lost ten straight playoff games—but three of those games were against the Royals in 1980 when we swept the Yankees (he was managing the Yankees). So, I remember catching the ball . . . Frank White was the first to greet me—he gave me a hug, and I hugged him back . . . walking off the field, high-fiving everybody. And then I handed the ball to Dick Howser, and I said, "It's about time you won a fucking game."

And that was the greatest game that I ever played—my greatest day in baseball—because it came at a time when someone had to step up and do something or we would have been eliminated in four games, and I had the greatest game of my life in such a meaningful situation. And we ended up going on to win the World Series. But that was by far the greatest game I ever played in my life. . . .

I never knew how good it would feel to get 3,000 hits—until you actually do it. I never knew how good it would feel to win a world championship—until you actually do it. I didn't know how great it would be to be a father—until I actually saw my wife give birth and I'm in the room, three times. Those are things that you can think about and get goose bumps and get teary-eyed, but you don't know how you'll react until [it] actually happens to you. And hopefully in 1999 I'll be inducted into the Hall of Fame. . . .

The feeling of accomplishment of 3,000 hits was, "Yeah, well, I played a long time, I should get 3,000 hits. . . .Wow, I'm glad that's over—now I can go out and relax and play." And once you get it, it's more of a relief. Well, in the playoffs, there was no relaxation—you try to relax, but you can't do it.

So my best day . . . no, I don't want my best day to be a relief; I want my best day to be full of excitement. And that's the most excited I was—running off the field after that game, Game 3 of the '85 playoffs.

That was the most excited I've ever been, because I really felt that I generated the win for us. I generated the win. I did something extraordinary. I did something very special in a situation where the team really needed someone to step up and take charge—to take control of the game. . . . And that's a feeling of accomplishment.

JACK BUCK

While space considerations made it impossible to include every great announcer's greatest day in this collection, Jack Buck was definitely essential. The voice of the St. Louis Cardinals for almost the entire second half of this century, Buck is as much a part of the team's storied history as Lou Brock, Bob

Gibson, Ozzie Smith, and other postwar stars, whose achievements he chronicled for the fans.

I've had seventy-two years of greatest days. I'm sure I have to pick more than one. One would be Gibson's no-hitter, over in Pittsburgh. After everything he had done as a pitcher, establishing himself as one of the greatest pitchers, the greatest competitors to ever play the game . . . He had no no-hitters until then, and he pitched one in Pittsburgh against a very good hitting line-up that included Willie Stargell, Al Oliver, Manny Sanguillen.

It was a thrilling moment for me. First of all, to broadcast a no-hitter is always fun—especially when you get someone like Gibson doing it against a ball club like that. That has to be one of my biggest thrills.

Then, of course, when Lou Brock broke Maury Wills's record in stolen bases. Number 104 and 105—he stole them both in the same game against Philadelphia. The thing about Brock was, not only was a he a base stealer, but he had more than 3,000 hits. And you knew when he was on base he was intent on stealing, and they couldn't stop him. The first basemen frequently played out of position, holding him close; pitchers paid a lot of attention to him; the infielders always cheated towards second base.

He was a good student of the game—the audacity with which he played was always very impressive to me. In addition, he was tough and happy and a challenging player. So that particular night, when he stole 104 and 105, was thrilling for me.

Then, of course, Ozzie Smith's home run in the playoffs in 1985 against the Dodgers. He had never, ever, ever hit a home run in the big leagues left-handed. He hit one that won the game, and I was on the air at the time, and I told the folks to go crazy! It was really a moment. So that has to rank there as well.

The first year I was with the ball club—in 1954—working with Harry Caray, Stan Musial hit five home runs in a doubleheader. How can you top that for a memory? . . .

Broadcasting for the network, I saw Kirk Gibson hit that home run against the Oakland team, managed by Tony LaRussa. It was such an unexpected and shocking event that I said, "I don't believe what I just saw!" The more you know about baseball, the more improbable that home run was. So, that's a list of my greatest days in baseball.

The beauty of radio was that you could add color to the game, and be dramatic, and sometimes be overdramatic and build it up. . . . You could put all the drama you cared to into a no-hitter, Brock stealing the base, or whatever.

BERT CAMPANERIS

Throughout his long career, Bert Campaneris was a middle-infield magician—a shortstop with great range who made acrobatic plays, hit for average, and was a tough clutch hitter as well. Many fans remember him as the first player to play all nine positions in a single game—in one of Charlie Finley's most memorable (and successful) promotional stunts—but Campaneris was also one of the key cogs in the Oakland A's championship teams of the early 1970s.

My greatest day? I've got a few. My greatest day is my first time in the major leagues—I hit two home runs in Minnesota. The first time at bat I hit a home run, and then later in the game I hit another home run.

The second greatest moment was when I played in the World Series, in '72, '73, '74. And I played all nine positions, too, for the Oakland A's. Charlie Finley, he knew I did it in the minor leagues, so he came to me and asked me if I wanted to do it in the major leagues. So I told him yes.

He promoted the game for two months, a month-and-a-half. I did it—I played all nine positions. It was September 8, 1965. In my country, I always played every position, you know, when I was a kid. . . . My entire spring training the manager told me, "If you want to play every position you can catch, play center field, play right field, first base." I just said, "OK," and I did it. None was any tougher than the other—basically they were all the same, because I had played them all.

The first home run I hit off of Jim Kaat, off the first pitch that he threw. I told Orlando Pena, the first pitch he threw I was gonna swing. Jim Kaat threw me a fastball right down the middle, and I hit a home run. Later in the game, in the fifth or sixth inning, I hit another home run—it was off Jim Kaat again. The second time it was a breaking pitch; I hit a curveball.

The second time, I wasn't afraid about him coming inside. I got

July 23, 1964

KANSAS CITY	AB	R	H	RBI	MINNESOTA	AB	R	H	RBI
Matthews, cf	5	0	0	0	Rollins, 3b	5	0	1	0
Campaneris, ss	4	2	3	3	Oliva, rf	5	1	1	0
Colavito, rf	4	0	0	0	Hall, cf	3	1	0	0
Gentle, 1b	5	0	1	0	Killebrew, lf	4	1	1	3
Harrelson, lf	4	0	0	0	Grant, pr	0	0	0	0
Alusik, lf	1	0	0	0	Mincher, 1b	5	0	0	0
Tortabull, lf	0	0	0	0	Battey, c	4	0	0	0
Edwards, c	5	1	2	1	Versalles, ss	4	0	1	0
Charles, 3b	4	0	2	0	Goryl, 2b	3	0	0	0
Shoemaker, 2b	5	1	1	0	Kostro, ph	1	0	0	0
Segui, p	3	0	2	0	Kindall, 2b	0	0	0	0
Wyatt, p	1	0	0	0	Kaat, p	3	0	0	0
					Worthington, p	0	0	0	0
					Arrigo, p	0	0	0	0
					Allison, ph	0	0	0	0
Totals	41	4	11	4	Totals	37	3	4	3

Kansas City	100	000	200	01 — 4
Minnesota	000	003	000	00 — 3

five stitches over my eyes, I got a broken cheekbone, but I wasn't afraid that he was gonna knock me down.

Of all the World Series games, in '73, where I do everything to win the MVP, and they took it away from me. They gave it to Reggie Jackson . . . so that really hurt. Fielding, hitting— I hit a home run in the seventh game, and I got the winning RBI of the first game, too. . . .

That one really hurt me for the Hall of Fame, because when you do something good like that, everybody says, "Wow, he was an MVP in the World Series." That hurt me a little bit for being in the Hall of Fame. I've still got a chance for the Veteran's Committee, but it's gonna be . . . somebody's gonna have to push.

I need a lot of push, but I have a good record. I helped the Oakland A's win five Western Division titles, the World Series—I did a lot of things. I played all nine positions. I did a lot of tough things, so I need somebody to push, to push me, you know, so they can put me in the Hall of Fame. I deserve it. I worked so hard all my life to be there like everybody else. I hope some day it happens.

HARRY CARAY

Perhaps more so than any other broadcaster in history, Harry Caray was thought of as an integral part of the game he described. His daily Wrigley Field rendition of "Take Me Out to the Ball Game" was the stuff of legends. Caray is a part of baseball history, as he so vividly illustrated in this version of his greatest day, which harks back to a time when clubs traveled by train and road trips were a piece of genuine Americana. Caray also made a significant contribution to the future of the game, as three generations of the Caray family have broadcast baseball. Baseball lost one of its great personalities when Caray passed away in February of 1998.

My greatest day in baseball? That would be easy, it would have to be the day that Stan Musial got his 3,000th hit. Not so much because I was there, but because what took place after was something that could never be recreated and will probably never happen again.

I was broadcasting for the Cardinals at the time, and it was late in the season. The Cardinals were playing the Cubs at Wrigley Field. Musial was kept out of the game because they wanted him to get his 3,000th hit in St. Louis, but the Cardinals were trailing by a run late in the game, and they got a couple of runners on base—I think it was either in the seventh or the eighth inning.

Fred Hutchinson was the manager, and, naturally, he wanted to win the game. So he stands up on top of the dugout steps and whistles for Musial to come in as a pinch-hitter—he was sitting out in the sun in the bullpen in right field in Wrigley Field. And Musial comes in and whistles a double down the left field line, and the tying run scores, and the winning run scores, and the Cardinals win the game.

Nowadays you hear about it all over when a player gets his 3,000th hit, people make a big fuss about it, but this was in the days before television and even radio—not all of the clubs had all of their games broadcast on radio. You traveled by train in those days, and there were about ten stops in between Chicago and St. Louis—I think it was the train line that Dizzy Dean used to sing about, the old Wabash Cannonball.

May 13, 1958

ST. LOUIS	AB	R	H	RBI	CHICAGO	AB	R	H	RBI
D. Schofield, ss	2	2	0	0	T. Taylor, 2b	4	0	1	0
D. Blasingame, 2b	5	1	1	1	L. Walls, rf	3	2	2	2
J. Cunningham, 1b	3	0	0	0	E. Banks, ss	3	0	0	1
I. Noren, lf	4	0	2	2	W. Moryn, lf	4	0	1	0
W. Moon, cf	4	0	1	1	D. Long, 1b	4	0	0	0
C. Flood, cf	1	0	1	0	S. Taylor, c	3	0	2	0
K. Boyer, 3b	4	0	1	0	B. Thomson, cf	3	1	0	0
G. Green, rf	5	1	1	0	J. Goryl, 3b	3	0	1	0
H. Smith, c	4	0	1	0	C. Tanner, ph	1	0	0	0
S. Jones, p	2	0	0	0	M. Drabowsky, p	2	0	0	0
S. Musial, ph	1	0	1	1	P. Smith, ph	1	0	0	0
F. Barnes, pr	0	1	0	0	T. Phillips, p	0	0	0	0
B. Moffett, p	0	0	0	0					
Totals	35	5	9	5	Totals	31	3	7	3

St. Louis	001	004	000 — 5
Chicago	101	010	000 — 3

We got to the first stop, and the entire railroad platform was full of people who had come out just to see Stan Musial. When you think about it, it was truly amazing—these were fairly small towns, and it seemed like the entire community must have been out there, standing at the railroad station. They came back in the car and got Stan—it was almost like he was a presidential candidate—and he went out to see all the people who had come out to see him.

Now Stan was the kind of guy who was always the life of the party—he did card tricks and played the harmonica, and he was very friendly, and people just seemed to sort of gravitate to him. And he began to entertain these people and shake hands with them—I think it was around the third stop that he pulled out his mouth harp and started to play songs for them. And that was the way it went at every stop until we got to St. Louis. All of these people in these small towns just came out to honor Stan because he'd just gotten his 3,000th hit.

I think it's my greatest day because it's something that will never happen again. I mean, nowadays, why would all these people come out to a railroad station? They'd probably just stay home and watch it on TV or listen to it on the radio.

Now if you ask me about my greatest day personally, that would have to be the day I was inducted into the Hall of Fame. [Editor's note: Caray received the Frick Award as a lifetime achievement in recognition of his contribution to the game in 1989.] I don't mean to be braggadocio about it, but I've gotten a lot of awards—but that day was just very special. I went in with Johnny Bench, Carl Yazstremski, Red Schoendienst, and Al Barlick, and it was just blazing hot on the day of the induction ceremony. And I think they had the largest crowd they'd ever had in the history of the ceremony at the time.

I was up on the platform, and my son and my grandson were there, and as I got up to make my speech the realization hit me that we had three generations in my family broadcasting major league baseball. . . . That had never been done before, and it may never be done again—it was something that was completely unique. And that realization just came to me as I stood up—that I was there, and my son was there, and my grandson was there, and we were all broadcasting baseball. Who could be more blessed than that?

STEVE CARLTON

Along with Sandy Koufax, Steve Carlton remains the dominant lefter of the postwar era, a power pitcher who struck out over 4,000 hitters and won more than 300 games in his long and illustrious career. For his greatest day, Carlton talked about his nineteen-strikeout game against the New York Mets in their miracle year of 1969—a game he ironically lost.

My greatest day in baseball . . . the day I retired, right? [Laughs.]

There's two stories that really stick out in my mind. In '69, when I struck out nineteen guys for the first time, which was never done. That night was an interesting night because I was kind of feeling feverish or sick the whole day. I was thinking about not even going to the park that day. I was gonna call in . . . [but] I thought, "Well, I'll go down there anyway."

So I laid around down there on the training table—didn't take batting practice, didn't even hardly go out on the field I recall. So I was in question until the very end, and I decided to go out and pitch.

I started to warm up. I was really throwing the ball better than I'd ever thrown it in my life—just speed, things were really jumping, you know? The slider was more powerful and dynamic than it had ever been at that time, and my curveball was dropping off the table. So I said, "Geez, coming from not feeling too well, this is pretty good stuff."

I started the game by striking out the first four guys. . . . Then we had an hour-and-twenty-minute rain delay, and I come out, and I'm feeling good after that. I come back and warm up and [am] throwing maybe even a little bit better—I was really surprised at how well I was throwing it. I went out to the game, and Swoboda hits a slider off me for a two-run homer, and he hits a fastball off me for a two-run homer. We lose 4–3, but I struck him out on the same two pitches—I struck him out on a slider, and I struck him out on a fastball.

It was one of those freaky things, like they were destined to be the world champions that year. . . . I remember Amos Otis—I struck him out four times—I forget the innings I struck him out in. He

September 15, 1969

NEW YORK (N.)	AB	R	H	RBI	ST. LOUIS (N.)	AB	R	H	RBI
Harrelson, ss	4	0	1	0	Brock, lf	4	1	2	0
Otis, lf	5	0	0	0	Flood, cf	5	2	2	1
Agee, cf	4	1	1	0	Pinson, rf	4	0	3	1
Clendenon, 1b	3	1	1	0	Torre, 1b	4	0	1	1
Swoboda, rf	4	2	2	3	McCarver, c	4	0	0	0
Charles, 3b	4	0	0	0	Shannon, 3b	4	0	0	0
Grote, c	4	0	2	0	Javier, 2b	4	0	0	0
Weis, 2b	4	0	1	0	Maxvill, ss	3	0	0	0
Gentry, p	2	0	0	0	Browne, ph	1	0	0	0
Pfeil, ph	1	0	1	0	Carlton, p	3	0	0	0
Gosger, pr	0	0	0	0	Gagliano, ph	1	0	0	0
McGraw, p	1	0	0	0	Nossek, pr	0	0	0	0
Totals	36	4	9	4	Totals	37	3	8	3

New York	000	200	020 — 4	
St. Louis	001	020	000 — 3	

NEW YORK	IP	H	R	ER	BB	SO
Gentry	6	7	3	3	4	3
McGraw, W	3	1	0	0	1	3
ST. LOUIS	IP	H	R	ER	BB	SO
Carlton, L	9	9	4	4	2	19

laughed about it in later years, but I just had dynamic stuff. It was fabulous! The ball was just jumping out of my hands. I felt like I never threw that well, ever, in my life.

It's funny, because two times previous to that—I think Koufax had the record at eighteen, a couple times he'd done it, maybe more than that, even—but I had struck out sixteen in eight innings on the road. . . . But on the road I never got a chance to pitch the ninth, so I just ended up three times at sixteen strikeouts in eight innings—this was the third time—but I got the chance to pitch the ninth, and I struck the side out in the ninth.

It was a great feeling. I knew because I had approached it before two other times—so I knew what the record was, and I knew where I stood on that record. But I was really just pouring everything into it I had, ninth inning, all the energy I had into it. Striking out the side in the ninth inning's pretty good, because it's late in the game—you throw a lot of pitches striking out that many.

The crowd was really excited. You could hear Harry Caray over the intercom—he was hollering and screaming about it and everything. The fans were really excited. My teammates were really . . . you know how they get in a no-hitter, they leave you alone. But it happened, I pulled it off. It was the third time I'd been in that position.

You knew you were doing it as you were doing it—there wasn't anything that was hidden. It was really exciting—you do the post-game show with Harry and Jack Buck, and they were just really excited. Just to come from not even gonna come to the park that day to set a record like that, just feeling great during the course of the game, have an hour-and-twenty-minute rain delay and come back throwing hard and pitch nine and strike out the side in the ninth inning. It was exciting. It was one of the best days in your life in your career.

Seaver came second with nineteen against San Diego a couple of years later—I was already caught—and then Ryan did it a couple of times at nineteen. You know those records aren't going to last because of the caliber of the talent you had at the time. And Clemens comes back and does it, his overpowering stuff. You hate to be knocked out like that, but you know it happens. When you set records those always seem to be broken some time. . . .

I really didn't prepare in the fashion I would have in 1969, because I was sick and I just laid around the training table. . . . There was somebody that was gonna be a backup pitcher that night. Red

Schoendienst was the manager at the time—he had somebody ready to go as a backup, one of the fifth starters or whatever. It's funny how that happens.

Tug McGraw got the win. . . . He kidded me in later years when he was with the Phillies about it, doing that, the little rascal.

The other story's in 1972, the great year I had in '72 with the Phillies winning twenty-seven games that year. It was a game early in the year, the first trip to the West Coast—we were playing San Francisco. The other games are kind of like excess, but this is really the economy of pitching. I think the '69 game I probably threw 150, 160 pitches to strike out [nineteen].

But this game, I pitched a one-hitter against the Giants. Chris Speier leads off with a double down the line. Somehow he got thrown out, either going to third on an infield grounder or he got thrown out at home, I forget which it was. I retired the next twenty-seven guys in a row. I threw 102 pitches and struck out fourteen. It was just a phenomenal amount of strikes.

Usually a game where you have high strikeouts the pitch count is high, too. Guys pitch lower amounts of balls, but they don't strike a lot of guys out, they get ground balls. It was just such an economy of pitches and so many strikeouts. To face twenty-eight batters . . . actually I only faced twenty-seven batters because we got Speier out, but I did give up one hit. It was almost a perfect game scenario, twenty-seven batters. That really stands out. We weren't really aware of pitch counts and those things back then, but when I found out how few pitches I threw and having that many strikeouts that's pretty neat, for the economy of strikes I threw that day and how few batters I had faced.

I forget the score—I don't know if I won that one 1 or 2 to nothing. It was just such a breeze. The game went quickly, it was over obviously in less than two hours, and all the strikeouts and how everything just flowed so well. It was typical Candlestick, cold and windy. I don't know if it was a night game or not. At Candlestick it's always cold, so I don't know if you're paying attention to whether the lights are on or not. It's really funny I can't remember that—I was really focused, I guess.

I thought just the way there were so few pitches and to have such dynamics with it, I thought that was pretty cool. . . .

But yeah, postseason play, that's great too, but where you put it in the context. In postseason play, even though we won the World Series, I didn't really have an outstanding game, a memorable game.

The overall picture is very memorable, but as far as your own self-performance, there was never really anything outstanding. We won, but we didn't win in any great fashion—the whole event is memorable, but not the specifics of it.

I think the S. Ray Hickock Award as the most outstanding athlete of the year is the most memorable award. So you're up against the whole field of athletes. In 1972 I won the S. Ray Hickock Award along with the Cy Young. The S. Ray, you're out of your own particular sport, you're across the board of all the sports. I think a jockey won it one year, Ali has won it in the past, so it's that sort of award that encompasses all of the particular sports, that's why it makes it more outstanding. You're against all the spectacular years that people have. I think in 1972 Mark Spitz was right there, too.

The S. Ray Hickock was probably the most prestigious award. The award itself is beautiful, but when you find out what you're up against to win it, it's a really special feeling.

The Hall of Fame is obviously very special, too. Obviously anyone who gets elected into the Hall . . . but that's a post kind of thing, and I thought this was more or less about during your career. That's the culmination of a lot of things—that's obviously very special. I think anybody you ask would probably have that same response. I went in with Scooter, Rizzuto, and Durocher was elected that year, too. It was great. . . .

Those are the two games that really stand out in my mind. There's some other moments, but I don't think the caliber, that special feeling you have, matches up to those two events.

JOE CARTER

© MIKE RUCKI

Up until Saturday night, October 23, 1993, Joe Carter was known as one of baseball's more underrated stars, a power-hitting outfielder from Oklahoma with a penchant for driving in 100 runs on an almost annual basis. Carter came up with the Cubs, then made his mark after being traded to the Cleveland Indians before a one-year stopover in the National League with the San Diego Padres.

He subsequently signed as a free agent with the Toronto Blue Jays and was an integral part of Canada's first championship team when the Jays beat the Braves in 1992.

But the best, as they say, was yet to come. In the sixth game of the 1993 World Series against the Philadelphia Phillies, ahead three games to two, Carter got to live the dream of every boy who grows up following the game: he won the last game of the Series with a home run in his team's final at-bat.

The thing about the Series [up until that point] is that we'd come out on top—we were ahead three games to two. I'd had a home run and three sacrifice flies, so I wasn't having a bad series, but I wasn't having a great series either. . . . It was guys like [Paul] Molitor who were hitting the ball really well. [Juan] Guzman pitched well, [Pat] Hentgen pitched well—they were pretty much doing the job along with Molitor and Rickey Henderson—those guys were the ones that were excelling. A guy would get on third base, I'd get a sacrifice fly to get him in—just doing the simple stuff, but really nothing spectacular.

I had a couple of errors, but they were tough errors. [Darren] Daulton hit me a line drive the first game in Toronto that short-hopped on me, and I got handcuffed in the outfield. In Philly I got one when I was going down the line on a double by John Kruk, and with the wet turf and everything I just couldn't get there in time. It ended up hitting off my glove, but it would have been tough even if I'd been able to get to it to hold him to a single. They were questionable, but that's neither here nor there. The good thing is that the last one didn't lead to any runs, because Hentgen struck out the last two guys [in Game 2] with the bases loaded to end the first inning.

The thing I remember the most is when I woke up I was telling my wife that I didn't know what it was, but something was going to happen in threes, the number three. That was a vision or a dream I had—that I hadn't done too much in the World Series, but that this was going to be my day. When I first saw a three I thought of Reggie Jackson, with the three home runs in the World Series, that's what I was thinking about. When I thought of threes I thought of three home runs.

We had lunch, and as I went to the ballpark it was around 3 o'clock—I went to the ballpark a little bit early. My mom and dad were there, [along with] my father-in-law, and my sister was there, and I remember distinctly telling them that, hey, watch out tonight, that we were going to win it tonight, and that something great's going to happen, I'm going to do something great tonight.

When I got to the ballpark, I was pumped up. Today was going to be the day that we were going to win the whole thing. I had told Darnell Coles, Dave Stewart, Rickey Henderson. I said, "Hey, I got my saddle on. You guys hop on. Today's gonna be the day." I distinctly told them that.

My first at-bat—we came up in the bottom of the first inning, they didn't score—and Molly [Molitor] hits a triple that knocks in a run, I think Devo [Devon White] was on base. I came up the first at-bat and hit a long sacrifice fly to make it 2–0. Then Olerud gets a base hit, and Robby [Alomar] gets a double to drive in Olerud, so we're up 3–0. Right then and there, that's exactly when it hit me—we got the three runs there in the bottom of the first to put the pressure on them.

So I'm in right field, and there weren't too many balls being hit to me, so I was basically just jogging in and out. The next couple of at-bats, I can't even remember what I did. We got shut down there, and Molitor's home run in, I think it was the fourth or fifth inning, made it a 4–1 or 5–1 ball game. We pretty much felt we were in the driver's seat, we were cruisin'. There wasn't gonna be any need for any kind of dramatics or anything.

Then Dykstra came to the plate in the seventh inning, I believe, and he hit a three-run homer. And then it was like, uh-oh, we kind of counted our eggs too quickly. Stewart was pitching that day, and he had won all of those games in the ALCS. In the World Series it was back and forth, up and down, but he had still pitched well for us. He gave up the three-run homer to Dykstra, but we just needed to settle down—we were still up by a run—it made it 5–4.

And then Danny Cox came in, and the doors just opened up. Mariano Duncan hit a high chopper over the mound, they ended up loading the bases. [Pete] Incaviglia gets a sac fly off of Al Leiter, and when he came up I think the game was tied, and I was thinking, "Hey, this is a good guy to strike out. We need a strike out right here. He doesn't handle the high stuff too well, he's a low-ball hitter." The first pitch is a fastball down and in, and he hits a fly ball to center field—I can't remember if that tied the game up or if they got another run to go up 6–5 after they loaded the bases up.

So we're coming into the eighth inning, and we knew we needed get it going even though we didn't score. I think I had made the last out in the seventh inning, or close to it, and I wasn't sure I was going to come up. But we loaded the bases up in the eighth, and Pat Borders came up against Larry Anderson, and he pops it up with two outs. We were a little dejected because we had our chances, but we just looked at each other at said, "Hey, we've got Rickey leading off." So the main thing is to go out there and have Leiter hold the guys down, and Leiter shuts them down in the ninth.

All of a sudden I'm in the outfield thinking, "Look, the first World Series [against Atlanta in 1992] ended with me, in Chicago [during the 1993 ALCS] the last out was to me," and I said, "It's gonna happen, something's gonna happen." I thought about winning it defensively, but then we got behind, and I said to myself, "You can't do it that way, with the last out coming to me, so I'm gonna do it with the bat."

I was fourth up, and I hadn't been on base. In the pictures of my home run I have a huge dirt spot on the back of my leg, and I was trying to figure out how I got that, because I wasn't on base at all in that game—I hit a sac fly and I was 0 for 2 after that. But I remembered where I got it from—I was sitting down on the steps that last inning, and Rickey was hitting, and I was waiting, and that's where all the dirt was. Mitch Williams comes in, and I hadn't faced him in the playoffs. I hadn't faced Mitch since his days with Texas, which was three, four, five years ago. I knew that he had thrown the ball well for Philadelphia, but I knew he didn't have the velocity he had early in the season, mainly because he was pretty much tired.

October 23, 1993

PHILADELPHIA	AB	R	H	RBI	TORONTO	AB	R	H	RBI
Dykstra, cf	3	1	1	3	Henderson, lf	4	1	0	0
Duncan, dh	5	1	1	0	White, cf	4	1	0	0
Kruk, 1b	3	0	0	0	Molitor, dh	5	3	3	2
Hollins, 3b	5	1	1	1	Carter, rf	4	1	1	4
Batiste, 3b	0	0	0	0	Olerud, 1b	3	1	1	0
Daulton, c	4	1	1	0	Griffin, pr–3b	0	0	0	0
Eisenreich, rf	5	0	2	1	Alomar, 2b	4	1	3	1
Thompson, lf	3	0	0	0	Fernandez, ss	3	0	0	0
Incaviglia, ph–lf	0	0	0	1	Sprague, 3b–1b	2	0	0	1
Stocker, ss	3	1	0	0	Borders, c	4	0	2	0
Morandini, 2b	4	1	1	0					
Totals	35	6	7	6	Totals	33	8	10	8

Philadelphia	000	100	500 — 6
Toronto	300	110	003 — 8

I told the boys when Mitch came walkin' through the gates, "This is it boys, something's gonna happen." Sure enough, after the first pitch Rickey calls time out, steps out, and Mitch is looking, he winds up, fakes a throw to first, then to home. The umpire went to the right, Rickey went to the left, and Mitch is holding the ball there, and there was just something about that. Rickey got on—and I knew he was gonna get on—he didn't even swing the bat [Henderson walked].

Devo works the count 3 and 2, cuts his swing down, and he pops up—a fly ball to left center field. And then up came Molly. Usually Rickey would have stolen second, but Mitch has a pretty good move. He had to stay there—he didn't want to make a senseless out with the top of the order coming up.

Molly had had a great series. This was his second series, but it was the first time he really had a chance to win it. . . . He gets a 1–1 pitch—I think he threw him a fastball down and in—and he hit a little short fly ball to left-center field for a base hit. And so here I come.

I'm looking for my strength, which is down and in, and I know he's gonna throw me fastballs. One thing I wanted to do was relax, because your nerves are pumped up, and the main thing I like to do to relax the best is to take until I get a strike. Usually, you think, "Hey, I'm going up here with a chance to win the ball game," but I was never thinking home run. I never thought about the home run, it was more or less just get a base hit and keep the inning going and everything. We've got one out. I wanted to put the ball in play somehow. I said to myself, "Don't hit into a double play and hope we can get a base hit to drive Rickey in," and I know there's still a chance Rickey can steal third base.

The first pitch he throws me a fastball for a ball—I'm taking all the way. The next pitch is a fastball away—ball two. So I said to myself, "There's no way I'm going to swing. A walk is as good as a hit right now, and with his control you never know." Sure enough, the 2–0 fastball is right down the middle of the plate. It always happens that way. When you take it, it's down the middle. If you say, "I'm gonna give it a good pass," then it's down in the dirt, or it's a bad pitch. Throughout the season I rarely swung on 2–0, and I was geared up for the fastball, but most of the time I'm really aggressive in that area of the count. It was a big game, the World Series, and I wanted to put the pressure on him to make him throw me a strike, because then he'd have to come back and throw me two more.

Now I'm looking for my pitch, a pitch I can drive. Mickey

Morandini moved over toward second base—they were really worried about keeping Rickey close at second so he wouldn't steal third—a sac fly would score the run and tie the game up. When he moved over he got right in the path of the pitcher. The way Mitch delivered the ball, he was right where the ball would be delivered, and I don't like when umpires stand there—if it's left-handed I want the umpire on the shortstop side because I don't like all that interference right there.

He threw me a slider that I lost completely. I saw it and thought it was a fastball, and I was swinging and I had committed, and it was a slider that was low in the dirt, and I looked really bad on it. So I kind of hit myself in the head, and I thought that if he throws that pitch again I've gotta be ready for it and bear down and at least pick up the ball. So I was looking for the same pitch, the slider, and I'm thinking, "Base hit, just put the ball in play, not a double play ball. If you strike out you strike out—you've still got one more out." I knew that if he throws that pitch again, it's gonna be a tough pitch to hit.

So he winds up, and I'm looking slider, and he does something that he had never done before—he gives me a slide step. Usually he's got a high leg kick, and when he does that he's got a little more velocity on the ball, but he gave a slide step because he's worried about Rickey stealing. When he did the slide step he threw me a fastball down and in that I thought was a hard slider because it cut down and in on me. Here I am thinking slider—and if I'm thinking fastball like I normally do a lot of times I'm gonna hook the ball way foul, because it was in my zone right where I hook it foul, and to this day I don't know how I even kept the ball fair, because I've hooked a lot of balls way foul throughout my career—because I was looking for the slider my hands were more relaxed, and I was looking to drive the ball up the middle.

I wanted to stay on the ball. Mitch didn't have that great control—he could walk you and throw four balls away or throw three balls on the inside corner for strike three, you just never know—so in that situation I'm always gonna look for my strength. I can't afford to expand my zone for him, because then I could swing at anything. So my idea was to swing at a good pitch that was in the zone, and after that one bad pitch I was really concentrating. . . .

He threw the fastball down and in, and it was all reaction. I've watched the replay so many times. Because I was looking for a slider I kept my head down, and when I hit it I knew it was a fastball—a very good pitch, it wasn't a bad pitch on his part. It just happened to be in my zone, down and in, and when I hit it, I had my head down. I saw the ball hit off my bat, and I faltered, and then I raised up and looked. I never saw the ball because of the lights—I immediately saw the bank of lights—and watching the replay, Daulton shields his face with his glove because he can't see the ball either.

So I didn't know how hard it was hit. I knew I hit it good; I didn't know if it would get out of the park because it had a lot of topspin on it. So I take one, two, three steps, and I look up and I see Pete Incaviglia, and he's running back to the wall, and all of a sudden I see him slow down. That's when I caught the flight of the ball, and I saw it hooking down, and once the ball went over the fence I literally jumped as high as I could. I had to stop because I wanted to make sure I touched first base, because I was halfway in the air when it landed and as I came down I altered my steps. It was almost like long jumping, I almost came to a complete stop to make sure I touched first base.

My helmet came off, and as I'm rounding the bases the first thing I thought was that this can't be true. You look around, and you see the fans jumping up, yelling. I saw my teammates come out of the dugout, jumping up, yelling, screaming, and high-fiving everybody and jumping into each other's arms, and I'm looking around like I'm waiting for something else to happen.

I touched second base, and I remember thinking, "Man, this really happened. I hit a home run to win the World Series." And I said, "Man, if I could do cartwheels . . ." I would have done cartwheels all around the bases.

As I got to third base I jumped up and gave Nick Leyva, our third base coach, a high-five, and I can remember coming to home plate, and Jack Morris was the first guy that I saw. I gave him five as I ran by. Pat Borders was there, and then Woody Williams. There was a helmet down around home plate, and Woody was picking it up so I wouldn't trip over it, and when I touched home plate I had a head rush.

Everyone clobbered me, and I went down. You try and fight it, but my legs got weak. It was a very teary-eyed moment; you could never imagine what it was like. When they got me up off the ground Tony Fernandez was the last guy in the pile—I think Guzman was on top of me—and then Tony Fernandez finally picked me up and everything. And then Danny Cox and I believe it was Al Leiter put me on their shoulders. As I looked up, I thought about what had just happened, and then I thought about the threes right then and there, and I said, "Wow, it was a three-run homer." And then I lifted up my head and said, "Thank you Jesus," and I pointed towards Him to acknowledge Him, "Thank you, Lord."

Then I kind of pointed into the stands toward where my wife was sitting, because of what she had been through. The wives were all sitting up there just holding hands whenever one of their husbands came up. She always tells me she gets very nervous whenever I come up. She didn't want me to make the last out. She didn't mind when I hit the home run, she just didn't want me to make the last out. All that flashed through my mind, how she was feeling also.

It is true what people say—that you don't know how big a moment it is until you're away from it. When it happened, it was great. They carried me off the field. I went into the locker room, and the TV announcers were there, and they gave us the World Series trophy, and all of a sudden they whipped me down to the interview room, and I'm talking about it, and I'm exhausted and everything. I come back, and I'm ready to celebrate, and there's nobody in the clubhouse. I didn't get to pour champagne on anybody. All the families had moved to our eating area, and I was like, "Where'd everybody go? There's supposed be a celebration!" We just missed everything.

The first one [championship] in Atlanta, we had so much fun. After the game we went back to the hotel. We had a party at the hotel. They had everything you could believe. They put it on in the spur of the moment, but it was a festival, it seemed fitting. In Toronto, we couldn't go out and party with the crowd. We couldn't go out in the streets. We probably would have got mobbed, so we were more or less confined.

In Atlanta, we had a lot of fans right at the hotel. They all came down—there was probably about two or three thousand people in the hotel—and we had the ballroom down there. I can remember Winfield up there, singing and dancing; Olerud's up there. Everybody had a great time. . . . We had such a good time that a few guys like David Cone missed the plane the next day. That was probably the most fun, the most excitement we had of the two championships.

Winning in Toronto we couldn't go out and really celebrate. It was like, "OK, we won it, it's over, now what do we do?" Everybody went to their houses and that was about it until we had the parade the next day. In that sense, winning on the road was probably better for us than winning in Toronto, but we couldn't have picked a better way to win it—the way we did, with the home run—and that can never be taken away. That excitement will live on for a long time to come.

So I went upstairs, and they had a little dinner for us after the game, and it was more like a relief. Everybody was just cool and calm, like it really hadn't sunk in. I got home at four or five o'clock that morning, and I had to do an interview at seven o'clock in the morning for "Good Morning America." It really wasn't until I got home . . . My neighbors had somehow got a hold of my garage door opener, and they put blue and white balloons in there. They cut "29" [Carter's number] into the yard with a lawnmower; they had signs up and everything. They did all of that very quickly, because I came home the next day.

It started to sink in then, but when it really sunk in was when I got the tapes, when I could sit back and watch the World Series videos. CBS sent me a tape from about twenty different angles—hitting the home run, showing my teammates, Alfredo Griffin behind me, the fans. That was probably the most touching moment, because in a team game you always want to come through.

And for that one time I could feel them pulling for me. And they showed me hitting the ball, and they immediately showed Devon White, Borders, Olerud, Darnell Coles, and they run out and they're jumping up and down. And watching the fans hugging and kissing one another—people who'd never even seen each other. I was watching the kind of excitement it caused in Toronto and the disappointment of the Phillies fans.

That was probably more special to me than me rounding the bases and the moment I hit the ball, the way it all turned out. I mean, it was . . . a picture's worth a thousand words.

I know that it will always be replayed everywhere. When you think about World Series, it's only happened twice before. The first year it happened was the year I was born. [Editor's note: During the 1960 World Series, Bill Mazeroski's home run powered the Pirates over the Yankees in the ninth inning of Game 7.] You think about it, and I remember watching the World Series last year—watching and wondering if it can happen again. But then I said "Nah, it won't happen for another thirty or forty years." It's amazing that it's only happened twice. It's something special. I'm thankful to God that I was chosen to do that, but it was the accumulation of a lot of team effort. I was just in the right spot at the right time, and I happened to come through.

I'd like to be remembered not only for hitting the home run, but it gave people a better insight as to what I've done throughout my career, the consistency I've had, playing every day. I don't really miss any games unless I'm really hurt, and there are times when I'm really hurt that I still play. Every year I drive in 100 RBIs—I'm almost close to averaging a hundred RBIs for my whole career. Things like that are very important to me—hitting 300 home runs, 2,000 hits. The one way that I would like to be remembered by the fans, my peers, is as a guy that had a lot of fun, who didn't complain about anything, who was consistent and always thought about his team first, and played the game as hard as he could. That's the way I want to be remembered.

WILL CLARK

PF SPORTS IMAGES

Will Clark has provided more than his share of thrills for fans in San Francisco and Texas, but his own biggest day was his debut against the Houston Astros in 1986.

My first big league at-bat, first big league day. Everything was completely new. I had come from A ball, and the first guy we're facing on Opening Day in 1986 is Nolan Ryan. I've got all my family there—it's in Houston.

I walk up to the plate, you know. Here's Nolan Ryan, "The Express," throws the fastball. First pitch he threw me was a curveball. So I started laughing, giggling a little bit when I backed out of the batter's box. It was a strike.

The next pitch was a fastball for a ball. The next pitch was a fastball that I hit out over the center field fence. When I hit it, I didn't know it was gone, but I just kept going and going and going. I was running, thinking, "Double." I don't ever stop . . . that's not my ball game. I was taught "don't do that."

You know when they're gone, but that one right there you didn't know, because center field in the Astrodome, that's a long way . . . Well, it used to be a long way. And after it went over the fence, I remember . . . I don't even remember touching second or third, because I was just in a state of euphoria. Touched home plate, came back toward the dugout, pointed toward my parents, and that was it.

April 8, 1986

SAN FRANCISCO	AB	R	H	RBI	HOUSTON	AB	R	H	RBI
Gladden, cf	4	0	1	0	Bullock, lf	3	0	0	0
Clark, 1b	4	1	1	1	Pankovits, lf	1	0	0	0
C. Davis, rf	4	1	0	0	Doran, 2b	2	1	0	0
Leonard, lf	4	1	1	2	Walling, 3b	4	0	1	0
C. Brown, 3b	4	1	1	0	G. Davis, 1b	4	1	1	2
Brenly, c	3	2	1	1	Bailey, c	4	0	0	0
Thompson, 2b	3	1	1	0	Bass, rf	4	1	2	0
Uribe, ss	2	0	1	1	Walker, cf	3	0	1	0
Gulden, ph	0	1	0	0	Hatcher, rf	1	0	0	0
Wellman, ss	1	0	0	0	Thon, ss	1	0	0	1
Krukow, p	2	0	0	0	Ryan, p	3	0	0	0
Driessen, ph	0	0	0	0	Calhoun, p	0	0	0	0
Maldonado, ph	1	0	1	3	Garner, ph	1	0	0	0
M. Davis, p	1	0	0	0					
Totals	33	8	8	8	Totals	31	3	5	3

San Francisco	100	110	311 — 8
Houston	210	000	000 — 3

Everybody came up and high-fived me. Crowd was . . . that was a pretty good crowd, that was when Houston was in contention, so it was a pretty memorable moment. I'll never, ever forget that one. . . .

I pick that because it was my first day in the major leagues—it was a pretty good way to break in. Postseason stuff is a lot of fun, but that'll never, ever compare with your first day in the big leagues.

ROGER CLEMENS

Mention Roger Clemens and the 1986 season, and most baseball fans will immediately think of Clemens's twenty-strikeout performance against the Seattle Mariners, a prelude to a storybook season in which he won both the MVP and Cy Young awards in the process of leading the Boston Red Sox to the brink of a World Series victory against the New York Mets.

What few people remember is that going into the 1986 season, Roger Clemens was a major question mark. The twenty-three-year-old phenom had posted a 7–5 record with a 3.29 ERA, and he'd given Red Sox fans a glimpse of the future with seventy-four strikeouts in ninety-eight innings. But Clemens also spent almost a month on the disabled list in midseason, and shortly after being disabled again on August 21st with a sore shoulder, Clemens underwent surgery for a torn rotator cuff on August 30th.

This interview was conducted at Fenway Park in August of the 1996 season, with the Red Sox coming off a division championship and a playoff loss against the Cleveland Indians. No one could have anticipated that a scant few weeks later he would duplicate his historic twenty-strikeout performance in a late September game against the Tigers in Detroit—then leave the Red Sox to sign as a free agent with the Toronto Blue Jays.

I would say that my biggest day would have to be the twenty-strikeout game, but that entire year was just a big spin for me. It went by so fast. Everything continued to happen to me day after day, start after start, from the beginning of '86 on it was just incredible.

I had a lot of expectations. There were a lot of areas where I was really going to have to prove myself, so my expectations were high. But for my teammates there was a big cloud hanging over me, because I was coming off an arm injury. But Dr. Andrews [the Red Sox orthopedic surgeon] said, "You're not gonna have any problem with this." Any surgery for a pitcher is a major thing, but he said, "Yours is fairly minor." He cleaned me out and said, "Your cuff looks good." This is where I was really introduced seriously to arm exercises for my rotator cuff. Basically, I lifted just like I did in football with football weights, and he said, "You're gonna be bigger and stronger than ever, so go get 'em."

So I came through spring training, and I really got beat up pretty good. I knew I had to hold back, and guys were hitting balls that usually don't hit me that well. I don't know that it hurt my confidence as much as it did build theirs. You never want to have a guy get that much of an edge on you. Then, in about my second-to-last start, I decided it was time to go with it.

Anyway, I came out and started from game one. I just spun off fourteen [wins in a row], and everything just started happening. I think the fourth or fifth one in was the twenty-strikeout game in April, and it was just an incredible scenario. I remember that day I got up, Deb fixed me breakfast, and we were always real active—I think that day I think we went and just hit the tennis ball around. Our first [son] was on the way. If you're talking about a big day, [Koby's birth] was probably the biggest day I ever had—forget anything about playing sports.

I was real conscious of the injury. I kept switching back from right arm to left when we were playing tennis; I just started messing around. Then on the way in we got caught in traffic. I usually get to the park about two-and-a-half hours before the game, but there was something going on around Boston Common. I thought it was no big deal because I was within two miles of the park, but then we only went one or two car lengths in twenty minutes.

So now the heart rate starts pounding a little bit, and I start panicking. My pitching coach at the time was Bill Fischer. I started looking down at my watch, and the game started at 7:35, and I usually warm up at 7:10, and it's about 6:40. So now I'm panicking. I pulled up on the curb, and as I pulled my car up onto the curb, Deb was gonna get over and drive to the park. I took my boots off—I had some jeans and some cowboy boots on—I took them off and got some running shoes on out of the trunk and proceeded to get ready to take off.

Right after I got my stuff on . . . a motorcycle policeman pulled up and said, "What are you doing? You know your car's on the curb?" And he looked at me, and he did a double take, and he goes, "Aren't you . . . ?," and I go, "Yeah, I am, but I'm not gonna be if I don't get to the park." And he says, "Follow me," and basically splits the sea like Moses and drove us right up into the ballpark.

I jumped out, came into the clubhouse at five after seven. They were within minutes of naming a new starter. Everybody was panicking. All eyes turned on me—it was like an E. F. Hutton commercial when I flew through that metal door. I was already lathered because I was a nervous wreck. I threw my uniform on and did a couple of stretches here and there, and then I was in the bullpen warming up.

I had nothing in the bullpen. I don't know if I threw a strike. I was all over the place. My heart was still racing. Basically, I felt like I was doing quantity instead of quality in my warmup, just to get my arm loose. Every time I bent over to pick up dirt or the resin bag I had the worst headache in my temple, I mean my head was just splitting.

So I came in and got a drink of water and ran out there and here we go. I think the second pitch of the game I threw right at

Spike Owen's head, and Spike just went crazy. He was yelling at me, you know, "What are you doing?"

After that it just started happening. When I see the film of it today, it's still just an unbelievable feeling. It seemed like it happened so fast. It was similar to a no-hit game in that nobody was talking to me after about the fourth inning. Geddy's [catcher Rich Gedman] comment was that he never caught a game where there was no such thing as a ball—they were all swinging and missing. [The plate umpire] Vic Voltaggio, he got into it. He said he'd never seen that type of command. He said that he even had to ice his arm down he was calling so many strikes.

Mike Moore for Seattle was matching me pitch for pitch, he was pitching a great game against me. The biggest moment was late in the game—I don't remember what inning, but I know I was trailing. I realized I had a lot of strikeouts, and I knew I was coming up on a Red Sox record when I was in the teens somewhere, and I got a 3–2 count against Gorman Thomas. I remember that was one of the ones where I was really trying to strike him out, and it caught up with me. He hit the ball into the center field bleachers, and I was trailing 1–0. The crowd was extremely loud. I knew we were getting close to something—and then it just got so quiet, like somebody just put a lid right on top of the stadium.

I was upset with that. I came off the mound and got in the dugout, and I fired some stuff around because I got out of my rhythm. Then Donnie Baylor dropped a ball at first base—to this day he says he did it on purpose—that allowed me to strike out Gorman or Dave Henderson, I'm not sure who it was.

The biggest lift I got was when Dewey [Dwight Evans] hit the three-run homer off Mike Moore to put me ahead for good. I remember grabbing Dewey and almost tackling him when he came into the dugout. I have no idea why I did that, sometimes I react differently, but it was just an emotional game, and I had no idea what was about to happen. Nobody would sit with me in the dugout. I wanted to talk to Hursty [pitcher Bruce Hurst] and some of the other guys, but nobody would come near me.

I remember I switched jerseys in the ninth, and Al Nipper was back in the clubhouse. He was pacing up and down, and I said, "What's the deal, man?" He said, "I gotta tell you something," and I said, "What are you talking about?" He said, "I don't think you know, but you've got eighteen strikeouts, you get two or three this inning and you set the all-time record." I said, "What are you talking about?" And he said, "You've already got the Red Sox record. You can tie three Hall of Famers if you blow the ball right by 'em and just get two more. I don't want to mess you up, but . . . ." And I just thought, "Wow."

But I didn't take it out there like I was grinding. I still just kind of floated and let it happen, and I ended up gettin' Spike and Phil Bradley—that's that one right there. [Clemens points at a photo above his locker in the Red Sox clubhouse.] And Geddy and I were so into the game—we won 3–1—that we didn't even think about gettin' the ball. Thank God the next hitter, I think it was Dave Phelps, he hit a ground ball to shortstop, and we got the ball.

Then the guys just started going crazy. On the replay I see Hurst and Oil Can [Boyd] and Nip and Marty [Barrett]. [Steve] Lyons was in center goin' crazy, and everybody's just clappin' and stuff in the dugout. It was incredible. I've talked to Seaver and a couple of the guys that have done it and lost their game with nineteen, and it's amazing just to think that you struck out everybody but seven guys.

April 29, 1986

SEATTLE	AB	R	H	RBI	BOSTON	AB	R	H	RBI
Owen, ss	4	0	1	0	Evans, rf	4	1	2	3
Bradley, lf	4	0	0	0	Boggs, 3b	3	0	0	0
Phelps, 1b	4	0	0	0	Buckner, dh	4	0	2	0
G. Thomas, dh	3	1	1	1	Rice, lf	4	0	1	0
Presley, 3b	3	0	0	0	Baylor, 1b	3	0	1	0
Calderon, rf	3	0	0	0	Stapleton, 1b	0	0	0	0
Tartabull, 2b	3	0	1	0	Gedman, c	4	0	1	0
Henderson, cf	3	0	0	0	Barrett, 2b	3	0	0	0
Yeager, c	2	0	0	0	Lyons, cf	3	1	1	0
Cowens, ph	1	0	0	0	Hoffman, ss	2	0	0	0
Kearney, c	0	0	0	0	Romero, pr–ss	0	1	0	0
Totals	30	1	3	1	Totals	30	3	8	3

Seattle	000	000	100 — 1	
Boston	000	000	30X — 3	

SEATTLE	IP	H	R	ER	BB	SO
Moore, L	7.1	8	3	3	4	4
Young	.1	0	0	0	0	0
Best	.1	0	0	0	0	1
BOSTON	IP	H	R	ER	BB	SO
Clemens, W	9	3	1	1	0	20

But overall I think the biggest stepping stone for me that season and for my career was just to show my teammates that I was healthy, that we could go forward.

When I first thought back to it was at the end of the year. We had the World Series, and it was just incredible, the amount of people that met us at the airport in Boston even though we lost. I think there was about 400,000 down there—the governor, the mayor—they met us at City Hall Plaza.

So I get home, and all the awards from my peers were coming out—The Sporting News Player of the Year and all these kinds of things. Then they hit me with the Cy Young first on a Thursday in November. We expected it, but you still want to see it be unanimous. The way they voted me in and all, to go in with Palmer and people like that was tremendous.

Then the next Thursday I get a phone call. I found that someone was going to be calling me about the MVP. I had no idea. I wasn't even around—I think I was out on the golf course or something—and my heart just stopped. I couldn't believe it, because I knew that as a pitcher I'd done something that was just incredible and awesome. And then the very next Thursday my child was born. So it all just boom, boom, boom, just like that until the day I had Koby.

Having him put everything in perspective, and it still does, all the way from Korey and Kasey and now Kody. So now Deb's saying Koby gets the first Cy Young, Korey's getting the second one, and Kasey gets the third one, so now I need to win another one for Kody. Deb wants the MVP, and basically she is our MVP for living in Boston permanently during the season with me and four boys that drive her crazy. . . .

I guess that would have to be it other than all the other awards, which have been great.

It's like a chain, where the game and the awards are just linked to one another. Every time I go home in my weight room I see the Cy Youngs and the MVP. Shoot, I can't leave out a part of that chain, which is the All Star game in Houston, and that was the same year. If you're talking about one big day—I woke up in my own bed, and pitched in my own city, where I really didn't get a chance to pitch except for my high school All-Star game, and I got slighted for that. So it was just an extra thrill to go there as a professional and win the MVP there.

DAVID CONE

David Cone has won the Cy Young Award, and he's played with teams in both New York and Toronto that won the World Series. But Cone's greatest day in baseball is something we've all done—his first trip to a major league baseball game.

My father took me to a Kansas City Royals game in 1969. I was seven years old, six years old. Lou Piniella was a player for the Royals then . . . Bob Oliver, and Spanky Kirkpatrick . . . It was the first time I'd ever been to a major league baseball game, and it was the first time I'd ever been to [Municipal] Stadium.

I ran down to get Lou Piniella's autograph, and he stopped signing right when I got there. And I never forgot what that felt like, to miss out on an autograph. But nonetheless, I still enjoyed the day, enjoyed the game. The Royals ended up winning that day—Bob Oliver got a big hit late in the game to win the game.

I remember how beautiful the field looked. George Toma was the groundskeeper—he's still one of the best in the world. I remember seeing how green the grass was. This was the old ball park, down off of Brooklyn St., downtown.

I remember that game that day almost like it was yesterday, just the look of the field. It was the first time I'd seen a major league field, ballpark—the green grass, the crack of the bat, and the attempt to get my first autograph, which failed, a failed attempt. I remember my dad teaching me how to keep score, showing me the line-up, how exactly that you keep score. I remember eating popcorn that day. I remember having a Coke. I remember eating a hot dog. Just the simple things that I remember . . . my first experience, I remember that day vividly.

Obviously there's been days when I played that were great days—that was the first one, that's where it all started.

As far as playing days go, obviously the most recent memory is last year: winning the World Series, coming back, down 0–2, pitching Game 3—we won Game 3 to get back into the series—having all my family there at the game. Having gone through what I went through last year, injury-wise with the aneurysm, then coming back and pitching in the World Series.

That night was such an emotional night—to have all my family there, and to come out on top and win that particular game—it
was such a must-win situation. The only comparison I could draw is
my father being there and enjoying that game as much as any game
he's probably ever been to.

Contrastingly, I would say that just going from that first day I
ever went to a ball park, just being totally relaxed and enjoying the
game—to having so much stress, so much pressure, so much relief
after the game was over, for having won the game.

I don't talk a whole lot about that first game with him. Every
now and then we'll mention it. I still remember finally getting a
chance to meet Lou Piniella, and telling him about that experience,
telling him, "No offense, but I hate you. . . . You didn't sign my autograph when I was nine years old." He laughed, we kind of had a
good laugh about it. Of course Lou was my favorite player, a great
guy. I still respect him a lot.

And now, being a major league player, I understand how tough
it is to sign everybody's autograph. You sign a hundred, and you miss
the 101st, and that kid's gonna be disappointed. I have a much better understanding of what goes on in the autograph world now.

I don't know what he'd say if he knew that was my greatest day.
I think he'd be very proud. The reason I go back to it is that it's still
so vivid, so it must be something that really stuck with me all these
years—just the impression it made on me that particular day, just the
influence my father had on me. He was such a sports fanatic. He
introduced me to the game. I'll never forget that. I wouldn't be here
today without him.

He taught me how to pitch as a youngster, that's where it all
started. He was the coach of my Little League team. He would take
me out in the backyard, and he would teach me the mechanics of
throwing a baseball and teach me how to throw strikes. Everything
that a lot of fathers do with their kids at that age.

I owe a lot to him. I'll never forget being introduced to the game
by him, and I'll never forget that day. I'll never forget how bright,
how vivid the green field was. That was a tribute to George Toma,
because he had by far the highest-rated field, playing surface, in the
major leagues, even back then.

I finally had a chance to meet George Toma, and I told him
about that—the old ballpark, how beautiful the grass was, the field.
He's widely respected in the industry as the best groundskeeper. And
even back then, Kansas City was the best ballpark—the most beautiful playing surface in the major leagues.

Going back to Kansas City was probably the other greatest day, my debut for the Royals. Having grown up in Kansas City, and then finally getting a chance to run out on the field and pitch in a major league game, knowing that my father was in the stands. That would be neck-and-neck with that first day that he took me out to the ballpark.

I never thought I would make it to the major leagues. I spent five or six years in the minor leagues, and I never thought I was gonna quite get over the hump. I finally did that day, and I remember the feeling—running out on the field from the bullpen. It was almost as if it was in slow motion. Everything was kind of a blur, it was almost surreal.

I remember getting out on the mound and warming up—my legs were kind of wobbly, I was so nervous . . . knowing that my father was up in the stands watching. I got in trouble, I gave up a run, and then I got out of trouble. It was a decent day. It wasn't a great day, but the thing that stands out was just that trot—from the bullpen to the mound. It was like I was running through water. It was like I was never going to make it through the mound. I'll never forget that feeling.

RYNE DUREN

A rendering of "greatest days" from Yankee players who participated in World Series victories would probably constitute a book in its own right. Former Yankee closer Ryne Duren provided one with his memory of the Yankees triumph in 1958 over a powerful Milwaukee Braves squad.

I pitched the sixth game of the 1958 World Series. I think it was in the fifth inning when I came in . . . Turley relieved me for the last out, and we were really without pitching that day. So I did a hell of a job for 'em.

Finally, I think it was MacDougald that hit the home run to put us up—it was a tie game all the way. MacDougald hit the home run to put us up, and I think they got a run off me in the bottom of the tenth with two out. Turley came in to face Frank Torre—I got up to see him last year in the Series because he was in the hospital getting the heart transplant at the time, and that also was the last time the

October 8, 1958

NEW YORK	AB	R	H	RBI	MILWAUKEE	AB	R	H	RBI
Carey, 3b	5	0	0	0	Schoendienst, 2b	4	1	2	0
McDougald, 2b	5	1	2	1	Logan, ss	2	1	0	0
Bauer, rf	5	1	2	1	Mathews, 3b	5	0	0	0
Mantle, cf	5	1	1	0	Aaron, rf	5	0	3	2
Howard, lf	5	1	2	0	Adcock, 1b	4	0	1	0
Berra, c	4	0	2	1	Mantilla, pr	0	0	0	0
Skowron, 1b	4	0	1	1	Crandall, c	4	0	0	0
Kubek, ss	2	0	0	0	Torre, ph	1	0	0	0
Slaughter, ph	1	0	0	0	Covington, lf	4	1	2	0
Duren, p	2	0	0	0	Pafko, cf	2	0	1	0
Turley, p	0	0	0	0	Bruton, cf	2	0	0	0
Ford, p	1	0	0	0	Spahn, p	4	0	1	1
Ditmar, p	1	0	0	0	McMahon, p	0	0	0	0
Lumoe, ph–ss	1	0	0	0					
Totals	41	4	10	4	Totals	37	3	10	3

New York	100	001	000	2 — 4	
Milwaukee	110	000	000	1 — 3	

NEW YORK	IP	H	R	ER
Ditmar	3.2	2	0	0
Duren, W	4.2	3	1	1
Turley	0.1	0	0	0
MILWAUKEE	IP	H	R	ER
Spahn, L	9.2	9	4	4
McMahon	0.1	1	0	0
Ford, 1.	1	5	2	2

Yankees played the Braves in the Series. So anyway, Turley, he got Torre to line out softly to second base.

I didn't make an appearance in the seventh game. Turley was the MVP of the Series. Had I gotten Torre out, they may have had to give it to me. I saved a game before that, and I probably pitched more innings in that Series than Wetteland did in the entire season.

And then there was another day, 1961. They traded me to the Angels, and as soon as the Yankees came to town again I had the ball. In fact, I got a hit off of Turley—we were losing 1–0, bottom of the sixth, two out, and Rigney let me hit, and I got a hit off him. Then Albie Pearson followed it with a home run, and I was the winning pitcher. I pitched eight innings, I think, and struck out twelve and gave up three hits. So I remember that.

But I don't know how many times I walked out there—like one night in Chicago I struck out eight out of nine guys, and many times I can remember coming in to relieve and I would strike out the side. Then I was in Boston, and I set the American League strikeout record. For a while I had it at seven in a row, until a rookie by the name of Yazstremski broke up the streak.

From another standpoint . . . I now had been around, '57 they sent me to Denver [Triple AAA]. And I went out to Denver, and my very first start in pinstripes I pitched a no-hitter. And it was the only no-hitter that had ever been pitched in Denver, and it stayed that way until last year when Nomo of the Dodgers threw his no-hitter in the new stadium.

So that had to be another great day, and I didn't realize how great it was, because it was my first start. I didn't know about the Denver air, how high that was, and how significant that was. So I guess you can take your choice of any of those things.

But now they didn't bring me up at the end of the year. Bob Halsam said they'd have had a riot in Denver had they taken me out of there. I lost twice, 1–0, and I was 13–2, and I saved a lot of games. They wanted to bring me up, but they just figured they couldn't take me out of Denver, and they brought up Sal Maglie instead.

Now, the next spring I made the club. I guess I was a shoo–in cinch. And now we're coming out to Yankee Stadium, and I see the Stadium. I'd been there before and seen the Stadium, but now I'm a New York Yankee, and you have to pause and say, "I'm a member of the New York Yankees." Emotionally, I think that may have been my greatest moment.

CECIL FIELDER

Of all the dominant power hitters who have played the game, few have had a more unique career than Cecil Fielder. After an abundance of talent made him the proverbial "odd man out" early in his career with the Toronto Blue Jays, Fielder played in Japan for several years before excelling for the Detroit Tigers. He got his first World Series ring in 1996 with the New York Yankees.

Game 6, we all got to run around and jump on top of each other, and just seeing the way New York reacted to having a World Series champ, that was the ultimate day. Being in baseball for as long as I have, and not really getting the opportunity to play in the post-season, and then to get that opportunity, and it goes the way you expect it to go.

Every day was a rush, being in the World Series. It was kind of tiring because of the fact that it was every day. You came to the ball-park, and you understood what was on the line. That whole scenario was probably my biggest moment in baseball.

It was a tense situation for us from the jump. We get off to an 0–2 start against the best pitching staff in baseball, and then to be able to go to Atlanta and turn in spades what they had done to us at our ballpark—we won three there. So I think that gave us a big boost going into Game 6. In a series like that, you don't want to go to Game 7, because in Game 7 anything can happen.

We had O'Neill at third, and Joe Girardi came up and hit a triple, and I think everybody on that bench and everybody in that stadium knew that we were gonna do this. It was just very emotional just knowing that—alright, you finally get the opportunity to do something very special that not everybody in the game gets the opportunity to do. I got the opportunity and I made the best of the opportunity.

I think during the whole World Series I hit every day. I hit almost .400 in the series. But I think the turning point was when we had Charlie Hayes on third base against John Smoltz down in Atlanta [in Game 5], and I hit the double to drive in the only run of the game. I think that was large. You had two pitchers out there, Pettite and Smoltz, just battling it out—you know, 1–0 ball game 'til the end.

I think for me, that was the turning point for us as a team. But personally that was a good feeling, knowing, "Hey, I got an oppor-tunity to drive a man home, and I was able to do it." I think by the time I came up that time I was already 2 for 2 against John—and you know John, he's coming at you—so I knew he was gonna try to come at me and get ahead of me right away. He threw a couple of pitches out of the strike zone, and then he had to come in with the fastball, and I hit the ball down the left field line for a double.

I just, for some reason, I don't know what it was, maybe it was determination—it was just the fact that I just felt great at the plate. I wanted to get that done. In that situation, with a man on third base and less than two outs, you know, you can't leave it up to the next man to get it done, you gotta do it yourself. I was the man up at that time. I got it done, and we won.

I don't know what it was about me and Smoltzie during the series. The first game, he pretty much handled us in New York. I just think that up 'til that point, we had sat around for so many days waiting for the series to start that they had the advantage coming into that series, because they'd just come from St. Louis [in the NLCS]. They were hot. They scored thirty runs in two games and then came to our place and scored a lot of runs. . . .

I felt good about going to Atlanta. I didn't feel like we were gonna be able to go in there and win three games, but I felt good about we were gonna make it back home. That's what everybody was thinking about . . . just winning two ball games and coming home and having a chance to beat 'em in our own ballpark.

[For box score, please see interview with Wade Boggs.]

ROLLIE FINGERS

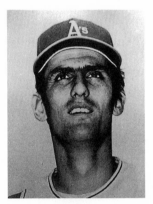

As the first closer to go into the Hall of Fame, Rollie Fingers's place in baseball history is secure. One of the great clutch pitchers of all time, Fingers helped lead the Oakland Athletics to three consecutive World Series victories in the early '70s, before copping the Cy Young Award as well near the end of his illustrious career with the Milwaukee Brewers.

I would probably have to say getting Pete Rose to fly out to Joe Rudi in left field for the final out of the '72 World Series. I'd come in the inning before with Johnny Bench up, and I think there was two outs, maybe it was one, I can't remember exactly. I ended up intentionally walking Johnny Bench, and then I ended up getting out of the inning. I think I got Denis Menke to pop-up to Campaneris for the final out of the eighth inning.

Going out into the ninth inning—this was the first World Series, so I was a little bit nervous, especially in the seventh game with a 3–2 lead in Cincinnati. The first guy hit a little soft pop-up to Bert Campaneris for the first out. The second out—I believe Dave Concepcion hit a ground ball to Dick Green for the second out.

And then they pinch hit for somebody—I don't know who it was, but they pinch hit a lefthander, and I hit him in the foot and put the winning run at the plate with Pete Rose. And at that time, Dick Williams came out of the dugout to the mound. He had Vida Blue warming up in the bullpen, and I think he wanted Pete Rose to hit right-handed instead of left-handed.

And Dave Duncan, our catcher, met Dick Williams at the foul line and told Dick to leave me in. This was before he made a motion to the bullpen. So Dick finally got to the mound, and he told me, "Look, I'll let you pitch to Pete, and I want you just to keep the ball away from him. Don't give him anything to pull. If he hits the ball to left field, fine."

I said, "OK," and the first pitch was a fastball, up and away, and he hit a nice little lazy fly ball out to Joe Rudi in left field for the final out.

It was kind of one of those things where when you're a kid, you dream of being on the mound, last game of a seventh game of the World Series, and getting the final out, that was like a dream come true.

I was just hoping, "Joe, don't drop it." That was all I was thinking, "Don't drop it." And then once it hit in his glove—it's like someone's taken an anvil off your shoulders. You've kind of gotta be there.

I can't remember how many times I faced Rose. I know I only faced him in the World Series. I pitched about twelve innings in the series, so I'm sure I faced him a few times. He got a hit off me in Game 5 and beat me—a fastball in for a base hit over second base—and they ended up winning the ball game 5–4. But prior to that I can't remember. I'm sure I got him out somewhere along the line.

I remember afterward, there are people jumping all over you. I remember Dave Duncan getting to me first and grabbing me, and then Sal Bando jumping on top of me, and by that time the whole dugout was on top of me. It was a lot of fun. . . .

I think that helped me out for a lot of reasons, especially for the rest of my career, because I was thrown into a seventh game of a World Series and pitched in six games at a young age. And so everything after that was kind of ho-hum . . . I mean, how can you top that?

Even the following years, '73 and '74, you know, the pressure really wasn't that bad as it was the first year. So after going through it and being able to be successful, it just became old hat.

In terms of the Milwaukee years, it was probably striking out Lou Whitaker to get us into the playoffs. It was the next to the last day of the season, and we had to win, and I came in in the eighth inning with two outs. I got a fly ball to get out of the inning. We were ahead 2–1. And then in the next inning I got a fly ball to left field, then struck out Champ Summers, and then I struck out Lou Whitaker, so that was another big celebration.

It was pretty close to the other day, but not as great—seventh game of the World Series is the ultimate.

I was on my way out of baseball, I thought, because I was a starting pitcher in 1971, and Dick Williams had seen enough of me as a starter. He put me down in the bullpen, and we were playing the Yankees in New York, and we were getting beat like 11–2 or something, and by the eighth inning we were all of a sudden ahead like 13–11, and I was the only guy left in the bullpen.

Dick had to bring me in, and so he brought me in, and I pitched two great innings, got a save. The next night, same situation. We were up by a run, I came in, pitched another inning, got another save. So he called me in and said, "From now on, in game situations, you're gonna be my short man." And I said, "Great," because I was getting to the point in my career where I was gonna be either in long relief or back to the minors. That's where I was at. That kind of saved me.

I had the type of arm where I could go out and throw one or two innings every day—more or less a rubber arm. It didn't bother me. I didn't get stiff real easy. I usually iced after I pitched, so I still felt strong the next day. I think there was one point in my career where I pitched in nine straight ball games.

So I was able to do that, and I also liked the idea of being able to come to the ballpark with an opportunity to get in the game. I hated starting and getting knocked out in the second inning and then waiting four more days to get knocked out in the second inning again. I think being a relief pitcher, I was more adapted to that.

Receiving the Cy Young and the MVP in '81 would be the greatest day as far as awards. That year was one of those dream years where you just kind of throw your glove out there, and you can't do nothing wrong. I won the Cy Young, the MVP, the Fireman of the Year, made the All-Star team—the whole nine yards. I remember going to the banquet and receiving the award, making a little acceptance speech.

There had never been a relief pitcher in the Hall of Fame, so I had no idea what the sportswriters would look at as far as statistics. I didn't know if I had the credentials and the stats to get in, and when I retired in '85 I really didn't even think about it. I didn't think I'd get as many votes as I did on the ballot. And I think about a year before I got on the ballot, sportswriters started asking me what I thought about going into the Hall of Fame, and I never even thought about it up until that point, because I had nothing to guage my statistics on.

And then in '91 I was on the ballot, and I missed it by about thirty votes, which was a pretty good surprise to me. And then I figured, well, if I missed it by thirty votes this year, maybe there's a better chance next year for me to get in. And then I made it by thirty votes. That's definitely the ultimate for any ballplayer, to get into the Hall of Fame—at least being voted in by the sportswriters, because I think there's only like a hundred of the guys that are in there that have been voted in there by the sportswriters. The rest of them have been by the Executive Committee.

I remember giving speeches . . . You stand up there, and it's very emotional—giving a speech and thanking all the people in your career who had anything to do with getting you into the Hall of Fame, having your family there. It is a very emotional moment, and probably more emotional than any ball game I ever pitched in.

I went in with Tom Seaver and Hal Newhouser. That was a great day, I'd have to pick that one over the World Series greatest day. It's something I wish every ballplayer had the opportunity to experience.

WHITEY FORD

As every sportswriter knows, sometimes players answer a question in the way they refuse to answer a question. That proved to be the case with Yankee great Whitey Ford, who pitched in more World Series games than any other hurler in baseball history.

People have asked me that before, and there's no certain day, or week, and I just don't have an answer for it. I always say that the only thing I remember is that we were in thirteen World Series in my first fifteen years with the team.

Going into the Hall of Fame was great, that was something I kind of expected. It was great going in with Mickey, that was nice, going in the same time as he did. And then they'll say, "Well, what was your favorite game?" And I said, "Well, I have no favorite game or special game. I just like winning World Series."

TOM GLAVINE

When the Atlanta Braves beat the Cleveland Indians in Game 6 of the 1995 World Series in Atlanta to win the Series four games to two, it seemed appropriate that it was a masterful performance from starter Tom Glavine that put them over the top. Not only had Glavine suffered through World Series defeats to the Minnesota Twins and the Toronto Blue Jays with the Braves, he'd also been a member of the clubs that had lost 100 games in consecutive seasons. Glavine compared those days with winning the World Series and copping the Cy Young Award in 1991.

I would have to say my greatest day would probably have to be Game 6 last year [1995] of the World Series. Obviously, first and foremost, winning that game, us becoming world champions, which was something that we had been close to doing but had been very elusive for us for one reason or another. We finally achieved that as a team, and for me to be the guy that went out there and pitched the game—I was ultimately the winning pitcher—it was probably the biggest day in Atlanta Braves franchise history.

It's something that I'll always remember, something I'll always be proud of—both for the performance that I had and for the fact that it was such a strong goal for this team and this organization, and up to that point it had been so hard for us to get.

As far as the day went, I just tried to relax as much as I could, not think about it a whole lot, not put any more pressure on it than there needed to be. I really just spent the day relaxing. I obviously talked to Greg Maddux about what he thought, what kind of adjustments Cleveland may or may not have made in Game 5. I certainly thought that the biggest adjustment that I would hopefully make would be that my stuff was gonna be better in Game 6 than it was in Game 2, and that that would be adjustment enough.

Specifically, it was just consistency and location, control . . . In Game 2, I struggled with my control. I got myself in trouble a lot, and I was fortunate that when I did get in trouble I was able to make good pitches. I just wanted to go into Game 6 and make more good pitches, not get myself into a situation. . . .

So I was hoping that my location was gonna be better and enable me to do that. And I figured it would be, because in Game 2 it had been about ten days or twelve days since I had pitched—it was hard to stay sharp in that period of time. I knew that with getting back in the routine of starting four days later, hopefully everything was gonna be a little bit better, and that's what it turned out to be. I was hoping that that was gonna be a big enough adjustment that I wasn't going to have to go out there and do anything different than what I'd been doing all year long.

Everybody was fairly relaxed, fairly quiet about everything. I remember it being a Saturday. There were a lot of college football games on, guys were watching. Really it wasn't anything out of the ordinary from what we'd been doing all year long. That probably helped enough, the fact that everybody was relaxed enough. The worse thing you can do in that situation is put more pressure on the game, or think you have to do better than you've done all year long, because then you go out there and you try to do those things, and then nine out of ten times you fail.

I felt it in the bullpen, but you don't know coming out of the bullpen how things are ultimately gonna be. I've had times where I've thrown real well in the bullpen and had a bad game, and I've had times where I've thrown poorly in the bullpen and then had a good game. I didn't put a whole lot of stock into it, other than that I knew warming up that I warmed up better than I did for Game 2.

Once I got out on the mound in the first inning, it was just a matter of trying to get as comfortable as I could right away, and really just try[ing] to figure out what kind of stuff I had. I knew right after that first inning that I had good stuff, I had good location.

I didn't do anything a whole lot different. There again I just think in Game 6 I was hitting my spots better, so I was pitching ahead in the count better. I was probably more aggressive. I think the thing you look at in that line-up is that, obviously, whenever Kenny Lofton's leading off an inning you want to keep him off base, not let him utilize his speed.

Then you try to keep Albert Belle out of a situation where he can beat you as much as possible. And even still, if you're in that situation, you've got to get Albert to try and hit your pitch and not anything other than that. I didn't really care if I walked Albert. I was determined that if Albert Belle was gonna hit a home run off me or beat me, it was gonna be on a fastball or a changeup away from him that he's gonna have to hit out to right or to right-center field, and if he's gonna do that, I'll tip my cap to him.

Those are probably the two guys that you really key in on, for those reasons, then you just try and be as aggressive with everybody else and get those other guys out as best you can.

When you're in a tight ball game like that, obviously, it's easier to keep your concentration. You know you can't afford to go out there and have any mental lapses that translate into base hits or home runs, whatever the case may be. Sure, I would have liked to have had a little bit of a cushion to work with, but that wasn't the way it worked. But I kind of knew early on that if I kept my concentration and kept my focus, I had the kind of stuff to win that ball game. It was just a matter of me maintaining that concentration throughout and not having any lapses.

Really, I just remember the chaos of it all after the game ended—people just running everywhere. What a great feeling it was to run out on that mound and jump around with everybody as world champions—the sense of accomplishment, a sense of pride, a sense of relief, all those things. And then once it carries into the clubhouse, it really was kind of hard to totally enjoy yourself because there's so many people in there, there was so much media in there.

That part was almost disappointing, because you go through the year with this group of guys, working so hard to get to where we were, that you kind of think that when you finally do it, we're all gonna be in [the clubhouse] celebrating together. But that wasn't the case, because there were so many other people in there that you hardly got to enjoy it with your teammates.

Eventually we did, everybody started clearing out, it was a little bit more the guys, but by then the celebration had lost a little of its luster. We started to calm down a little bit more and just realize, hey, we just achieved what we wanted to achieve, and we became world champions. But it was still fun. It was great to be able to do all of that in our home ballpark, ultimately, with our own family and friends there.

I think, ultimately, it meant more to those of us who had been around—just from the sense of realizing where we'd come from and how far we'd come. There's a lot of guys in here who were here when we were losing a hundred games a year, guys who had been here when we came close to being world champions—we lost two times. I think any time you go from one extreme of losing a hundred games to being so close to being world champions and losing and then ultimately win it—it's like anything else in life, you appreciate it more because of what you had to put in to get there.

October 28, 1995

CLEVELAND	AB	R	H	RBI	ATLANTA	AB	R	H	RBI
Lofton, cf	4	0	0	0	Grissom, cf	4	0	1	0
Vizquel, ss	3	0	0	0	Lemke, 2b	2	0	1	0
Sorrento, ph	1	0	0	0	Jones, 3b	3	0	2	0
Baerga, 2b	4	0	0	0	McGriff, 1b	4	0	0	0
Belle, lf	1	0	0	0	Justice, rf	2	1	2	1
Murray, 1b	2	0	0	0	Klesko, lf	1	0	0	0
Ramirez, rf	3	0	0	0	Devereaux, lf	1	0	0	0
Embree, p	0	0	0	0	Lopez, c	3	0	0	0
Tavarez, p	0	0	0	0	Belliard, ss	4	0	0	0
Assenmacher, p	0	0	0	0	Glavine, p	3	0	0	0
Thome, 3b	3	0	0	0	Polonia, ph	1	0	0	0
T. Pena, c	3	0	1	0	Wohlers, p	0	0	0	0
Martinez, p	1	0	0	0					
Poole, p	1	0	0	0					
Hill, p	0	0	0	0					
Amaro, rf	1	0	0	0					
Totals	27	0	1	0	Totals	28	1	6	1

```
Cleveland   000   000   000 — 0
Atlanta     000   001   00X — 1
```

CLEVELAND	IP	H	R	ER	BB	SO
Martinez	4.2	4	0	0	5	2
Poole, L	1.1	1	1	1	0	1
Hill	0	1	0	0	0	0
Embree	1	0	0	0	2	0
Tavarez	.2	0	0	0	0	0
Assenmacher	.1	0	0	0	0	1
ATLANTA	IP	H	R	ER	BB	SO
Glavine, W	8	1	0	0	3	8
Wohlers, S	1	0	0	0	0	0

We talked about it a little bit that night. We talk about it more as time goes by, because that's something that a lot of our younger guys will never be able to appreciate probably or hopefully ever go through. I hope we never lose a hundred games around here again. That's something I don't want anybody to go through, but I think there's no question that it gave us a better appreciation for it.

There's not a whole lot of difference between the teams that won and the teams that got close. When it came down to it, we just executed better in the situations where we had to. I think the '91 team was probably the best fundamental team we had here, maybe the least talented, but the best fundamental team. We had an opportunity to win that World Series, Game 7—we had the bases loaded, didn't score, and, ultimately, we lose 1–0.

In '92 we probably got outplayed a little bit by the Blue Jays. We didn't deserve to win that series as much as we did against Minnesota. But even though we finally won against Cleveland, there wasn't a whole lot of difference between us being world champions and us losing. There were some tight games in Colorado that we ended up winning, we swept Cincinnati, and really, the first two games in that series could have gone either way.

I do subscribe to the theory that there's a window of opportunity for a certain group of guys to a certain degree. I subscribe to it because I think in this day and age, as a group, it's harder and harder to keep a talented team together. So from that standpoint you have to wonder how long can they keep this team together, thereby giving us this opportunity year after year to win.

As far as what ultimately boils down to you winning and losing, I don't think there's a whole lot of difference, I really don't. Like I said, it may be a matter of one or two times when you execute as opposed to not executing means you're world champions or it means you lose the World Series and you go home.

Again, I don't think there's that much difference, it's just that last year we made the plays we had to make when we had to make 'em, we scored the key runs when we had to score 'em, and those are the differences in the ball game. In a short series like that, that makes a big, big difference because you don't have a lot of time to recover from the mistakes.

Individual awards, to me, are nice—they mean that you've obviously accomplished something that you set out to do, and that you've done something well—but to me there's nothing like that feeling of being a world champion. I said it in '91—I'd trade my Cy Young award in for a World Championship ring. I meant it at the time. Now that I've got a World Series ring, I probably mean it even more and understand why I said it.

You play this game because you want to be the best at what you do, and in order to do that you've gotta be world champions. Not many people get the opportunity to do that. There are so many great players who played this game who never even got to a playoff game, let alone a world championship. We're all in here obviously on an individual basis, to have good years, because that's what keeps you around, that's what keeps you playing this game for a long time is to do something special individually.

But it's a different feeling, and to me it's a better feeling, to have a group of guys all working toward the same goal. . . . It's just so hard and so rare to be a part of that, that all that hard work from twenty-five guys that came together and made that one goal happen, that one common goal for everybody.

I think that it was just a lot more fun for me than as an individual being able to go out and win twenty games and say, "Hey, look, I won the Cy Young award," because it ultimately left you an empty feeling of not being a world champion.

There's gonna come a point in time where age starts catching up with your skills, and you just can't do the things you want to do, and that's gonna happen. I think the thing that keeps me going is, number one, I'd like to do everything all over again. I'd like to win another Cy Young award just to show that the first one wasn't a fluke. I'd love to win as many world championships as I can, because there's nothing like winning. I don't ever want to go back to losing again, losing a hundred games a year. That wasn't any fun. What we did last year was so much more fun. That keeps me going.

I just think that, for me, I'm the type of person, I always feel like I can do something better, I always feel like I can learn. I guess, ultimately, I just have this tremendous fear of embarrassment . . . I don't ever want to go out there and have a bad game and embarrass myself. That's a fear of mine. It's not any fun to go out there and get embarrassed. . . .

I think I've always been that way. I always wanted to be good at what I do, and a lot of that comes from my parents. They always taught me to work hard and be the best you can be with what you've got, whether that meant being a Cy Young award winner or a fifteen-game winner, or a ten-game winner, whatever the case may be. If that's the extent of your ability, do everything you can to make that happen and get the most out of yourself. Because someday I'm gonna have to look back and say to myself, "Did I give it everything I had? Could I have gotten better? Could I have worked harder?"

I don't want to ever get to the point where that day comes, where I look in the mirror and say, "Well, you could have worked harder," or, "You could have been better." I've always used that fear as a motivator. . . . I think when you try to weed it out you get to the point where it doesn't affect you . . . it depends on how you use it. For me, my fear of embarrassing myself means I'm gonna go out there and work harder and try to make good things happen. At the same time I can't let that fear consume me in that I become tentative—I'm afraid to make mistakes, I'm afraid to throw pitches, that kind of thing.

You have to be relaxed about it, you have to be aggressive, you almost have to get to the point where you confront that fear and say, I'm just not gonna let that happen. If you do that, then you're gonna go out there and be aggressive, you're gonna go out there and trust yourself. But yeah, if you get to the point where you're saying, oh, my God, I don't want to embarrass myself, I gotta be perfect, I gotta do this, I gotta do that, you're gonna make mistakes.

As long as you don't cross that line from being aggressive to being afraid of making mistakes and ultimately embarrass yourself, if you approach it head on and say, I'm gonna be aggressive about this and not let it happen, then you're gonna be OK and you're gonna go out there and do good things.

I think being around these guys and being on this pitching staff made it easier for me and for everybody else to be successful. To a certain extent we coach ourselves, Leo's a great pitching coach, he helps us out a lot. But I think to be truly successful the way you want to be, you have to recognize some things that go wrong out on the mound and be able to make adjustments from pitch to pitch and not have to rely on your pitching coach who's sitting in the dugout to tell you what's going on. Because if you do that, by the time the inning is over, you may have given up four or five runs. You should be able to nip that before it gets to that point.

So I think we all understand ourselves and the adjustments we need to make during the course of a ball game to get the success that we want. Again, being around these guys, it takes a lot of pressure off of you individually to feel like you're the guy that has to go out there and win. Every team has their "ace," and when that guy goes out there he feels like he's gotta win because who knows when you're gonna win again with the four guys that are coming behind you.

Here, with the four guys we run out behind each other, none of us feels we're the guy that absolutely has to win. When you take that pressure off of each other, it ultimately helps each of us to relax, and if you go out there relaxed, you're gonna do good things.

JIM "MUDCAT" GRANT

Even if he hadn't been a great pitcher and the first African-American pitcher to win twenty games and then a World Series game, Jim Grant would have been remembered for having one of the greatest nicknames in baseball. But the affable hurler had far more than a nickname going for him when he took the mound.

Well, the greatest day, one of the greatest days I've had, was the day in Frank Lane's coaching room when I signed my first major league contract. I was in spring training, and they decided that I was good enough to go, and I signed that contract, and I put that contract underneath my pillow—and they say that if you put anything underneath your pillow it gets ingrained until you never forget it, and I never did forget that.

I think the minimum at that time was $5,500, and if you stayed past thirty days they gave you another $500. Big day, eh? Yeah, big day.

But the reason the day was such a big day is because it goes back to the time when we were on the porch of Mrs. Eppie Johnson, and we had heard the news that Jackie Robinson had signed to play with the Dodgers. So here, about eleven years later, or something like that, I became a major league ballplayer.

And the next biggest day I had was in Baltimore when I became the first black pitcher to win twenty games in the American League. I never will forget that, too. That was 1965. I was a few years ahead of Downing, and, in fact, I was the only pitcher in the league that did that for about a year-and-a-half or two years, so I was ahead of Al Downing, Earl Wilson, all of those guys.

First, naturally, before the game there's conversations about the day, that [it] was about to happen. It's OK when you discuss it before the game, but to be honest with you, during the game nothing else comes in except the game. And for several hours after, nothing gets out but just the game.

So I didn't get a chance to enjoy that, even though Howard Cosell ran on the field and said [imitating Cosell], "How do ya feel about being the first black pitcher to win twenty games?" And I said something stupid, because I wasn't ready, you know. I had to hit myself upside of my head and say to myself, "Answer the question." I said that I am happy just to be a pitcher that won twenty games. Now that was stupid. Actually it wasn't stupid—it was ill-conceived at that time.

And then I had to hunt him up later on after I started thinking about it, I said, "Howard, that's not the answer that I really want to say. I want to say that I am very proud to be the first black pitcher to win twenty games in the American League, and that it is a milestone that I can always tell my children and my grandchildren . . ." and so forth and so on. I gave him a much better answer—a true feeling, of course.

I don't know the score; I won it. Tough line-up, but it was a well-pitched game—it might have been 3–1, might have been 4–1 or something. I had won my nineteenth game on that road trip in Boston—I shut them out 2–0.

And then the next greatest day was when I won the first World Series game for a black pitcher. That was wonderful. So those three days I remember most. And I would imagine the fourth day was the night that they told me I was rooming with Larry Doby, who was the first black American to play in the American League. So those four days were some great days for me.

I remember a lot about the World Series. Washington hadn't been in the World Series for a long time, probably never, and this was the old Washington Senators ball club. It was a great ballpark, and Minneapolis is a great city. I remember Senator Humphrey was there, and we talked a little bit about the game I was to pitch.

I remember that, thanks to Mr. Yom Kippur, that I didn't have to pitch against Sandy Koufax on that particular type of day. I pitched against Drysdale, and I remember that we were up for the Series. Everybody expected us to lose, but we were up for the Series, and Earl Battey was up for the Series.

Other than that, it's a World Series game, alright, but you've gotta remember, if you focus . . . it's a game. It's an important game, but it's a game, you've gotta do the same thing that you've been doing all along all season. You've gotta go out there, you've gotta be tough, you've gotta throw strikes, you've gotta throw good strikes. You've gotta be ready to make double plays and so forth, and that's how I felt about it.

Rooming with Doby was a great experience, because Doby wasn't the type of guy to say a whole lot. But as his roommate, I got to hear a whole lot. I got to hear about all of the misnomers and uncorrect press conversations, who did this and who did that. . . . He did stay up late at night. I was very quiet in the room all the time. If he wanted to watch TV, we watched TV—if he wanted it off, it was off.

We did talk about when he came into the league, how he was traded. And certainly I've heard about all of his disappointments. But then on the other hand I heard about all the good things—him getting the opportunity to play. He taught me about credit. He taught me about colors and clothing. He taught me about discipline. He taught me about the fact that I should be very careful in what I do and what I say, because we were role models for children, and he reminded me about that.

He told me about going out at night—you can enjoy yourself, but because you're an athlete, alcohol was not the best thing to do, or any kind of drugs. He taught me how to appreciate other skills of other people, no matter on what scale those skills were.

There's no doubt that he was my mentor. I remember him taking me about to a spring training speaking engagement, and he said, "I don't like to put accolades on anybody, but this kid is gonna be one hell of a pitcher." I remember him saying that, and Larry Doby almost never said anything like that.

And generally speaking he just taught me about life, like a father. And I enjoyed myself with Larry Doby, even though it was short.

KEN GRIFFEY, JR.

When it comes to greatest days, brevity runs deep in the Griffey family. For all his tape-measure home runs, spectacular catches, MVPs, and Gold Gloves, Ken Griffey, Jr.'s greatest day was definitely a family affair.

That's an easy one for me—my greatest day in baseball is the first day I played with

August 31, 1990

KANSAS CITY	AB	R	H	RBI	SEATTLE	AB	R	H	RBI
Seitzer, 3b	4	0	0	0	Reynolds, 2b	5	0	1	0
McRae, cf	4	0	1	0	Griffey Sr., lf	4	1	1	0
Tartabull, dh	3	0	1	0	Griffey Jr., cf	4	1	1	0
B. Jackson, lf	3	1	1	0	A. Davis, dh	2	3	2	1
Macfarlane, c	4	0	1	0	P. O'Brien, 1b	3	0	0	0
Eisenreich, rf	3	0	0	1	Buhner, rf	3	0	2	1
Pecota, 1b	3	1	1	1	E. Martinez, 3b	2	0	1	1
F. White, 2b	3	0	1	0	Schaefer, 3b	2	0	1	1
Jeltz, ss	3	0	0	0	S. Bradley, c	4	0	1	0
					Vizquel, ss	3	0	0	0
Totals	30	2	6	2	Totals	32	5	10	4

```
Kansas City  020   000   000 — 2
Seattle      300   010   10X — 5
```

my father and every day after that that I had the chance to play with my father. My dad had nineteen years in the big leagues, and he hung around through everything—the strikes, the labor agreements—he hung around to get a chance to play with me.

We don't even really talk about baseball. If I do something, he'll mention it, but we talk about other things more than baseball. He's a father first and then a baseball player and coach second. He makes sure that I'm OK, and then if I'm OK and we have time, we talk about baseball and things that I'm seeing and things that I'm doing wrong. Just keeping me on an even keel, that's the biggest thing he's done for me, not letting the highs get too high and the lows get too low, to stay consistent in what you do day in and day out.

No matter what anybody says about what I do or what he did, it was the first time that a father and a son stepped out on the same field. Just being able to run out in the outfield with someone that you've known all your life, not someone that you've met in professional baseball. This guy, he raised me, and you can't say enough for that.

KEN GRIFFEY, SR.

Anyone who thinks that Ken Griffey, Sr.'s greatest contribution to the game was his son never saw him play. An integral cog in the "Big Red Machine," Griffey talked about playing with Junior, as well as

his pivotal contribution to Cincinnati's victory in the 1975 World Series against the Boston Red Sox.

Well, the only thing I can tell you is that the greatest day I ever had is when I played with Junior. Just getting the opportunity to play out in Seattle with him. . . .

We hit back-to-back singles. We won that game. There weren't very many at-bats, but that was probably my greatest moment—one of 'em. The other was just getting the opportunity to play in the '75 World Series.

What stands out is just the fact that I was playing with him, throwing and tossing baseballs with him. You know, I was looking at him out in the distance in center field, and he looked like he was twelve years old again—and all of a sudden he walked up on me, and he was 6' 2". So that was one of the things that stands out.

It was the first time we played together—we never played together until that moment in August on the 31st. I was in the big leagues. He came up in '89. I was already there, and it was his rookie year in '89. That was probably the greatest moment in my career.

The back-to-back home runs was probably another special moment. Just the idea that I hit a home run first . . . coming in from third base, and he was standing at home plate to greet me, and I kind of had one of those suspicions that he was gonna hit one too, then. It was off Kirk McCaskill. We never talked about it.

I hit one, and he was right behind me, doing the trot. I think that was his doing more than anything. I didn't worry about it, because I didn't think it was gonna happen. But it did, and it was a great feeling. I enjoyed the same feeling that he did—those two were just a little more special.

1975 was just an opportunity to play every day on a championship team in my first full year in the big leagues. And we went to the World Series and won in seven games. That whole year was probably special for me.

I guess the greatest day would probably be the second game of the World Series in '75, when I got a double to win the game. Top of the ninth inning—Bench leads off with a double, Concepcion singles him home to tie the game up, then Davey steals second, and I drive in Davey to win the game. That was probably the most special.

October 12, 1975

CINCINNATI	AB	R	H	PO	A	E
Rose, 3b	4	0	2	1	1	0
Morgan, 2b	3	1	0	0	4	0
Bench, c	4	1	2	9	3	0
Perez, 1b	3	0	0	8	0	0
Foster, lf	4	0	1	2	0	0
Concepcion, ss	4	1	1	2	4	1
Griffey, rf	4	0	1	2	0	0
Geronimo, cf	3	0	0	3	0	0
Billingham, p	2	0	0	0	2	0
Borbon, p	0	0	0	0	0	0
McEnaney, p	0	0	0	0	0	0
Rettenmund, ph	1	0	0	0	0	0
Eastwick, p	1	0	0	0	0	0
Totals	33	3	7	27	14	1

BOSTON	AB	R	H	PO	A	E
Cooper, 1b	5	0	1	10	1	0
Doyle, 2b	4	0	1	2	5	0
Yastrzemski, lf	3	2	1	1	0	0
Fisk, c	3	0	1	5	1	0
Lynn, cf	4	0	0	5	0	0
Petrocelli, 3b	4	0	2	0	0	0
Evans, rf	3	0	0	2	0	0
Burleson, ss	4	0	1	2	4	0
Lee, p	3	0	0	0	0	0
Drago, p	0	0	0	0	0	0
Carbo, ph	1	0	0	0	0	0
Totals	33	2	7	27	11	0

Cincinnati	000	100	002 — 3
Boston	100	001	000 — 2

What I remember about the at-bat was that the manager changed pitchers just so this guy could pitch to me instead of leaving the other guy in. He was a fastball pitcher, and I knew I was a fastball hitter, and I looked for a mistake—Drago, I think his name was. Drago was a hard thrower, but I faced all those the whole year, and I didn't have any problem hitting him.

When they brought him in, I guess the special part of the whole day was that they kept talking about the "Green Monster," and it was the first time it was hit. I hit a double off the wall, the "Green Monster," and that was what most of the talk was about. . . .

TONY GWYNN

PF SPORTS IMAGES

A National League batting title seems to be an annual award each season for Tony Gwynn, who is arguably one of the best hitters to ever play the game. But for the great San Diego Padres outfielder, his greatest day took him back to his first season in 1984, when the Padres defeated the Chicago Cubs before losing in the World Series against the Detroit Tigers. As the Padres drove toward another postseason appearance in the NL playoffs in September of 1996, Gwynn talked about Steve Garvey's phenomenal performance in Game 4.

For me that would have to be the first time I made it into the postseason—which is the only time I ever made it into the postseason—which was in my rookie year in 1984 when we played the Cubs in the NLCS. I think I hit something like .350 that year, and I guess that was the first time I won the batting title. But it wasn't even my game that stands out, because it was Steve Garvey who put on just one of the most incredible performances I've ever seen to win a game for us that we just had to win.

He had four hits and drove in four or five runs, and I was on first base when he hit a homer to win it in the bottom of the ninth. That was one of the most incredible experiences I've ever had, just being on base and being a part of that when it happened.

We had lost the first two games to the Cubs in Chicago. The first one was like 13–0—I mean, we just got our butts kicked. And then they beat us again. So we were coming home, down 2–0, and I can remember how quiet the plane ride home was after those first two games. That was a long, quiet ride—guys just didn't say anything. We knew what we had to do, and we knew what we were up against.

What sticks out for me is just the whole experience. We won the first game back in San Diego without too much trouble, and I remember what it was like in San Diego—the place just full of people. I mean, man, that place was rockin'—people pounding on cars when we were leaving the parking lot after the game. I've played in San Diego a long time now, I'd never heard it like that. It was the loudest that stadium had ever been.

So the fourth game things went back and forth a lot. We got out to a lead, and then they came back and tied, then they went ahead—I mean, the whole game was just like that. What I remember is Garv just coming up with so many big hits when we needed them. I know one time he doubled, and he was just there every time he came up with men on base.

Scott Sanderson started for them—he was the guy with the really good curveball, kind of a junk ball kind of guy. I drove in a run off him with a sac fly, and then later they brought in their lefty, Warren Brusstar. I actually scored before the ninth inning, too. I walked, and Garv drove me home with a single.

They came back and tied it up—I think it was the eighth inning. And then we couldn't score, and they couldn't score. So we come up in the bottom of the ninth and this is it—if we don't win the season's over. We don't go back to Chicago. We don't go anywhere. I guess everybody just goes golfing or something.

So I come up in the ninth inning against Lee Smith, and at that point in his career he was just throwing gas—ninety-five, one hundred miles an hour. I remember thinking about the home run in the

October 6, 1984

CHICAGO	AB	R	H	RBI	SAN DIEGO	AB	R	H	RBI
Dernier, cf	4	0	1	0	Wiggins, 2b	4	1	1	0
Sandberg, 2b	3	1	1	0	Gwynn, rf	3	2	1	1
Matthews, lf	3	1	0	0	Garvey, 1b	5	1	4	5
Moreland, rf	4	0	1	1	Nettles, 3b	3	0	0	0
Cotto, pr–rf	0	1	0	0	Kennedy, c	4	0	1	0
Cey, 3b	5	0	0	0	McReynolds, cf	3	0	1	0
Davis, c	4	1	3	3	Salazar, ph–cf	1	0	0	0
Durham, 1b	3	1	1	1	Martinez, lf	4	0	1	0
Bowa, ss	3	0	1	0	Templeton, ss	4	1	1	0
Hebner, ph	1	0	0	0	Lollar, p	1	0	0	0
Smith, p	0	0	0	0	Hawkins, p	0	0	0	0
Sanderson, p	2	0	0	0	Flannery, ph	1	1	1	0
Brussler, p	0	0	0	0	Dravecky, p	0	0	0	0
Lopes, ph	1	0	0	0	Brown, ph	0	1	0	0
Stoddard, p	0	0	0	0	Gossage, p	0	0	0	0
Veryzer, ss	1	0	0	0	Summers, ph	1	0	0	0
					Lefferts, p	0	0	0	0
Totals	34	5	8	5	Totals	34	7	11	6

Chicago	000	300	020 — 5	
San Diego	002	010	202 — 7	

on-deck circle, but when I got to the plate I thought back to the earlier at-bat when I hit the fly ball, thinking I might have been trying to do too much. So I just tried to hit the ball hard and put it in play, that was my game anyway. And I got a single—I think it was up the middle to center field—that brought Garv up.

I remember seeing the ball go out—he just met it and the ball took off to right field, right over my head. And then it was like time just kind of stopped when I was going around the bases—all the noise, everybody coming out from the dugout toward home plate. The funniest thing I remember about that was that the first guy to meet me when I got there was my Nike guy, my rep from Nike. And then everybody else came out, there was the pileup, and the celebration.

The thing that stands out from the whole experience was just the feeling of it, the whole postseason feeling. And the amazing thing for me is that it happened in my rookie year. I mean, I can remember guys sitting in the clubhouse for hours after the game—having a beer, watching the video, talking about the at-bats and the different situations, things like that. It's just not like that during the regular season. This is more of a day-to-day grind; you really have to grind it out. And things have changed, guys don't do that kind of thing any more. That's what I really miss.

People talk to me about the batting titles and the Hall of Fame, all the people I'm getting close to—Stan Musial, Rogers Hornsby, those kind of guys—but I really don't think about that. They tell me about my place in history—what I've accomplished, what I'm gonna feel like, how I've got a chance to be one of the best hitters that ever played, all those kinds of things—but right now none of that matters to me. What I really want is that feeling again—that comes with going to the postseason.

I think before my career is over I'll be able to say that, but right now the ultimate is to win the ring. That's what this game is all about. When you go to spring training, nobody says, "Oh, I'm gonna hit forty home runs and win a home run title," or, "I'm gonna win a batting title this year, or lead the league in homers, or win a Triple Crown." Nobody says that.

So when it gets right down to it, if you don't win, your year wasn't what it should've been or what you wanted it to be. The batting title's like a consolation prize. It's like, "Hey, you didn't win the division, but here, you earned this batting title." It looks good in the trophy case, and it's nice to talk about, but it's not really what the game is all about.

When you haven't won one, sometimes your focus is easy to shift over to other things. That first year for me, I played in the World Series, and it just sticks with me—the crowd, the feeling that you felt as you left the ballpark, 20,000 people banging on your car as you drive off—that sticks with you. All the other stuff is nice. It sounds good, it looks good, it'll pay for the media guide and all that stuff, but it doesn't give you that same feeling. That's what I'm searching for, that same feeling that I felt that night.

I've waited a long time. Maybe this year will be that year. Maybe it'll be next year, or whatever, but I'll eventually get it before my career is out. I'll be able to feel that again. Nobody in here will know what I'm going through, nobody else, 'cause I can try to explain it, I've tried to explain it. I brought in a tape of the [1984 NLCS] game and showed it here—guys said, "Who's that guy? Who is Warren Brusstar? Who was that guy?" They don't even know who these guys are.

For me it's about winning. Early in my career, sometimes I knew that's what it was about, but sometimes you put other stuff ahead of it. But as you get older you start to realize that this game's about winning, it's not about all the other stuff. I reached that point when I was about twenty-seven. When I started playing in the big leagues I was twenty-four, and when I was twenty-seven I just realized that's that what it was all about.

So I just put all the other stuff on the back burner for now. It's nice, but I'm trying to win.

People have said that I'm different—"He's different. He ain't worried about all the other stuff"—and really I'm not, but you'd have a hard time convincing people. Everywhere you go they want to talk about the batting titles, how many do you got? It's hard to convince people. But if we get to that point again, I hate to even think about it, because I found out a lot about myself after that game.

I found out a lot about myself, because I realized that that's the environment you want to play baseball in. Sure, during the regular season you gotta grind it out, but to me the good players have always stepped up when it's been time to step up. Watching Garvey that night, you couldn't have been any better than he was—he got four two-out hits and all of them drove in runs.

That's when you find out about people. Slumps are part of the game. When you're going good it's easy to talk about what you're doing, how you're doing it, why you're doing it. But when you're horseshit, you ain't hittin' the ball worth a damn, that's when you find out about yourself. You will either let all that adversity get to you, or you will put it aside and grind it out and try to do what you want to do to get to that place you want to get to.

That night I grew up, and I think I learned a lot about the game of baseball. That's why, to me, that's my greatest moment—and it wasn't even my moment. But after that game was over, I learned a lot about the game of baseball.

KEN "HAWK" HARRELSON

As a player, Ken "Hawk" Harrelson was known for his prodigious home runs and his flamboyant colorful style, and he's had an equally great second career as a Chicago White Sox broadcaster for WGN. The former Red Sox and Cleveland Indian slugger also has a soft side that came through in this interview, which was conducted in the broadcast booth in Fenway Park in 1997. Many players interviewed for this book talked about the father/son relationship that baseball seems to promote and nourish, but few if any had Hawk's eloquence when he described his mother's role in his career.

My greatest day ever . . . I was fortunate enough to play on the "Impossible Dream" here in Boston, I played in the World Series, played in the All-Star game, hit three homers in a game. . . . A lot of good things happened.

But there's no question to me what my greatest day in baseball was, that was . . . I don't recall what day it was, either. My mom—I was always a momma's boy—lived in Savannah [Georgia], and she came up to Kansas City to watch me play in the only big league game she ever saw me play in person.

In fact, Jaime Navarro's dad, Julio Navarro, was pitching for the Tigers, and I wasn't supposed to be in there, because I was in a slump—this was '63. She came up, and I got called downstairs before the game, and I got tickets—great tickets, right there by the on-deck circle and everything. And the first time I went to the plate, Navarro hung me a curve ball, and I hit it about 500 feet into left-center field for a home run.

And when I came around the base paths, she was just like she always was. She was just smilin', and she had tears—I could see the tears coming down [from] her eyes. That, without question, was my greatest day in baseball, because I was so close to my mom.

She was divorced when I was eight, so she raised me, and we had just an unbelievable relationship. And any time anybody ever asked me what my best day was, it wasn't playing in the World Series, it wasn't that. It wasn't All-Star. It was the first at-bat my mom ever saw me in the big leagues.

It was wonderful being with her afterward. There may have been some guys as close to their mom as I was, but nobody was ever closer. She used to drive from Savannah to Atlanta—this was before they had four-lane highways, two-lane roads. We'd play in a basketball tournament there. She'd drive back and forth, because she had to work.

Absolutely just a thrill for me, because the only thing she ever wanted me to do—she didn't want me to work when I was a kid. She was only making fifty-six bucks a week. She worked as a secretary in a meat-packing company, and I used to tell mom, "You know, I'll get a job," because I'd see her sittin' down crying all the time, the bills. She was robbing Peter to pay Paul. We had grits like six times a week—a lot of times we'd have 'em for dinner, because that's all we could afford.

And she'd never let me do that. She said, "No, I want you to play sports—baseball." And she really and truly paid the price, physically and mentally, for me to go out. When everybody else maybe had a summer or a part-time job, I was out on the baseball field, because of her.

We had, as I said, a very special relationship, and the irony of things is that I was in such a slump. Shit, I couldn't hit the ground.

I remember one time in high school we were getting ready to play for the state championship in basketball—I was an All-American in basketball, so I was a stud, you know?

So she'd been driving back and forth, and it was a long way from Atlanta—it was 250 miles on those two-lane roads. We were getting ready to start the game, and the funny thing about it was that everybody knew how close my mom and I were, everybody in the state. In fact, I used to go to some arenas out of town, and they'd have big signs that said, "Momma's Boy," and I loved it.

But we were getting ready to tip off—and she always wore this one red wool suit during basketball season, it was what we called our good-luck suit—and I didn't see her. We were at Georgia Tech Coliseum, and Rick Miller was the coach, and I said, "Rick"—and this is only like two minutes to tip-off, we're standing around having a little meeting, what you're gonna do and all that shit. And I'm looking around and I couldn't see her, and I said, "Coach, I'm gonna call the state police."

And he never even hesitated. He said, "OK." He didn't say, "No. Where are you going? We've got a game to play," because he knew. And now, going over to go to the telephone, as I'm doing that, here she comes down the exit going, "Son, I'm here."

RICKEY HENDERSON

Flamboyant and controversial, Rickey Henderson is perhaps the consummate base stealer of all time, as well as one of the best leadoff hitters ever to play the game. Henderson chose the day he set the single-season record for stolen bases as his greatest day.

I'd probably say my greatest day was the day I set the season record for stolen bases. To me it stands out more than the overall record because it's just one year. You've got time after it happens to look back. You have years and years to just go over it.

We were playing in Milwaukee. It was about the fourth or fifth inning—actually, it was the fifth inning. I drew a walk. I got five pitches tossed to first base—I definitely remember it was five. I went on the sixth pitch. It was a bang-bang play. The pitcher stepped to home plate and I got a decent jump—I think it was Sundberg who might have been catching. Milwaukee had a lot of catchers at the time. I had decent luck off him, but it was during a time when I got on, I was just going, whatever the circumstances were.

Either Robin Yount or Jim Gantner received the ball and caught it in front of the bag. It was Yount, actually. He made a wiping tag, and to me it was really closer than it should have been. If he had caught the ball at the bag there wouldn't have been a play, but he caught the ball in front of the bag and wiped back real fast. I beat the tag, and that was the record.

Lou Brock was there—he was traveling for about a week with me. He told me he wasn't going to go back until I got it, so I had to do it that day. He told me he was tired and he wanted to go see his family. I talked to him every day; we discussed everything. I had met Lou back when I first started my career—back in '79 when I got to the big leagues and I stole a hundred bases and met Lou Brock and we became friends.

I just picked his mind on what he did, got his assessment of what I needed to learn for me to have success. He felt that I was gonna be the guy to break his record and to break the all-time record, because I had the desire and the aggressiveness to go out there and not worry about failure. It just so happened that that was true.

We talked about it over and over, and Lou was good to me. He did a lot for baseball, and I always wanted to be the one in the next generation to carry it forward, to keep it going. The biggest thing I learned from him was to really analyze on how many steps it took to get to second base. He told me to always keep that in mind—that when you steal, you take that many steps, and then you just go into your slide no matter where you're at, just go into your slide and you should be where you want to be, that's what he taught me.

He taught me a lot about reading pitchers. I used to have trouble with left-handed pitchers, and he used to have a walking lead off of left-handed pitchers—most of his assessment went into getting a walking lead. It seemed like every time I went out to use a walking lead I never could get back on the right foot or start on the right foot—I'd use a stutter-step. I really wanted to figure out how I do what I do, but it never really came to me, 'cause I always was a push-off guy—I always pushed off to get my jumps, and he always had a walking lead.

When I stole the base and broke the record it was really a big relief. I think that I had so much pressure on myself to get that one base to break the record, all the rest of the bases were almost easy compared to that. I had so much pressure on that one base. When I stole that base I had new life—it was a new world, the beginning of a new thing. I was relieved. I was happy that it was over. I had too much pressure and tension. That's what I remember the most was that the pressure was finally relieved.

I saw Brock after the game, and he said his speech—he was just happy that I had achieved this, he was a big fan of Rickey. We talked about just continuing to go out and do what you're capable of doing, not to let anybody put the fear in you that you can't go out each and every day and steal a base.

It was a lot of wear-and-tear, because I was running a lot more. I got picked off probably thirty times, and then I got caught stealing some—I think I got caught a total of forty-three times. Between that and the pickoff throws, I was out there maybe 200 or 300 times just hitting the dirt. I had nagging bruises in my shoulders. By the last few games in the season I really couldn't throw the ball. I had to hand the ball off to [A's center fielder] Dwayne Murphy. It was a lot of pounding, and then I had to regroup and put my body back through training to get rid of the pains.

I think that's what makes me keep going to continue to steal the bases, because once it's over, if you go back and train your body to get back in shape, it takes away the aches and the pains, and you can go back out there and do it again. You have to go out and train. I do a lot of running and a lot of swimming, mainly for my shoulders. I very rarely do a lot of weight training. I do a lot of pushups, situps, and flexibility exercises. I went to karate class to force the mental part, to learn how to relax the body, and that's what I think it takes—it takes a lot to just find out about your body, how to bring it back up.

I would feel joy if somebody broke the record. I would feel that somebody's continued and took my style and my aggressiveness on the bases and put it to another level, like I did with Lou Brock's record. It would be an honor to both myself and Lou Brock that we could see the stolen bases being used to affect baseball, to see that continued—that's what I would feel joy about.

Lou Brock did all his running. And before that there was Ty [Cobb] and [Maury] Wills and all the rest of 'em. But there was a period where it was eliminated—stealing bases wasn't really a part of the game, and it didn't have an effect on the game until I came along and took it to another level. And now stolen bases are a big part of the game again, because if you can get a player in scoring position, you'll score a lot more runs. They're trying to figure out a way of stopping that or slowing it down until the next guy comes around. I hope that when the next guy comes around he can continue it, the trends just keep going.

Right now the main guy is Kenny Lofton. I think that when he came in the league he came to me and learned from me just the way I learned from Lou Brock. Now I look over my shoulder and see the great things he's doing on the bases, and that makes me proud. I can't say he's the guy that would break the record. He has the potential to do it, but I think nowadays the pitchers use a little more slide step. They're paying a lot more attention to the fast runners, so it's very difficult right now to get 100 or 130 stolen bases.

You never know if it'll happen in these modern days. They [said] Lou Brock's record would never be broken, and I came along and did it. So I'm always gonna say there'll be somebody, somewhere, that's gonna give their best shot and might have a chance to break the record. I don't feel that there's too many players out there that are gonna break it.

The aggressiveness and the confidence that I had is what allowed me to set the record, not being afraid to run. That's what Brock said it was. He told me that what he saw was that when I stole a base, if I got thrown out, I got right back up and went out and stole the base again. He said that's what he thought would allow me to have success—you can't be afraid of getting thrown out.

Most guys, like Willie Wilson and the guys back in my day, they got thrown out, and they wouldn't attempt to steal again. He felt I had the aggressiveness to just get back up and go again, and I think that's what any great base stealer has to be doing, is to just go out and just not worry about being thrown out, to just have aggressiveness on the base paths.

I think that aggressiveness is an individual thing. You take a lot of pounding, you have to want to be a base stealer, you have to want to be the one to go out there and take that pounding. It's individual, it's not required. It's not like in baseball they want you to go out and steal bases and have that be your only job so that you can be a star and get paid the money. I think it's the kind of thing where an individual feels that this is what he wants to do and achieve. It takes a unique guy who comes along once every ten or twenty years and says, "Hey, when I was a kid, this is what I idolized, and this is what I want to do."

I idolized Lou Brock and Maury Wills and Ty Cobb. All I did was look at film of guys like that. I like the aggressiveness of Ty Cobb—he didn't have any fear, and he would try to punish the guy at second whenever he tried to steal the base. Lou Brock had the technique and the art and the science and all that—how many steps it takes to get to the base—and he was aggressive and feisty.

What made me really want to be a base stealer when I was in high school was that my counselor, Mrs. Wilson, used to give me a quarter to steal bases. She's my favorite. She was there when I broke the record. Right now she's a little sick, but she still tries to follow what I'm doing. Wherever I'm at, she's just pulling for me to steal another base.

OREL HERSHISER

When it comes to records, Orel Hershiser is best known for breaking Don Drysdale's mark for consecutive scoreless innings. But he also had a reputation as a great clutch pitcher, and in his most memorable clutch performance he added some timely hitting to his hurling, which always makes the experience unforgettable for any pitcher.

My greatest day would probably be, statistically, the day that I threw the shutout in '88 against Oakland in Game 2 after [Kirk] Gibson hit the home run in Game 1 to win. I went out and threw a three-hit shutout and got three hits myself. That was a lot of fun. To hit two doubles, and then I think I got another RBI, a single, and to throw a three-hit shutout in the World Series in Dodger Stadium is like—that's a dream come true for anybody. So that would have to be the greatest day for me.

It relieved a lot of pressure, Kirk hitting the home run. I can remember sitting there in the ninth inning, with Eckersley on the mound. . . . I'm thinking, "We're going down 0–1, and I'm gonna have to go out and get us a win." It was a lot of responsibility, because of the resume that I brought into that game, with the fifty-nine scoreless and the possible Cy Young, so I felt like the pressure was on me. And then Kirk hits the home run, and it took a lot of pressure off me, because now it's 1–0, and we're gonna leave L.A. 1–1 or 2–0, so I felt great about going into that outing.

I was so excited after the game that I forgot to take my scouting tape home. I had to go back to the ballpark early the next day, which broke my regimen of things I like to do the day before I pitch and the day I pitch, because here I am thinking, "OK, I've gotta get my scouting tape." I'm taking notes on the hitters, doing everything I want to do to get ready.

And Kirk hit the home run, and we're just jumping all over the place, and I forgot my scouting tape. I forgot my scouting notes. I got home that night, and I couldn't go to sleep because I was so excited. And I get up the next day ready to scout and read over my notes, and they're not there. So I had to go to the ballpark early, and that broke my routine a little bit, but it seemed not to affect it.

I remember Dave Parker hitting me well. He might have got all three of Oakland's hits, because he was an ex-National Leaguer, and maybe knew me a little better. So I was more surprised by the Oakland hitters; they hadn't seen me yet. I remember having a consistent, good, sinking fastball again—pretty much the kind of pitch that you could say, "It's coming," but it's still hard to hit.

And then the breaking ball was just a big surprise. When you have a pitch that's dominant and up, when you throw it well in the right spot, and they know it's coming, it's still hard to hit. It's very hard because the hitter cannot do anything but think of that pitch. And then if you throw something else, you have it. That's what's neat—to watch dominant pitchers pitch if they're in a groove. If they've got their location plus their dominance, it looks like it's pretty easy out there. That's why people who make mistakes get hurt.

I was developing that pitch in the minor leagues, hoping that I could be able to throw it eight out of ten times. You know, you throw it four out of ten times, and then the next year you throw it five out of ten times and it's still good, and one time it's flat and one time it sinks. And then you get to the point where you say, "Hey, I've got the hang of this thing, and it really is a good pitch." And I'd say that finally came along where I knew I had a really good, solid sinker that I could execute most of the time—probably in 1984, '85, right in there.

First year in the big leagues was '83. In September '84 I pitched pretty well but really didn't know how to pitch yet. I think the beginning of '85 I really started to think that I could execute this pitch and live with it.

I think the number one hit I remember from that game was a slash double down the right field line with Alfredo Griffin running at first base, and he ended up scoring. . . . That was a lot of fun. I also got a base hit up the middle, I remember, a line drive right over the pitcher's head. I can't remember my first hit right off the top of my head—it might have been a ground ball double down the left field line. It's definitely a lot of fun. I think I'll remember when I watch the highlight film.

I'd rather not talk about my approach—I don't want to tell a secret. Well, I don't know if it's a secret, but there's definitely a way I try to go about it, and that really is just to put the ball in play, and good things happen. If you put the ball in play ten times, maybe two or three times it's gonna fall in. If I strike out four out of those ten times, now I've only got six chances to put the ball in play, and only one falls in, that's ten percent. If I put the ball in play ten times, I've got a chance to have it fall, no matter how hard I hit it. It's like today [in a spring training game against the Cardinals]. I just blooped it in—but I put it in play, first at-bat, just put it in play.

I think there's ways to set pitchers up. I think you can look stupid on a pitch and then just sit on it because you know they're gonna throw it again. I think you can look like there's no way you can reach an inside pitch, but in your mind you're sitting on it. It looks like there's no way you can reach the outside pitch, and in your mind you're going there. So you're trying to play the game.

I think the play from some of the guys that really didn't have big years stands out from the rest of the Series—that guys we really didn't count on, guys like Mickey Hatcher and Mike Davis, kind of

October 14, 1988

OAKLAND	AB	R	H	RBI	LOS ANGELES	AB	R	H	RBI
Lansford, 3b	3	0	0	0	Sax, 2b	4	1	1	0
Henderson, cf	4	0	0	0	Stubbs, 1b	2	1	1	1
Canseco, rf	4	0	0	0	Woodson, 1b	1	0	0	0
Parker, lf	4	0	3	0	Hatcher, lf	4	1	2	1
McGwire, 1b	3	0	0	0	Marshall, rf	4	1	2	3
Hassey, c	3	0	0	0	Gonzalez, rf	0	0	0	0
Hubbard, 2b	2	0	0	0	Shelby, cf	4	0	0	0
Weiss, ss	3	0	0	0	Scioscia, c	4	0	0	0
S. Davis, p	1	0	0	0	Hamilton, 3b	4	0	0	0
Nelson, p	0	0	0	0	Griffin, ss	4	1	1	0
Polonia, ph	1	0	0	0	Hershiser, p	3	1	3	1
Young, p	0	0	0	0					
Plunk, p	1	0	0	0					
Honeycutt, p	0	0	0	0					
Totals	29	0	3	0	Totals	34	6	10	6

```
Oakland       000   000   000 — 0
Los Angeles   005   100   00X — 6
```

OAKLAND	IP	H	R	ER	BB	SO
S. Davis, L	3.1	8	6	6	0	2
Nelson	1.2	1	0	0	1	1
Young	1	1	0	0	0	0
Plunk	1	0	0	0	0	3
Honeycutt	1	0	0	0	0	2
LOS ANGELES	IP	H	R	ER	BB	SO
Hershiser, W	9	3	0	0	2	8

had an off year but ended up hitting a home run in the World Series. You know, Kirk only gets one at-bat in the World Series, and it's a huge one. Guys like Tracy Woodson and Franklin Stubbs, guys that aren't household names, that had a really good World Series and made big contributions.

And it was definitely a team effort. I remember Bob Costas saying, you know, that we don't even belong on the same field with the Oakland A's, because we were all banged up—Sciosia got hurt so Dempsey's catching, Gibson's out so we've got a different left fielder. We've got people out there—it was really our second-division split squad—that kind of thing, from spring training.

I remember Costas in the pregame show said that we didn't belong on the field with them, and Tommy Lasorda was in the locker room when that was on, and he turned it up and made sure all of us heard it. And it kind of inspired us to go out there and play a little harder in that Series—and we won. I think that definitely was an inspiration.

I think you just understand when it seems like it's David against Goliath that everybody's gonna have to do every single thing for the good of the team, and nobody can let their concentration down for one moment, because the giant will beat you. We saw them as people that really had unbelievable ability, that could beat us at any moment, so we had that jungle-like mentality that anything can attack from anywhere—when you've got eyes in the back of your head, and you're listening, and every sense is at a finely-tuned pitch. Maybe they didn't have that, I don't know—I wasn't over on their side.

I guess I pick that one because I like hitting. I like hitting. You tell me any other pitcher that went three-for-three in the World Series and wouldn't like that day. I want to meet that guy.

The day we won the world championship was awesome. The day I broke Drysdale's record was awesome. And when I came back from my arm surgery that I wasn't supposed to come back from. And every day I have a baseball is a greatest day, because I'm not supposed to be here.

Great things happen in people's lives, and [one] of the first questions you hear [is], "Can you repeat?" So they don't let you really enjoy what you've just accomplished. . . .

I didn't really enjoy it completely until the middle of the off-season, when you go back and you just relax for a while. Because when you go through it, and you're doing so well, the pressure is to keep going. It isn't like, oh, I'm doing so well, this is so much fun, I can relax. No. I'm doing so well, I have to continue to work as hard as I can to keep this up.

And so there's a lot of expectation around you, there's a lot of, "I can't relax," and "I've gotta remember what got me here." Will I continue to have a good sinker? Because people expect me to have a good sinker. I have to continue to think about how I stay in shape, because people are expecting me to stay in shape.

So everybody says, "Well, you must have been having a blast. You're in the zone. You're doing this, you're doing that." No. I did interviews and said, "This is not fun. This is work." And yes, I'm having a great time doing well after the work is over, but after the work is over and you guys are interviewing me about a shutout, I have to go back to work.

It doesn't last that long. Fifteen minutes after being out of the ice and doing the interviews, I'm going to [be eating] a plate of pasta and eating chicken and thinking, "Well, tomorrow I've gotta come in and lift weights, and I've gotta go get my rest, and I've gotta eat properly, and I've gotta come in here and work on my pitches, and I've got to go to the video room and study the hitters." So it's right back into the flow. It's not sit there and bask in the glory for five days and take a vacation. It's not going to last very long.

I don't think that second game was as big an accomplishment as the streak. If I had to sit back and say, "That was the greatest day, but how does that compare with other things that have happened in my life?" No, the streak just still boggles my mind.

Both of those things involve a combination. Because if you're a pitcher, especially if you're a pitcher the way I pitch, I need a defense. I don't go out and strike out fifteen, sixteen guys. The ball gets put in play a lot when I pitch. I just strike out—at that time, I was probably striking out an average of six batters. So . . . twenty-seven outs, six strikeouts a game—twenty-one times my team's helping me a lot.

And especially in the streak. I go back and watch the tapes of the streak, and I just go "Wow." I still get nervous, it's first and third with one out—you mean they're not gonna score here? This guy just can't hit a sacrifice fly? And then I see a ground ball double play. I see somebody make a good play . . . Even though I've lived it and seen it and done it, you still watch it at home and you go, "Oh, they're gonna score." It's just, I'm dreaming, pinch me, you know? That's how hard it is to do, when that happens.

Life for me is—you get up in the morning and you do your best, and that's how good things happen to you. Does anybody get up in the morning and say, "I want to have an adequate day," or, "I want to have a bad day"? I get up in the morning and say, "I want to have a good day." Even if they feel bad or don't think it's going to happen, they would like to have it happen. So take an active role in having that, you know? Go have one.

I really don't think about the Hall of Fame. . . . I get up today and I've gotta go be the best I can be today with what is put in front of me, and that's pitch a baseball still and raise my family and stay dedicated to my wife. To think, "What's the big picture here?" I don't think about the Hall of Fame.

Have I accomplished enough to get there? That's up to other people to decide. It's out of my control. I can't get up tomorrow and look in the mirror and say, "I'm gonna vote for myself for the Hall of Fame." But I can get up in the morning and say, "I'm gonna try my best to do what's in front of me." So I don't worry about that.

People come up to me and say, "You know, what do you think it's gonna take in your career for you to get in?" Maybe 200 wins. I'm 165 and whatever—I need thirty-five wins to get to 200. People have compared me to Drysdale and said—yeah, I think he had 206 or 210 or whatever—"You know, if you get to 200, that could be a magic number for you, with the streak and the World Series and the MVP in both leagues, and coming back from the shoulder surgery. If you get to 200 wins, you're gonna be a lock, because that's why Drysdale got in—200 wins plus the streak."

So if I get to 198, we can talk about it—199, maybe. But I'm thirty-five wins away. That's a lot of work. If I don't ever get to 200 wins, maybe they'll still think there's an opportunity, but it's not make or break in my life. . . . It would be more icing on the cake, and there's already icing on it—I'm not lacking any, and if people get too much icing, they get a stomachache.

RANDY HUNDLEY

The Chicago Cubs had some great clubs in the late '60s that never quite made it to the World Series. But they did have some great players, including nonpareil catcher Randy Hundley. A defensive standout who could also hit for power and drive in runs, Hundley also left his mark on the game in the form of his son Todd, who broke Roy Campanella's single season record for a catcher in his rookie year in 1996.

There have been two or three—a couple of 'em I guess are a little bit corny, people will think they're kind of corny. We played the Mets in a doubleheader in Wrigley Field one day. We'd lost the first game, and of course it was a big game in the second game—it must have been '71 or something like that. And I hit a three-run homer off of Tug McGraw to win the ball game—two outs, ninth inning. That was a big thrill. Actually, that may have been '72.

In '71, I had a real severe knee injury. I was in the hospital for about eight weeks. I had a pulmonary embolism—a blood clot broke loose, went through my heart, my knee was swollen up to this point at one time. They said I'd never play the game again. We didn't have programs the way they have now, I had to do it all on my own. And there was no 'scoping then, they cut me all the way down.

When I stood at home plate the next year to open the season, it was a real thrill to me. My career was over, basically, and I worked so hard to get back. I mean, I can't begin to describe for you what it's like standing there for Opening Day to open the season when they said I'd never play again. There were times when I had my doubts, but I said, somehow, some way, I was gonna do it, and I was able to do it.

Just being there, going through spring training and making the starting position—it's not given to you. I had played well enough in spring training, and I ended up catching 125 ball games that year, which was amazing. I was very fortunate to be able to do that, but it was a tough road back.

Sometimes, when I look at Todd—and first of all, just the mere fact that he's playing major league baseball—I don't even know how the heck he does what he does. First of all, just the mere fact that Todd's in major league baseball is an incredible feat. Although I've been there, it's almost like I can't relate to it. Of course, when you're doing it, you think nothing of it, and I don't even know if I could begin to explain that.

I come out on the field now—I was in there [in the locker room at the Legends game in St. Petersburg in spring training of 1997] getting dressed, and I was thinking I was freaking lucky. How many people would like to be in this locker room, to get to dress with these other great ballplayers? You dream about it when you're a kid, and when you're an adult, when you're a grown man, you'd have the opportunity to do it.

So on one hand, we take it for granted an awful lot. On the other hand, I really appreciated and just enjoyed the daylights out of it. And then to see your son do it and know what he has to look forward to. I mean, what more could you ask for, other than good health?

The day he was born, I hit a grand slam home run—that was out in San Francisco. He was born back in Virginia, and my wife knew that I didn't get my rest. He was born at 2:00 a.m. San Francisco time, and my wife waited until 7:00 in the morning to call me and let me know. And of course we had two girls first, and I thought, "Holy cow, I'm gonna get a boy." And then, when my wife told me, that day I hit a grand slam home run to win the ball game. That was a thrill.

This past season, Todd did an awful lot of things that just thrilled the daylights out of me. Just seeing him conduct himself very professionally and wanting to go and win ball games, and try to get better as a player and make his team better without much concern for individual records.

You know, a new season's starting now, so you can't rest on those laurels very long. You've gotta go strap it right on again and start all over and see if you can't do it again. That's one of the tough

April 15, 1972

PHILA. (N.)	AB	R	H	RBI	CHICAGO (N.)	AB	R	H	RBI
Bowa, ss	5	1	1	0	Cardenal, rf	3	1	0	0
McCarver, c	5	0	2	1	Becker, 2b	4	0	1	1
Montanez, cf	5	0	1	0	Williams, lf	4	0	0	0
Johnson, 1b	4	0	0	0	Santo, 3b	4	0	0	0
Luzinski, lf	3	1	1	1	Pepitone, 1b	4	0	0	0
Money, 3b	4	0	1	0	Hundley, c	4	0	1	0
Anderson, rf	4	0	2	0	Monday, cf	3	1	1	0
Doyle, 2b	3	1	1	0	Kessinger, ss	2	0	1	0
Carlton, p	2	0	0	0	Jenkins, p	2	0	0	1
Stone, ph	1	1	1	0	Hands, p	1	0	0	0
Hoerner, p	0	0	0	0	Hamilton, p	0	0	0	0
Totals	36	4	10	2	Totals	31	2	4	2

Philadelphia	000	100	102 — 4
Chicago	001	000	010 — 2

things about this game—you just have to keep going. You can't just kick back. . . .

The thing that I try and impress upon him is to just enjoy it, have fun, and give it every stinking thing he has every day. Because when you get back over here on this side, if you have to say, "You know, I didn't give it all I had"—that's gonna be a tough thing to do. You're really gonna regret it.

And I think he understands that quite well, and I'm proud for him for that.

TODD HUNDLEY

Usually it takes rookie catchers a couple of years to learn the league and their own pitching staff and to master the physical and mental demands of the position. No one's made it through the learning process faster than New York Mets catcher Todd Hundley (his father, former Cubs catcher Randy Hundley, must have pretty good genes), who in his first season accomplished the amazing feat of topping Roy Campanella's all-time record for home runs for a catcher with forty-one.

My greatest day in baseball? Has to be when I was called up to the big leagues in 1990 from Wichita, Kansas. I was playing for the Jackson Mets in Double AA, and I went from Double AA to San Diego. I met the team in San Diego, and that day, probably got my first major league hit, off of Bruce Hurst in my second at-bat. Then there was my first home run—off of Bill Landrum, against the Pirates—and then I'd have to say my forty-first home run off of McMichael to break Campanella's record.

The hit, my first big league hit, was facing Bruce Hurst. In my first at-bat, he threw me three pitches. I was fucking dumb, I had no chance at all. It took him all of three pitches to strike me out. All curves, all fucking bullshit—three backdoor curveballs and then sit down.

I said, "OK," so then my next at-bat, I went up and hit a double—third pitch, I hit a double down the left field line. He finally threw me a fucking fastball, and I hit it down that line. And Kevin

Elster was on first base, and he tried to come around and score, and they ended up throwing him out at home, and I went to third base on the play.

I hit my first home run off of Will Landrum at Shea. We were— it was kind of funny, but it was the bottom of the ninth—I hit a home run in the first game of a doubleheader, two outs, I hit the home run. It was '90. We were out of it by that time, it was late September.

A lot of guys were kind of mad more than happy for me, because it sent the game into extra innings, and we had another game. We had a doubleheader to play that fucking night. The first game ended up going about fourteen innings, so they were mad at me. They congratulated me and everything, but it was kind of like, "What the fuck, man? You're supposed to do this in the second game, not the first game." So it was kind of ironic.

The one off of McMichael, to break Campanella's record, was a very long day. I was tired as shit. It was a day game after a night game. Fastball down and away—I was sittin' on the changeup, he threw me a fastball down and away, and I went with it to left field. I knew I hit it, I knew I got it, I knew it was gonna be gone. Thank God I got all of it. I got all this pressure off my shoulders, got it done and got it over with.

I believe it was June, or late July. I hit one against the Reds, and it was my thirtieth—my thirtieth home run. And [Mets PR director]

May 18, 1990

METS	AB	R	H	RBI	SAN DIEGO	AB	R	H	RBI
Jefferies, 2b	5	0	0	0	Roberts, lf	4	1	1	0
Miller, cf	5	0	1	0	T. Gwynn, rf	3	0	1	0
H. Johnson, 3b	3	0	1	0	Alomar, 2b	4	0	1	1
McReynolds, lf	2	2	1	1	J. Carter, 1b	4	1	2	1
Strawberry, rf	4	0	1	0	Santiago, c	4	1	1	0
Marshall, 1b	4	0	1	0	Abner, cf	4	1	1	0
Elster, ss	2	0	1	0	Pagliarulo, 3b	3	1	0	0
Magadan, 3b	1	0	0	0	Templeton, ss	3	1	1	4
Hundley, c	4	1	1	0	Hurst, p	2	0	0	0
Viola, p	3	0	2	2	G. Harris, p	1	0	0	0
Carren, ph	1	0	0	0	Lefferts, p	0	0	0	0
Totals	34	3	9	3	Totals	32	6	8	6

Mets	011	100	000 — 3	
San Diego	040	010	01X — 6	

Jay Horwitz came up to me, and he said, "Todd, you know what the record is for catchers for home runs?" And I said, "No." And he said, "Forty is the record, Roy Campanella holds it." And I said, "No shit." And he said, "Yeah." And I thought, "Fuck, we've got August, September, couple days in October—I gotta figure in two months I can hit ten home runs by accident."

I got to that, and then I finally got to forty, I got to thirty-nine, it took me a couple weeks to get to forty. Once I got to forty it took me a couple weeks to get to forty-one. Before that, I was hittin' a lot of home runs, and then when I got closer to it, as the pressure mounted—I had to come to the yard a lot earlier, I had to talk to the media, try to give them their time, and then when they were done I would go do my thing, get my hitting in, do my stuff.

The adjustments I had to make was being a lot more patient, because they weren't giving me—I don't think anyone really wanted to give in to me, to say, "Aw, he hit it off me. I'm going down in the record books." I know Greg Maddux didn't, he told me that. He said, "I ain't givin' you shit to hit. You're not hitting it off of me, 'cause I don't want to go down in history for that fucking feat." And I knew it, guys just weren't going to give me a pitch to hit.

Defensively, I just went out there and did everything I could possibly do to help the team win. I'm more of a team player than I am an individual player. I worry about the team first, that's how I just went about my job. There was a lot of mental fatigue, you know? Catching is a lot of mental fatigue—it's just something that you just have to deal with and put up with.

But I just went out there and tried to get as many wins as possible, and that's what I concentrated on. I'm not out there to hit five home runs a game or whatever, I just do whatever. If we need a home run to win the ball game, yes, I would be swinging for it, but if we don't, if we need a single, I just try and get the base hit.

Winning the World Series would be the next greatest day for me . . . by far. It's been on my mind since day one, after I got to the big leagues. So now it's—the personal stuff, I've taken care of that—now it's a matter of getting there as a team, and playing in the World Series will definitely top it off.

JIM "CATFISH" HUNTER

When it comes to greatest days, few pitchers have more to choose from than Jim "Catfish" Hunter. Hunter selected a nice assortment,

from the perfect game he threw early in his career to his World Series victories with both the Oakland A's and the Yankees, then moving on to his landmark free agent signing with New York and entering the Hall of Fame before circling back to his big league debut.

Well, one of 'em was my perfect game in 1968. I was taking batting practice, and that was when the pitchers could hit, and Bob Kennedy walked out and said, "That's it, you don't hit anymore." I said, "No, I've got six more pitches." He said, "No, get out of the cage." I said, "No, I've got six more pitches."

He jumped in front of the batting practice cage and told the batting practice pitcher not to throw me any more. So I wrapped the bat around the cage and broke it, and I went on into the clubhouse.

And then as I pitched the perfect game, he comes up to me, and he says, "Nice pitching." And I said, "No, how 'bout my hitting? I went three for four, knocked in three of the runs, and scored the fourth one." And he said, "Well, you hit pretty good, too." I don't know who I got the hits off of, but I know I got three of 'em. Dave Boswell was the starting pitcher. . . .

The main thing was that I had real good control that night, no matter where the catcher held his mitt I could throw it and hit it. And if I thought the umpire missed a pitch, I thought, "Well, heck, I'll throw another one." Nothing bothered me that night. I knew I had good control and I had good stuff.

About the fifth or sixth inning, Mike Hershberger was sitting on the bench, and I came in, and I heard him say that somebody got on. And I knew that nobody had gotten a base hit, so maybe I walked somebody in the first or second inning or something. And I walked on down to the end of the dugout, and right on up until the end of the game I knew it was a no-hitter, but I didn't know it was a perfect game.

I went three-and-two on the last hitter and struck him out. Rich Reese. He fouled off seven in a row.

The next one would have to be pitching against the Cincinnati Reds in the World Series and winning the World Series in 1972, because we were the long-haired mustache gang that everybody said was lucky to be there. We beat 'em, and they still said they were better than us.

The first World Series you're in always sticks out in your mind, and I thought that was probably the best World Series we played. I would say the last game sticks out probably more than anything else, because I came in in relief of Blue Moon [Odom] in about the fifth or sixth inning. . . .

I pitched right on up through the eighth and ninth inning, and Dick Williams came out to take me out. He says, "You don't have anything, but you were the best that I had." He said, "I'm gonna bring in Rollie." And Rollie came in and saved the ball game.

In the clubhouse, we couldn't believe it. We just said we wanted to say the "Green Machine" instead of the "Red Machine." But I think everybody was happy and surprised and glad to be there. We were just glad to be there, because none of us had ever been there before, and we were just happy to win. That's one of my greatest days with Oakland, probably after the '74 World Series when we beat the Dodgers.

We beat three National League teams in a row, and still they were saying that we were lucky to be there. What stands out about '74 was when I came in relief for Rollie. Rollie and Blue Moon had had a fight just before the ball game, I don't know which game it was, fourth, fifth, somewhere along there, and Rollie had six stitches taken in his head, and the writers were sittin' there lookin', you know, they couldn't believe it, they just said, this team does fight. We did fight once in a while.

And we sewed him up, six stitches, and I think he pitched three-and-two-thirds innings, and there was two out in the ninth, and I'm down in the bullpen just messin' around, throwin' the ball, loosening up in case I get a start again. And Alvin Dark calls down and says, "How does Catfish feel?" "How do you feel?" they asked me. And I said, "I feel great." And I looked at him, and he's bringing me in the ball game. And I said, "Oh, my God."

So I walked into Dodger Stadium. I was walking to the mound, and that was the longest walk I ever walked in my life. I got there and Alvin Dark said—it was the catcher, Ferguson, for the Dodgers—he says, "This guy can't hit a curveball with a paddle. What are you gonna throw him?" I said, "Fastball." Alvin spit—he went, "Tooey." He said, "I said this guy can't hit a curve with a paddle. Watcha gonna throw him?" I said, "Fastball." "Why are you gonna throw him a fastball?" I said, "I don't have a curveball." And he walked off the mound.

And I threw five straight fastballs, and I struck him out. He came running out, and he said, "Boy, I'm glad you didn't throw him a slider or a curveball." I said, "Why?" He said, "'Cause he'd of hit it out of the ballpark off of you."

I guess my greatest Yankee day was probably when I was signing with them and then probably the last game I pitched in the World Series in 1978 against the Dodgers. Before the signing I didn't think I was gonna sign with the Yankees, but the scout who had signed me with the A's was working with the Yankees, Clyde Kluttz.

And Clyde said, "I'll meet you for breakfast before I go back home." We were talking, and he said, "What would it take for the Yankees to sign you?" He said, "Just write it down." I said, "I don't know, Clyde." And so I wrote down a figure, whatever, and I said, plus there had to be this and this and whatever.

He said, "Let me call Gabe Paul." He called Gabe Paul, and Gabe Paul said, "I think we can work that out. Get up here." So we went to the lawyer's office after we ate and talked to Mr. Cherry and everything, and we flew up to New York. And that was a great day, because I'd spent the whole fall trying to hook on with a club, or whatever, as the first free agent.

We signed on New Year's Eve, and that was a great day, being a Yankee right then. Then the first year it wasn't like being a Yankee, because we played at Shea Stadium. And then after that we started playing at Yankee Stadium, and '76, '77, and '78 we were in the World Series.

I would say '78, the last game that I pitched in the World Series—we won the sixth game. I remember I was in the clubhouse—we were in L.A.—and Piniella walked by my locker, and my jacket was hanging up in there. And he looked in my jacket pocket, and I had a plane ticket for that night right after the ball game to come home.

And Lou says, "Look at this guy, he thinks he's gonna win tonight. He's got his ticket." I said, "That's right, Lou, we're gonna win, and I'm gonna go home." And we won, and I come on home. That should have been the year that I retired, 1978, instead of 1979.

I was gettin' 'em out and everything, and I remember when I was taken out of the game—I think it was in the bottom of the eighth, I had one out or something, and Bob Lemon walked out, and he said, "Cat, I know you can get 'em out, but I don't want 'em to have another damn run." He says, "I'm gonna bring in Goose." I said, "That's fine with me," and I walked on into the dugout.

And I said right then that that should have been my last pitch in baseball.

I didn't ever think I'd be in the Hall of Fame. I always thought that all the Hall of Famers were a step ahead of me and everything. When they voted me in, I couldn't believe it. . . .

I went in with Billy Williams and Ray Dandridge. I remember Mr. Steinbrenner and Mr. Finley both were at the Hall of Fame that day in Cooperstown. And I thanked both of 'em—Mr. Finley for giving me the chance to play baseball, for signing me, and operating on my foot before I got to play, and then I thanked Mr. Steinbrenner for giving me enough money to retire on. . . .

Another would probably be the first time I pitched in Washington, D.C.—that my mom and dad could come up and see me. Our whole family I guess was up in Washington, and I got to play and pitch, and I hit a home run that day. And they were jumping up and down and yelling so much that I think one of my kinfolk lost a watch and everything—she didn't even know she lost it, she was jumpin' up and down so much. It seemed like I pitched a little bit better when my family was around.

REGGIE JACKSON

You don't even have to be a baseball fan to be able to guess Reggie Jackson's greatest day in baseball. If you get within shouting distance of a TV set in April and you're familiar with the expression "Mr. October," then you know what Reggie did against the Los Angeles Dodgers on October 18, 1977.

It's kind of obvious, isn't it?

I had a relaxing day—watched TV, relaxed around the house, did a lot of fun things in the afternoon. Had a nice lady, went to the ballpark completely relaxed, and I probably had the best batting practice I've ever had, or that maybe anyone's ever had.

I hit the last five minutes all the time. Dick Howser threw to me, and in fifty swings, I probably hit thirty-five balls in the seats within about a fifty-foot radius. Got a standing ovation at the ting practice. I've had some great batting practices, but never a.., thing like that.

I knew I felt good. I knew I had the bat going in the right way. I'd had a good day Sunday—I got a couple hits—and we had the day off on Monday. When I was hitting, the Dodgers were all in left field on the foul line near third base, waiting to take the field, and you could tell from the display being made that they were being wowed by the batting practice I was having.

First time up Burt Hooton went ball one, ball two, ball three, ball four, right around the strike zone—one up and away, one down and in, one low and away, you know. He never even came close to throwing a strike—he walked me. Next time up he threw a fastball in, and I hit the ball like a low two-iron. I was just hoping that the ball would stay up—I had a lot of top hand, the ball was hooking a little bit—went in the stands, hit on a line, deep.

Next time up, they changed pitchers—and I was swinging the bat well, that was pretty easy to see—and they brought in Elias Sosa, good fastball. I remember it was 2–2. I hit the ball in the same spot, and I hit the ball lower this time, and I was worried it wasn't going to be high enough, it was hit hard enough. I didn't know if it was going to be high enough. It went into the stands—boom, number two.

When I circled the bases that time, I really felt ecstatic. I had tied the home run record for most home runs in the Series. I was always a fan of Duke Snider's and Mantle, guys that had played and excelled in the Series. Snider had the record—I think he hit four homers in the Series twice.

Then the last time up, when I walked out of the dugout, people were excited—clapping, chanting, "Reggie . . . Reggie." They started the "Reggie" chant after the first one, but this time, I think it was the eighth inning—game was in pretty good hands, you know? I think it was like 7–3 at the time or something, and they brought in Charlie Hough.

I couldn't believe it, because I had so much success in my history against knuckleballers. You approach the knuckleball just like—it's all timing, a fully-extended swing that's timed at the speed of the ball.

He threw the ball at me, and it was just right there. I couldn't believe it. I was in a no-lose situation. The game was in the eighth inning, it was over. All I had to do was just do anything, and I was gonna be cheered. I wound up hitting a home run, and I couldn't believe it. I guess I could believe it—the way the night was going, I couldn't do anything wrong.

I remember Sutton and Garvey and somebody else—Lasorda came over and said it was the greatest performance he'd ever seen. I loved that. I remember being real—in fact, I remember sharing a lot of good moments with Billy Martin—him and I were, you know, enemies, really.

I remember my father in the clubhouse. I remember doing an interview with Bill White. I remember thanking God. I remember thanking all my friends and people that had stuck with me—what a day.

FERGIE JENKINS

Renowned for his consistency throughout his career, it's hardly surprising that one of Fergie Jenkins's greatest days would have to do with the phenomenal streak of winning at least twenty games for six consecutive seasons. But Jenkins also authored one of the most memorable All-Star performances in history during his first mid-season appearance in 1967.

I would have to say that I have two greatest days. The first was in Anaheim in 1967, which was my first All-Star game. I arrived in Anaheim on a Friday night, and I can remember going to a dinner and seeing all the great players on the team—Mays, Aaron, Clemente, guys like that. I wasn't really nervous, because I never really got nervous when it came to baseball—and besides that, I'd already pitched Opening Day for the Cubs. Billy Williams from the Cubs was on the team, as well as Ernie Banks, and Ernie was my roommate.

So we get to the game, and I was the second pitcher—I don't even remember who started, I think it was Gibson or Marichal. When I got into the game it was the bottom of their order that was coming up, and I struck out the first guy I faced—I don't remember who it was. And they announced their pinch-hitter, and it was Mickey Mantle.

The late Walter Alston, he was the [National League] manager, he came out to the mound, and he basically told me to just go after him, but that if I got behind I had first base open and that I could pitch around him. Alston went back to the dugout, and Joe Torre was the catcher, and he turned to me and he said, "You know who you're pitching to?" And I said, "Yeah, I know who I'm pitching to."

So I threw the first pitch—it was a fastball on the outside corner for a called strike. And I said to myself, "Shoot, I'm ahead in the count. I'm just gonna go after him and back him off the plate and see if I can get him out." At that point in my career I was still a thrower, I was really still learning how to pitch.

The next pitch was another fastball that was up and in, and he fouled it away on kind of a half-swing. Then the next pitch I threw was on the outside corner—it was a little high. I forget who the umpire was, but he called it a strike. And there it was, I'd struck out Mickey Mantle on three pitches.

Then I struck out the next guy to end the inning. And we come out the next inning, and I struck out all three guys—I don't even remember who I struck out. I also gave up a home run to Brooks Robinson—he hit a slider that stayed up high out over the plate. He hit it to left field.

That was significant because all the runs in that particular game came on home runs. Dick Allen hit one to tie it at 1–1, and the game went fifteen innings. And Tony Perez of the National League hit a home run to win the game, and Drysdale was the winning pitcher. And then somebody came up to me after the game and told me what I'd done, and they said that it had never been done before.

My other day would have to be the day I won my twentieth game for the sixth straight season in a row. I don't remember who I faced—I think it might have been the Phillies, which was kind of funny because I came up through their farm system before they traded me to the Cubs. I know it was early September, my record was 19–11, so I knew I probably had four or five starts to get it done. But I said to myself, "Shoot, I'm gonna go after it tonight and get it done so that I don't have to worry about it. That way everything I get over twenty wins is gravy."

I was always pretty relaxed when I pitched, and one of the things I always did was to take a nap in the training room before the game. On this particular day I went into a really deep sleep, and when I woke up I barely knew where I was. And I just remember thinking when I got up, "Damn, I have to pitch today."

So I'm running around trying to find the trainer, and I'm asking everybody what time it was, and somebody says to me, "Relax,

Fergie, you've still got twenty-five minutes." It was a day game. I think it was either a one o'clock start or one-thirty. I went out to the bullpen and threw for about ten minutes—that was another thing I always did. I threw all of the pitches I was going to throw in the game—fastball, slider, curve—and then I was ready to go.

I don't remember the score of the game—I know I gave up a run or two, but we won the game. The Cubs had some champagne on ice in the clubhouse after the game. And then my wife picked me up with the kids, and we went out and celebrated.

The Hall of Fame was a different kind of greatest day, because you wait for five years before you get elected. You know what you've done, what your numbers are, you have so many wins and so many strikeouts. But you're thinking about the way the fans perceived you, how the reporters are going to vote—that kind of thing plays in the back of your mind. And then there was the incident in Toronto when the articles were found in my suitcase. [Editor's note: Jenkins was later acquitted of a drug possession charge.]

The first time they voted was in 1988, and I was seventy votes short. Then the next year I came up thirty-five votes short—I needed 277. Then, finally, the third year I got in with Rod Carew and Gaylord Perry—I got in by two votes. I had always won games by close scores—2–1, 3–2, 1–0—so getting in on a close vote was nothing new to me. That was just the way things went for me during my career.

I can remember being in the room in Cooperstown, waiting to go to the ceremony, sitting in that room with Gaylord Perry and Rod Carew. We got out on the dais, and I can just remember the whole thing like it was yesterday—the color of the suit I had on, the exact color combinations that Gaylord and Rod were wearing.

It was really hot that day, and Rod Carew got up to give his speech, and you could see the sweat on the back of his trousers. I looked over at Gaylord, and his shirt is soaked. I mean he's just sweating like crazy. He's bald, you know, and he's wiping his brow and everything. I was barely sweating, and he looks at me as if to say, "Aren't you nervous?" And I said to him, "This is the greatest time of our lives, don't you think?" And he looks at me and says, "Yeah, but that's not gonna stop me from sweating bullets."

So Rod Carew was in the middle of his speech when he mentions Billy Martin's name, and all of a sudden out of the blue you could hear the thunder, and a bolt of lightning split the sky off in the distance. And he stops and looks up in the sky, and he says, "Billy must be up there listening to us." That got quite a reaction from the crowd, and then it was my turn to give a speech.

And then the most amazing thing happened. I pulled out the piece of paper before I got up to make the speech, but then when I got to the dais I just blanked out completely and forgot everything that I was going to say. That had never happened to me before—as an athlete you're conditioned and programmed to remember things through repetition.

When I was a student I studied drafting, and there was a lot of math and trigonometry—and trigonometry is all a lot of memorizing formulas—so I was used to mental preparation from that perspective as well. And as a pitcher, I used to mentally pitch the game the day before when I was in the dugout charting pitches. After a while you get so used to that kind of preparation that you don't even think that something like what happened to me could happen.

Then the man from the Hall of Fame gave me the award just before I got to the podium, and at that instant it all came back to me. So I thanked everyone—from my wife and family, the scout who signed me, the Phillies, and everyone from the Cubs.

I think it was putting on the Cubs uniform that was always special to me more than the Red Sox or the Rangers—and I won twenty-five games with the Rangers when everyone said I would wilt from the heat down there. So I always tried to give the best performance I could, because the Cubs were the team that meant the most to me throughout my whole career.

DEREK JETER

There's a certain element of peril to asking any second-year player what his "greatest day" might be, but given Derek Jeter's potential as one of the "shortstops of the future," it seemed like a good idea to get his thoughts about his phenomenal rookie year and his role in the Yankees' drive to win the 1996 World Series.

That's easy, the World Series—that and the parade. The last game sticks out. We were down 2–0—we came back, we knew we were in a good position to win Game 6. We had a lead going into the ninth inning. They got close, but it was just like the whole thing, everything was in slow motion. The last pop-up, it seemed like it took forever to come down. It's—winning the whole thing, it's just a dream come true.

The other thing I remember is how loud it was. I mean, we played in Seattle the year before—that's a dome, and it was loud, and I don't think it can compare to how loud it was in New York. It was something that—I don't even think you really describe it in words. It was like everything was vibrating. By far the loudest, even compared to the other games in the playoffs.

My greatest moment was probably just getting the hit and scoring the run in that inning we scored three runs. Joey [Girardi] got a hit, then I got a hit, and I stole second, and Bernie drove me in. I think that inning was the most exciting.

It was 2–0, and [Maddux] pretty much gave me a good pitch to hit, so I hit it up the middle. Just one of those things—it just seemed like everything went right for us that year.

The parade—I've never in my life seen that many people. I think if you add up all the people I've ever seen, it wouldn't have been that many people. It was unbelievable. It was overwhelming. I've never seen anything like it before. I didn't realize there was that many Yankee fans. I didn't realize there was that many people in New York, period. It was absolutely packed. Unless you're there, you really can't describe it. . . .

You always remember your debut and your first hit, but winning the World Series, I think that's something that every kid who plays Little League has ever dreamed of. Once you get it, it's like the ultimate dream come true. Nothing else can compare.

[For box score, please see interview with Wade Boggs.]

RANDY JOHNSON

When he broke into the big leagues with Montreal, this left-handed fireballer was an oddity—a 6'10" pitcher with a near 100 mile an hour fastball, a biting slider, and a lack of control that threatened the health and welfare of virtually every batter to step up to the plate against him, left-handed hitters especially. After harnessing his gifts, Johnson has gone on to pitch a

*no-hitter, set numerous strikeout records, and become one of the best
pitchers in baseball, helping to lead the Seattle Mariners to division
titles in both 1996 and 1997.*

I would say that one of my greatest days in baseball was just
making it to the major leagues, and my first major thrill in this game
was my first major league start when I was with the Montreal Expos
back in '88. My very first major league start was against the
Pittsburgh Pirates in Montreal, and I won the game. But it was a
game where one particular batter hit two home runs off me—his
name was Glenn Wilson.

I was just kind of in awe, because I wasn't sure if all the players were gonna be like this, or what. But that was my first major
thrill, that was when I really had butterflies. I've had a few more
thrills in this game. I've been fortunate enough to throw a no-hitter,
so that was a thrill in my career. And I also pitched a game that won
the American League West in 1995.

That was a complete game, so I got the thrill of being able to
make the last out and all that. I'd say those are probably my three
biggest thrills in this game. Hopefully there'll be many more, to go
to the World Series or something like that would obviously be a big
thrill. But to this date, those are my biggest thrills—my major league
debut, pitching the no-hitter, and pitching the '95 ALS championship game.

Back in '88, that's when Andy Van Slyke and Barry Bonds and
Bobby Bonilla and Glenn Wilson and all those guys were on the
Pittsburgh Pirates team at the time. I was in awe of pitching to all
these guys that I knew because I watched TV and had heard of them
and read newspapers and stuff, so it was just a great thrill for me. I
was in awe of being there and of pitching to major league hitters and
pitching in front of a relatively big crowd, bigger than I had pitched
to in the past.

I just remember not sleeping well the night before, having butterflies . . . Basically, at that time I think I was the only rookie on the
team. I was surrounded by veteran players on the team, so they made
it a little bit easier for me by just telling me to relax a little bit and
have fun.

I think that I was expecting to have a little bit more trouble
with Barry Bonds or Van Slyke or Bobby Bonilla, because I'd always
heard their names more than I'd heard Glenn Wilson's. Glenn Wilson
was the one that—I think he hit a home run off me in like the second

inning, and then he came up again maybe in the fifth or sixth inning, and he hit another home run off me.

I was just in awe of him—not because he hit 'em off me, but because I thought all the major league hitters were gonna be like this guy. I thought this guy was the next best thing since Babe Ruth. He hit home runs, and I was throwing my best pitches—the same pitches that I was getting out all these other big-name ballplayers with—I was getting them out, but I wasn't getting this guy out. I was just a little in awe of him.

After I got my first major league win, and I got a win that game, it was just a thrill. And ever since then, I've just always tried to have the most fun possible in this game. It's just something I've enjoyed doing ever since Little League.

The no-hitter was something. It was a game where I was very young—I think I had a little over a year of major league experience. It was in 1990, and it was a game where I was really wild—I think I walked seven guys—and so I think it was one of those games where I'd have the bases loaded and then get a pop-up or something like that.

I really didn't realize that I had a no-hitter until late in the game. And then the last out was Mike Heath, it was a high fastball—it was definitely not a strike, but he swung at it. I didn't really know what to do. I just kind of jumped up and down. My catcher at the time, his name was Scott Bradley, he came out, and all my teammates came out, and we were all jumping up and down.

It was just something that now I realize is hard to accomplish, because I've had a couple in the ninth inning and I lost 'em. So I realized I was very fortunate just to have that one, and that's one reason why that was probably one of my biggest thrills in this game.

The one-game playoff was against the California Angels, and it was if we win, we win the West, and if the Angels win, they win the West, so that was probably the biggest game I've pitched. Ironically, that was a game against the California Angels and the pitcher that I got traded from Montreal to Seattle for, Mark Langston. So there was a little riff there. It was kind of fun facing him. He pitched an excellent game.

I think it was like a nothing-nothing ball game for about six or seven innings, and then we finally scored a run, and then we finally broke the game open later in the game. That was a great thrill, because I knew the significance of that game, and it was obviously quite a thrill for all the fans. So that was probably my third-biggest thrill in this game.

There's no real comparison, because those were moments that I won't forget, my first major league start—obviously everybody remembers their first major league hit, or their first start—so that was much more significant factor in my career, getting to the major leagues. A no-hitter's something that's very hard to achieve, so that's something that they won't be able to take away from me. And then the one-game playoff was a situation that, hopefully, you won't have to be in a one-game playoff for that, but it was just the situation that we were in.

Maybe other significant games that I've pitched in, striking out 300 batters in a year, you know, it's there, and I enjoyed doing that— it was maybe a once-in-a-lifetime type thing that I'll do. Going 18–2 in '95 and winning the Cy Young Award, I don't put a lot of emphasis on that, it was a great year and everything.

I would say the 300 strikeouts was quite a thrill, because I may never accomplish that again. I'm one of, I think, twelve guys that have struck out 300 in a season, and so to be among guys that are probably in the Hall of Fame, that's quite a thrill. I remember the 300th— it was against Ruben Sierra. It was against Oakland in Seattle, and there was a person out in center field that had a big countdown.

When I got the 299th, everybody was standing up and clapping. And I got Ruben Sierra out on a slider, and everybody stood up and started clapping, and I got the ball and threw it into the dugout. I have that [ball] now, so that was quite a thrill. The fans, not only did I realize the significance of that, but the fans did as well, so they were very knowledgeable of what was going on and the significance of that.

Hopefully there will be many more thrills, but up until now those are the ones that were the tops of all of them.

JIM KAAT

In a remarkable career that spanned four decades (he's probably best known for his pitching in the '60s with the Minnesota Twins), Jim Kaat won almost 300 games, was a perennial twenty-game winner, a perennial All-Star, and a postseason standout. For his greatest day, however, Kaat chose an experience near the end of his career, when he was a relief specialist for the St. Louis Cardinals.

I'm kind of torn on that, but I think I would have to say, you know, scrapping an individual thrill for a team thrill would be the seventh game of the 1982 World Series, and I did not even participate in that game. In fact, I think a couple of my best days in baseball were days that I didn't even play. One of 'em was being a coach in Cincinnati when Pete Rose got the hit to break Ty Cobb's record, and the other was Game 7 of the World Series in 1982 when we beat the Milwaukee Brewers.

I had a lot of success from an individual standpoint. As all young players strive for, you want to prove that you belong and that you're good, and you want to make an All-Star team and win twenty games and be recognized as being one of the best at what you do. But then the longer your career goes on, you realize that the big thing in this game is getting a World Series ring. . . . Even after all these years, that year sticks out in my mind as my favorite year.

I had reached the World Series in 1965 with the Minnesota Twins, and we were still a fairly young ball club and figured we would be back many years. Now we did get to the playoffs a few years after that, and we might have been as good a team as there was in the American League in the '60s for the whole decade. The Yankees dominated early, and the Orioles late, but over the whole decade we were pretty solid. But we never got back to the World Series.

Then I went to the Phillies, and we had good teams there. Ability-wise I'd say a couple of those teams in the late '70s were the best teams that I had been on, and we got to the playoffs but never did get to the Series. So here it's 1982, and it's seventeen years since I've been to the World Series. I'm forty-three years old, about to be forty-four, and I'm saying, "This is it. This is going to be the last shot at it."

We whipped through the Braves in three straight, and the Brewers series goes back and forth, and we get down to Game 7— where we had to win Game 6 to force a Game 7. I just think that that day I had more thoughts flashing through my mind about what baseball meant to me and what it had done for me.

I recall the ninth inning. We had a three-run lead, I believe it was 6–3, and the guards and the police came down to the bullpen and said, "If you would like to go down to the dugout to avoid the fans running on the field, feel free to do that." And I was sitting down there with our bullpen coach, Dave Ricketts, and I said, "I'm not moving. I'm staying here."

First of all, if by some chance Bruce Sutter would get in some trouble—you know, we didn't anticipate that, he was our ace, and he usually got the job done—but I thought if in fact he did, I wanted to be down there ready to warm up. And secondly, I would say that once we took the lead—I think we may have taken the lead in the sixth or seventh inning—we fell behind early and then we came back and took the lead, and I started really kind of getting sentimental.

October 20, 1982

MILWAUKEE	AB	R	H	RBI	ST. LOUIS	AB	R	H	RBI
Molitor, 3b	4	1	2	0	L. Smith, lf	5	2	3	1
Yount, ss	4	0	1	0	Oberkfell, 3b	3	0	0	0
Cooper, 1b	3	0	1	1	Tenace, ph	0	0	0	0
Simmons, c	4	0	0	0	Ramsey, 3b	1	1	0	0
Oglivie, lf	4	1	1	1	Hernandez, 1b	3	1	2	2
Thomas, cf	4	0	0	0	Hendrick, cf	5	0	2	1
Howell, dh	3	0	0	0	Porter, c	5	0	1	1
Moore, rf	3	0	1	0	Iorg, dh	3	0	2	0
Gantner, 2b	3	1	1	0	Green, dh	0	0	0	0
Vuckovich, p	0	0	0	0	Braun, dh	2	0	1	1
McClure, p	0	0	0	0	McGee, cf	5	1	1	0
Haas, p	0	0	0	0	Herr, 2b	3	0	1	0
Caldwell, p	0	0	0	0	O. Smith, ss	4	1	2	0
					Andujar, p	0	0	0	0
					Sutter, p	0	0	0	0
Totals	32	3	7	2	Totals	39	6	15	6

```
Milwaukee   000   012   000 — 3
St. Louis   000   103   02X — 6
```

MILWAUKEE	IP	H	R	ER	BB	SO
Vuckovich	5.1	10	3	3	2	3
McClure, L	0.1	2	1	1	1	0
Haas	2	1	2	2	1	1
Caldwell	0.1	2	0	0	0	0
ST. LOUIS	IP	H	R	ER	BB	SO
Andujar, W	7	7	3	2	0	1
Sutter, S	2	0	0	0		

I thought back to the bus rides in Superior, Nebraska, and Missoula, Montana, and I thought, "Man, all these years I've been in the game now . . ." That would have been my twenty-sixth or twenty-seventh year professionally, twenty-fifth in the big leagues. And I thought back to all those bus rides and all of the highs and lows of my career, and I thought, "Here it is, three outs away, and I'm gonna get that feeling that I've heard so much about but I've never experienced."

I'll never forget—Bruce Sutter was known as a split-finger fastball pitcher, but he threw a fastball past Gorman Thomas to strike him out for the last out of the game. I would say that for that day, and for the next couple of days, when we had the parade in St. Louis, that was as high a high as I have had in baseball.

Granted, beating Koufax in Game 2 in the '65 Series and things like winning your twentieth game the first time or hitting your first home run and going to the All-Star game in '62 with a lot of great players when I was still a young kid, you know, Mantle and Colavito, guys like that, that was exciting, too. But I don't think anything topped that late October of 1982.

That year I was pretty much a part-time player. I think Whitey Herzog made me feel very good when we won the division, and then when we won the National League championship series, of which I did not even participate in. I wasn't needed. But he made me feel very good about, you know, we couldn't have won it without your contribution.

And there were some moments where I came in to save a game. And even in the World Series, I got a couple of outs in Game 2, and I got a couple of outs in Game 3 that helped us win the game. But there wasn't any command performance that I had during that year that really stuck out.

When I competed against Pete [Rose], you know, we competed pretty good against each other. He used to run over the mound and try to intimidate pitchers, and I used to try to get in his way or make him run around. And it was pretty flattering to me when he sent one of their batting practice pitchers over and said if he ever managed, he wanted me to be his pitching coach.

So after I got released in 1983, and I was just sort of inactive, trying to figure out what I was gonna do with my life, I hear over the news that he's gonna be the player/manager of the Cincinnati Reds. This happened in late '84, I want to say maybe August of '84.

I told my buddy . . . that I'm gonna get a call from Pete Rose tomorrow. And he said, "Ah, he probably told fifteen or twenty guys." And I said, "No, Pete is a loyal guy who wouldn't say that without meaning it." So sure enough, he called me the next day.

So I went in to coach for him the rest of the '84 season and all of '85, and as it got—I mean, I was very close to him and he was a playing manager, and he relied on me to handle just about all the pitching. And we hung out together, we ate together, and unfortunately in some cases, the story doesn't come off too well, but we went to a lot of horse races together, which probably helped get him in trouble. I can't say that I did—he's always been a horse track lover—but we kind of shared that love. So we spent a lot of time together.

I'd say those last two to three weeks [before Rose broke Ty Cobb's record] when the media started really following him and tracking that, it became very exciting just to watch every at-bat, it was almost like following a pennant race. I'll never forget the day. But the weekend before, we were going back to Cincinnati—this would have been maybe September 7, 8, 9 in 1985. We're playing the Cubs in Chicago, and Steve Trout is pitching, left-hand pitcher, and Pete never played against left-hand pitching. I think either Esasky or Tony Perez or somebody else played first base against left-hand pitching.

So he's on the bench and he's not playing, and it's a cold, miserable day and the Cubs have us beat. And all the writers are heading to the airport, they're going back to Cincinnati, because we're gonna be there tomorrow, and he's one hit away from the record. Lo and behold, we come back and tie it up and the Cubs bring up Lee Smith, and the pitcher's spot is due up.

And I'm standing next to Pete in the dugout, and he said, "What am I gonna do? If that spot comes up, I've gotta hit. I owe it to my team to try to win the game." And I'm looking in the stands, there's not 5,000 people left. It's dark and grey, and I thought, "Man, what a shame this would be. . . ."

And then of course he didn't, and we came back to Cincinnati. And he had a shot at it the first night against the Padres, and he went like 0–4. And I'll never forget Tommy Helms, his close buddy, telling him the next day, when Pete came to the ballpark—his nickname was "Scooter"— and Tommy said, "Scooter, that's the first time I've ever seen you at the ballpark when you didn't look like you were having fun." He was really uptight.

That night, the night that he did break it, he loosened up and he was a lot more himself, and of course he went up that day and he got the base hit off of Eric Show. I had written all that stuff down, I thought, "This is gonna be a memorable night." Carmelo Martinez fielded the ball, and Bruce Bochy was the catcher, and the late Lee Weyer was the umpire.

You seldom saw Pete show his emotions, but when he got around first base and realized what he'd done, and his son was there, and he ran out and threw his arms around him, and of course the whole team ran out on the field. There are moments that stand out in your mind, and we relate a lot of it to baseball—you know, like where you were when Fisk hit the home run, or Thomson, things like that. When I look back over my career that's just a stick-out moment. Having become good friends with Pete, and having so much respect for what he did in the game of baseball, to actually be there and be a part of it was a real highlight.

You know, there are games that don't necessarily have an impact on a pennant race—I pitched a game out in Anaheim, it might have been the last game I ever won for the Minnesota Twins in '73 before they unloaded me. I think I gave up a home run to Frank Robinson to lead off the second inning, and I got all the rest of the guys out.

It was like a 2–1 win over Bill Singer in an hour and thirty-seven minutes. In fact, Herb Karneal, the current voice of the Twins, loves to tell this story. We played a 6 o'clock game, because they were gonna have fireworks after the game. The game ended at 7:38, and they had to keep the fans busy for an hour until it got dark, because they couldn't shoot off the fireworks. And we were back at the hotel having dinner while the fans were still sitting out there waiting for the fireworks. As far as effective pitching, I probably couldn't have pitched too much better than I did that day.

The Koufax game, obviously, because it was Game 2 of the World Series, but I got a great boost in that game by Bob Allison's catch. It didn't happen in New York, you know, so it didn't get as much publicity, but it might have been one of the greatest World Series catches ever, which would have given the Dodgers the lead, and I doubt we would have beaten Koufax. He did catch it, and I went on to pitch pretty well, and yeah, that game stands out.

There are games where you know you're on top of your game, and it might be just one of those middle of June, middle game of a series that doesn't seem to be that important. You know, another one that probably stuck out was probably my first win in Yankee

Stadium against Whitey Ford. I pitched seven innings, gave up three earned runs, pitched pretty well, thinking these were the Yankees, and I was just a young kid. We ended up coming back and winning that game, that stood out in my mind.

As an announcer—the '91 World Series, the whole postseason. I was working for CBS, and during the World Series I was a field reporter, and I had to hold the postgame trophy presentation. Being right down there at field level, particularly at the Metrodome, when it seemed like I was almost playing first base, the spot I had was so close to the diamond. . . . To be almost on the field, right down up close for those, from a broadcast standpoint, was a real highlight.

I think as the years have gone by I probably get a little more cynical about the Hall of Fame. The first few years I was eligible I was anxious, I wondered where I would stack up. And then after a couple of years it became pretty clear to me that I had some support but I was not near, in the ballpark, in the opinion of most of the guys that vote. . . .

I would say that the two things that probably kept me out of the Hall of Fame for sure at this point were both base running incidents.

This is kind of unusual—in 1972, the year before the DH, I'm 10–2 on the first of July. Palmer and I are leading the league in everything. I slide into second base to break up a double play, and I break the navicular bone in my wrist. I'm shot for the rest of the year. The way I was pitching, you'd have to say I had an excellent shot at winning twenty, but maybe I would have come up and been seventeen or eighteen.

Now in 1976, I'm starting to roll along, and I think I finally got straightened out and I get to 10–6 or 10–7. And I'm sitting in the dugout in St. Louis, and out of the blue Danny Ozark says, "Go in and run for Luzinski." Here's Bull at twenty-nine years old, and I'm the old guy on the team at thirty-seven at the time. I'm sitting there in my turf shoes, no jock, not anticipating being in this game. I'd pitched nine innings the day before, and I'm saying, I don't want to cause a scene and tell the manager, hey, I don't want to go in to run.

So I do a couple deep knee bends, and I go in to loosen up. And lo and behold, Jay Johnstone hits a double on the first pitch, and I come truckin' around second toward third, and that's when they still had dirt in the infield in St. Louis, it wasn't solid turf, it was turf but then the base paths were dirt. There was loose dirt near third base, and I kind of half-slide and half-stumble into third. And when the inning's over, I get back to the bench, I look at my knee, and my knee is puffing up like a volleyball.

It ended up I had a little lateral hairline fracture of the kneecap, and I did pitch some after that, but not as effectively, and I think that really hurt me. Even in '77, it took a little while before my leg got to where I could land on that front foot the way I needed to. So I think those two injuries—probably there are a lot of players that could say that—but those two injuries in particular took a lot of opportunities away from me to maybe win some games.

The other thing, if I were to make a case for myself, the other thing that is a bit unusual about my career versus the rest of 'em is I think I'm still in the top ten or eleven in games appeared. I pitched a combination of starting and relieving. In terms of being a middle man, having nineteen saves, having 600 and some starts— I don't think there's any other pitcher, maybe Wilhelm, who started a lot and relieved, that pitched in as many different roles for as long as I did. And still, the last year I pitched, contributed to a World Series winner.

AL KALINE

Very few players become synonymous with the franchises they play for, but if you're a baseball fan and you think of the Detroit Tigers, you automatically think of Al Kaline. After a marvelous career that began when he donned the batboy's uniform, Kaline capped his achievements with some great clutch-hitting in the Tigers' drive to the title in 1968.

Certainly one of the days, the greatest day I ever had, was the first day I joined the ball club right out of high school and put on the major league uniform. To me that was the ultimate—to walk out on the major league field wearing a major league uniform. That to me was almost as big a thrill as I've ever had.

The other time was in 1955, when I hit three home runs in one game, two in one inning. That was an individual thing that certainly I remembered as one of my best days in baseball. Finally, the day we cinched the American League pennant in 1968, to finally get a chance to play in the World Series was a great thrill for me. I'd have to consider that a team thing and a great day in baseball for me.

And of course when I was out of baseball, the ultimate was an induction into baseball's Hall of Fame. That was a tremendous day even though I wasn't an active player. But still, I think that to be recognized as one of the best in your field is a great honor. It certainly was a big day for me, and I was very fortunate that my mother and father were still alive to enjoy that day also.

The first day, of course—I was born and raised in Baltimore and signed with the Tigers. I took a train to Philadelphia, and got to the hotel just in time to get to the bus and go out to the ballpark. I was not a very big guy at the time, and I'll never forget, they had to give me the batboy's uniform—I was only 150 pounds. Of course, it didn't say "batboy" on the back, but I remember that, not only because it was the first day I walked into a major league ballpark, but also because I had to wear a batboy's uniform.

I got in as a pinch-hitter in the eighth inning, I think it was, and I hit the first pitch to center field for an out. It was off of Harry Byrd, who was their best pitcher at the time. . . .

And 1955, the day I hit the three home runs, it was early in the season, I got off to a great start. I hit three home runs, two in one inning. . . . I went on to win the batting title that year, so that was early in the year, and it gave me a great start.

Of course 1968 was the year—we lost the championship on the last day in 1967—'68 was a great year, everybody on the Tigers came to spring training with one goal in mind. And that was really the only time I've ever played on a team where everybody was focused on one thing, and that was going out to win, because we all thought we should have won it in 1967.

So everybody was focused. We had a great spring. We went on and almost led wire-to-wire and had a great bunch of guys, so that was a great thrill to play on that team. What you learn is that if everybody focuses on doing the little things, and to not worry about individual statistics, that anything's possible. I think that's what happened. Everybody knew their role. We basically had the same bunch of guys, and we all thought if we can all do something a little bit better, each of us, then we could possibly go on and win this thing.

We got in the World Series and beat St. Louis in the seventh game to become world champions. We learned an awful lot about what was expected of you in 1967.

I can't think of any one day personally in '68, but I knew we

June 25, 1953

DETROIT (A.)	AB	R	H	PO	A	PHILA. (A.)	AB	R	H	PO	A
Kuenn, ss	4	0	2	3	2	DeMaestri, ss	4	1	1	1	2
Hatfield, pr	0	0	0	0	0	Philley, rf	4	1	2	1	0
Pesky, 2b	5	0	0	1	3	Robinson, 1b	2	0	1	5	0
Boone, 3b	3	0	1	2	0	Hamilton, 1b	1	0	0	5	0
Dropo, 1b	4	0	0	5	2	Zernial, lf	4	0	0	0	0
Delsing, cf	3	0	0	2	0	Suder, 2b	4	0	2	1	2
Kaline, cf	1	0	0	0	0	Babe, 3b	3	1	0	1	0
Nieman, rf	4	1	1	4	0	McGhee, cf	3	1	0	4	0
Souchock, lf	4	0	1	4	0	Astroth, c	3	0	1	9	0
Batts, c	4	1	2	2	0	Byrd, p	3	1	1	0	1
Marlowe, p	1	0	0	0	1						
Welk, p	1	0	0	0	1						
Mullin, ph	1	0	1	0	0						
Miller, p	0	0	0	0	0						
Lund, ph	1	0	1	0	0						
Totals	36	2	9	24	8	Totals	31	3	8	27	5

```
Detroit        000    000    002 — 2
Philadelphia   050    000    00X — 5
```

had a team that was never out of a game. We were a big-inning type of a team, and we knew eventually, late in the ball game, we were going to explode for as many runs as we needed. It was just a game to us—that sooner or later we were going to explode and score three, four runs in any one inning. It was the type of team that never thought they were out of the game, even going into the ninth inning, because we came from behind in many, many games in '68.

The Hall of Fame was certainly—you knew your time. It was ballots. A lot of people tell you that you're a cinch to make it, but you really don't know. There's been a lot of guys that have been disappointed and have missed it by a very few votes. I got the call and I went in on the very first ballot, and of course, what a great thrill.

I'll never forget the day I was inducted, being in the back before you make your appearance out on the stage at Cooperstown, being there with all the great players. I went in with Duke Snider and Mr. Yawkey, and I'll never forget sitting back there and just looking at the great players—Ted Williams, Stan Musial, Yogi Berra—I mean, I could go on and on and on and on. But just to sit back there and say, "My God, am I supposed to be thought of as being as good as some of these guys?" Certainly not the guys I mentioned, but what a great honor, for people to think that I belong in this category.

And then of course to be on the stage, and you see your wife and your kids and your mom and dad—the tremendous feeling that they must have, to know that their loved one is being thought of as one of the best in his field.

There's not much more I can say. I was very nervous about my speech, but I wanted to really express my feelings about the game. My whole life was involved as far as being young and playing baseball, and my only goal in life was to become a professional baseball player. I set my goals ever since I was twelve years old to somehow be a professional, not knowing that I would go on and do the things that I did.

I just wanted to sign a contract, go away, make a little bit of money, try to—when you get married—have enough money to have a house. But to realize a life, a goal that you set for yourself and do exacty what you want in your life—you know, not too many people in life can say that. I was very fortunate that I was blessed with a good body and a love for the game, and I had a great deal of pride in myself. So there's not much more I can say except that I've been blessed with the ability to do exactly with my life what I wanted to and play the great game, the greatest game in the world, I think.

Certainly the Hall of Fame stands out the most, but if I had to choose any one, it was the '68 team, when we won that last game that we needed to win to cinch the pennant and the World Series. I don't think you can say the '68 season without saying the '68 World Series. But to become world champions was the biggest honor that you can possibly have, and that's a team thing. I put that over everything else, with the exception of going to the Hall of Fame.

I was running out of time. I was thirty-six years old when I got into the World Series, and I thought time was running out for me. I knew my skills were starting to go somewhat. You keep worrying that year after year, am I gonna get a chance? To finally reach that goal, it really was the ultimate.

TOM KELLY

At the tender age of thirty-six, Tom Kelly became the youngest manager in the history of baseball to win the World Championship, leading the Minnesota Twins to victory against the St. Louis Cardinals in 1987. Kelly has also become a symbol of class and consistency during his tenure with the Twins, winning the championship again in 1991 in one of the most exciting World Series ever against the Atlanta Braves.

After giving it some thought, I think I'd have to go with the seventh game in the first World Series. That was quite a remarkable day, being thirty-six years old. At the time, you don't think about it as that, but it was pretty special. At the time, it was about winning.

I've thought about it in the past, and a lot of the players I had in the minor leagues played in that game, and they played well all that season. That was one of my favorite collection of players, and watching those players after the game was over was particularly memorable.

I think they made that trade for Baylor, that was Andy McPhail, and he helped win it for us in the playoffs. He really hadn't done much, but then he got that home run for us in the playoffs, and then you just try and write the names down and stay out of the way. It's like Sparky Anderson says: "You keep your feet up in the dugout, away from the aisle there, so that you don't trip anybody." He's right.

I think it might have come off Worrell? He had some real good at-bats off of Worrell, but I didn't know he had seven, eight, nine hits, and that he had aspirations of being the MVP. And then Roy Smalley walked, and I believe that loaded the bases, and Gagne hit the ball down the third base line. So when I sent Smalley up, I don't know if that was a big strategic move or not, to keep him in the game or pinch hit, but that's really the only move that I can remember. It didn't seem like that big of a move, but it's something that people remember. . . .

So much of what you do depends on the team, what you have. The last few years have been different, according to the team that you have and the position you think you're in. After the last few years, we're in a position where if we get this guy and this guy, we might be in a position to win. So we try to get to that position. . . .

My other two days—well, obviously when I got called up to the big leagues. That was a special day. I got called up, and I called my wife at the time, and she was on a trip with my parents, a mini-vacation. It meant a lot to me that my dad got to see me in the big leagues shortly after that, that was obviously a very special day.

The day we won the Atlanta series was a very special day

because all the games were very exciting, because all the games were a storybook. It seemed like a storybook game, it went into the tenth inning and the eleventh inning every game, except the one game we lost 6–5, Game 5—5 kind of got away from us at the end. It took all the sweat, every ounce of what we had, so that was very emotional and very serious. I was torn between Kirby's game and Game 7, when Morris pitched the extra-inning shutout.

The move we made in that game that turned out good was that we walked Justice to pitch to the guy that went to the Pirates—Sid Bream. We walked Justice to pitch to Bream, and we got the double play. Later in the game that backfired on us. There was a bunt, he hit into a double play, and we ended up with egg on our face.

The game ended, and it just seemed like everything sort of stopped. It was very stressful at the time. I remember about three weeks after the Series was over, I woke up in the morning and wondered who was pitching. I just woke up and thought about who was pitching. You make these moves, and people say different things at

October 25, 1987

ST. LOUIS	AB	R	H	RBI	MINNESOTA	AB	R	H	RBI
Coleman, lf	4	0	0	0	Gladden, lf	5	0	1	1
Smith, ss	4	0	0	0	Gagne, ss	5	1	2	1
Herr, 2b	4	0	1	0	Puckett, cf	4	0	2	1
Lindeman, 1b	3	1	1	0	Gaetti, 3b	3	0	0	0
Ford, ph	1	0	0	0	Baylor, dh	3	0	1	0
McGee, cf	4	1	1	0	Brunansky, rf	3	2	1	0
Pena, dh	3	0	2	1	Hrbek, 1b	3	0	0	0
Oquendo, rf	3	0	0	0	Laudner, c	3	1	2	0
Lawless, 3b	3	0	0	0	Lombardozzi, 2b	2	0	1	1
Lake, c	3	0	1	1	Smalley, ph	0	0	0	0
					Newman, 2b	1	0	0	0
Totals	32	2	6	2	Totals	32	4	10	4

St. Louis	020	000	000 — 2
Minnesota	010	011	01X — 4

ST. LOUIS	IP	H	R	ER	BB	SO
Magrane	4.1	5	2	2	1	4
Cox, L	0.2	2	1	1	3	0
Worrell	3	3	1	1	1	2
MINNESOTA	IP	H	R	ER	BB	SO
Viola, W	8	6	2	2	0	7
Reardon, S	1	0	0	0	0	0

different times, and one thing the fans just never understand about this game and never will is the emotion of this game. The emotion of this game is very overwhelming. The people who play this game are very emotional people, and the fan never gets to experience that.

The awards and all the achievements, those things are coattail. You have guys like Kirby Puckett, Frank Viola, Jeff Reardon, those players get you those awards. It's really the players—you don't have the players, you don't get any of those kind of awards, you don't even have a job. But I have had players, and I've had good players.

HARMON KILLEBREW

One of the game's consummate power hitters, Harmon Killebrew probably hit as many tape-measure home runs as anyone who ever played the game. A remarkably consistent player through his career, the former Minnesota Twins Hall of Famer also overcame considerable adversity in his career, coming back from a severe leg injury to cop the MVP Award in 1969.

You know, I've thought and thought . . . I don't know what was my greatest day in baseball, I really don't. I can say that there was a game that was voted as the most memorable thing in Twins history, in 1965 just before the All-Star break. I hit a home run off Pete Mikkelsen in the ninth inning with two outs that won the game for us. . . .

I fouled off several pitches, it was a 3–2 pitch with two outs, bottom of the ninth, Rollins was on first base. It was a sinker, and I hit it into the left field bleachers.

Another was the day I hit three homers in a row at Fenway— and I had a chance to hit the fourth one. I don't even remember what year it was, but I'd hit three in a row. They were all to left field, and the last time up I had a chance to hit four in a row, and I hit a 99-hopper to the second baseman.

The World Series also stands out, hitting a home run off of Drysdale, that was certainly—if you hit a home run in the World Series, that was certainly a big thing. We lost the game, actually. It was in Dodger Stadium, and it was two strikes and no balls, and Drysdale tried to throw a fastball by me, and I happened to hit a home run.

The significant part about playing in that World Series was that I had dislocated my elbow that year in a play at first base against the Orioles in Met Stadium on August 2nd of that year. Russ Snyder bunted the ball at third base, and Rich Rollins fielded the ball and threw it inside the line towards home. And I went off the bag, caught the ball, and Snyder hit me—it was right across his chest, and just completely dislocated my elbow.

I was out for the rest of the season, and I played the last ten games at third base, and then played in the World Series at third. That was a significant thing for me to be able to play in the World Series, after all those years of playing on clubs that were losing clubs. And then to hit a home run, that was a big thing for me.

Also in that Series I broke up a no-hitter of Koufax's. It was probably the fifth or sixth game, because Osteen started. We started the Series at home, and it was a Jewish holiday on the Opening Day, and Koufax didn't start—Drysdale started, and we beat him. Second day, we beat Koufax, and we went to the West Coast and, "Gee," we were thinking, "maybe we'll sweep this series."

Osteen was pitching, and we lost that game, and then the next two to Drysdale and Koufax, so that probably would have been the fifth game. I'm thinking it happened in the seventh inning, but maybe it wasn't that late in the game. It was just a little single into center-field. It was nothing spectacular, but he had a no-hitter going. He was throwing awfully well, but for some reason I had decent luck in that World Series.

Another thing I remember is that I got the last hit in that World Series—I guess that's another memorable thing, too. The seventh game of the World Series [Koufax] pitched on two days rest in Minnesota, throwing mostly fastballs, and I got the last hit in that Series, a line drive base hit to left field. And then with two outs, Allison struck out. So that's another one I'll always remember.

He had that great fastball that would seem to rise a little bit, so to lay off of that ball up around the letters, to me that was the one that was significant.

My 500th home run was certainly a significant thing, and the story on that was that the Twins had made a commemorative mug that they were going to pass out to I don't know how many fans, the first fans that came in. I don't know how many they made, but they thought surely that I'd hit my home run by that date. And that day came, and I hadn't hit my 500th home run.

They passed out the mug anyway, and then I finally ended up hitting my 500th, which seemed like it was about a month later. That was in '71, and I hit it off Mike Cuellar in the Met Stadium again, off a curveball. When I came to the dugout, Rigney was the manager, he said, "I hope it's not as long between 500 and 501 as it was between 499 and 500." And I hit my 501st the next at-bat.

It was sort of a mental thing, I guess—500 was just a number.

The MVP award in 1969—the thing about that season was that in 1968, I got hurt in the All-Star game in the Astrodome. I completely tore up my leg. People said it was a pulled muscle—well, it was a lot more than a pulled muscle. I was playing first, and Curt Flood hit a ground ball to Fregosi at shortstop, and Jim threw to first, and it was a low throw, not a bad throw at all.

And I just kind of caught the ball, and Flood was out, and my foot gave way, and I went completely over on top of my leg. I tore some things below the knee, and I tore the fascia, the covering of the hamstring there, and I tore a piece of bone away from the pelvis, where the hamstring attaches. It sounded like a rifle shot, and I could hear it, but I didn't know if anybody else could. And later on, guys in the National League dugout told me they heard it, the noise from that popping.

They carried me into the National League clubhouse, and of course I was out for the rest of the season—there were a lot of doctors who thought that maybe I was through playing. That winter I worked hard, and rehabilitated my leg, and the next year I had the best year I ever had in baseball.

That was the year that Billy Martin managed the Twins, the only year—a lot of people think he managed several years, but it was the only year he managed. Billy was interesting. He was probably the best manager I've ever seen in between the lines. He was an excellent manager; it was all the other stuff with Billy.

But we won the divisional setup, that was the first year, 1969. I'd led both leagues in home runs and RBIs. I hit forty-nine home runs and drove in 140 runs and got the MVP Award. Of course we lost to the Orioles in the playoffs, that was a significant thing there.

That was Opening Day the next year when I got the award, so that one stands out because it was Joe Cronin that gave me the award, and of course Joe was always one of my favorite people.

When your career is over, whatever you've done, you've done, so going into the Hall of Fame was certainly a memorable day for me. I told people I wasn't going to get emotional, but it was a very emotional thing, to be up there with your peers at the induction ceremony certainly was a big thing. That year I went in with Drysdale,

Rick Farrell, Luis Aparicio, and Pee Wee [Reese]. So it was a nice group to go in with.

Bowie Kuhn was the one that inducted me. I always had a special feeling for him, so that was nice, too. Since then I've had so many people say that they remember my speech, so the speech went quite well.

One thing I mentioned in there was about my father. My father passed away when I was sixteen, and I was recalling things about him, and I said that one time it was my father that really got me started in sports. He was a really fine athlete in Illinois. He went to James Milliken University in Illinois, which is now Milliken at Decatur. He was a fine football player—went to West Virginia West and played for Greasy Neal, who later coached the Eagles.

So anyway, I grew up in Idaho, and my brother and I used to play out in the yard—football, baseball, everything. We used to tear up the yard a little bit, I think, and one day my mother came out and was complaining to my father about the holes in the yard. And my dad said, "We're raising boys here, not grass." So that's what I think I mentioned in the speech, and I've heard so many people remember that and mention it to me.

July 11, 1965

NEW YORK	AB	R	H	RBI	MINNESOTA	AB	R	H	RBI
Richardson, 2b	4	0	1	0	Versalles, ss	3	2	1	1
Linz, ss	5	1	1	0	Rollins, 3b	4	1	1	1
Mantle, lf	4	2	2	0	Oliva, rf	5	1	2	0
Ramos, p	0	0	0	0	Killebrew, 1b–lf	4	2	3	2
Mikkelsen, p	0	0	0	0	Nessek, cf	3	0	0	0
Howard, c	4	2	3	2	Mincher, 1b	1	0	0	0
Lopez, rf	4	0	2	0	Hall, lf–cf	3	0	1	1
Pepitone, 1b	5	0	0	0	Battey, c	4	0	2	1
Boyer, 3b	3	0	0	0	Grant, pr	0	0	0	0
Repaz, cf	4	0	0	0	Zimmerman, c	0	0	0	0
Downing, p	2	0	0	0	Kindall, 2b	3	0	1	0
Baker, ph	1	0	1	0	Allen, 2b	1	0	0	0
Reniffe, p	0	0	0	0	Kaat, p	1	0	0	0
Hamilton, p	0	0	0	0	Worthington, p	2	0	0	0
Tresh, ph	1	0	0	0	Pleis, p	0	0	0	0
Moschitto, lf	1	0	0	0	Klippstein, p	0	0	0	0
					Valdespine, ph	1	0	0	0
					Fosnow, p	0	0	0	0
Totals	38	5	10	2	Totals	35	6	11	6

New York	100	020	101 — 5	
Minnesota	001	210	002 — 6	

CHUCK KNOBLAUCH

In his first season, second baseman Chuck Knoblauch of the Minnesota Twins got it all—the Rookie of the Year Award and a World Championship. Very few players could win the Rookie of the Year Award and then legitimately claim that they didn't have a very good year, but Knoblauch's numbers since then almost back up that contention from this now-perennial All-Star.

Right at this moment, I'd have to say that my greatest day would have been winning the World Series in '91, which was my rookie year. I know that's not quite a greatest day, but that's probably the greatest achievement, so it would have to be part of the greatest day—winning it and being a part of it, especially with it being my first year. It was very unexpected for me.

Going into my first year, not knowing what to expect—there were so many things up in the air, so many questions out there left to be answered. Not only just getting through the season, but getting to the playoffs and getting in the World Series and winning it. It was unbelievable for me.

There wasn't anything in particular from breaking in that stayed with me. What I'll remember from that year doesn't have anything to do with me being a rookie. We were something like 23–25, I think—that probably had to be about June sometime—and we were playing the last game in Kansas City before we went home for a ten- or twelve-game homestand. And I was thinking that if we could win this game and be one game under .500 going home, and then hopefully have a good homestand. . . .

We won that day, and we won all the games at home—that was when we won fifteen games in a row. We went from being in whatever position we were in to being in first place. . . . That fifteen-game winning streak will always be in my memory about my rookie year, because that was what turned everything around, when everything started to click.

Looking back on it, for me it wasn't that good of a year. I guess as a rookie it was a good year, but I was learning so much at the time that I really don't have any particular day that sticks out. I mean, I can remember the first game we played, in Oakland. Dave Stewart was pitching against Jack Morris, he was starting for us. I can remember the feeling I had that day, being in Oakland, and it was pretty close to a sellout, Opening Day out there. And I'll remember that as a personal thing, my very first major league game.

I was zero for three, and I walked. My first at-bat, I flew out to the warning track in left center—Rickey Henderson caught it. So that was my first at-bat. I don't remember the other two at-bats, and then I walked my last time, I remember that. I got my first hit the next day, against Bob Welch. It was the second at-bat, I think—I got a single to right. I was probably 1 for 4 that game.

We clinched it—we lost in Toronto on a getaway day, and we were flying to Chicago afterward. Chicago was behind us, and they lost that day, so that clinched it for us. I just remember we found out on the plane or on the bus or something like that. It was exciting.

We finished the year and then played Toronto. We split with them to start the series in Minnesota and went there and won all three games there. . . . So we partied it up in Toronto after clinching it that day.

We always had trouble winning there in the Skydome, but—I can't remember who pitched the first game, but we came out swinging and we scored some runs. They were good close games. One of those games in there, maybe the second or third there, I had a big hit. I had a double and scored two runs—that's a memory I have from

October 19, 1991

ATLANTA	AB	R	H	RBI	MINNESOTA	AB	R	H	RBI
Smith, dh	3	1	0	0	Gladden, lf	2	1	0	0
Treadway, 2b	3	1	1	0	Knoblauch, 2b	3	0	3	1
Pendleton, 3b	4	0	0	0	Puckett, cf	4	0	0	0
Justice, rf	2	0	1	0	Davis, dh	3	0	0	0
Gant, cf	4	0	3	2	Harper, c	4	0	2	0
Bream, 1b	4	0	0	0	Mack, rf	4	0	0	0
Hunter, lf	4	0	0	0	Hrbek, 1b	4	2	2	1
Olson, c	3	0	1	0	Leius, 3b	2	1	1	0
Belliard, ss	1	0	0	0	Pagliarulo, ph–3b	1	0	0	0
Blauser, ph–ss	2	0	0	0	Gagne, ss	3	1	1	3
Totals	30	2	8	2	Totals	30	5	9	5

Atlanta	000	001	010 — 2
Minnesota	001	031	00X — 5

there. I had a pretty good series. I think I was seven for twenty in that series with Toronto.

Then we opened the World Series in Minnesota against Atlanta, and we won the first two, and everything was looking real good, and they beat us three games in a row—two of those were extra inning games. Then I had some doubts about coming back after losing three on the long plane ride home. I was worried that we weren't gonna get it done. That's when Puckett had his big day, made the big catch, and he hit the winning home run. When we won that game, I knew for sure that we would win it. I had a real good feeling about Game 7, that we would win it.

We ended up winning it 1–0, we squeaked it out. Jack Morris was unbelievable that day. That was an unbelievable year, and I appreciate it more now than I did then, because, not knowing what to expect, and then going through it, just really the unknown that was going on for me. I was on winning teams growing up and in high school and college, and I was used to winning, so it was just another winning season.

But now, after '93, '94, '95, pretty much all losing seasons, it's really become more of a treasure, because now I realize what it takes, what we did in '91. I can appreciate how hard it is to win the division and win the playoffs and win the World Series. It's a lot more gratifying today looking back on it than when it was actually happening, because, like I said, I had no idea what was going on. You're just playing the game, and you're into the game, and they're pressure-packed games.

It's much more gratifying now because it seems so far away. That only goes to show you that you never know—that might be the only time that I get to the playoffs or the World Series and win the World Series. You never know when you'll have a chance to win, when you're on the right side, when it's all said and done.

The first game of the World Series, I was three for three with a walk, so I got three hits in my first World Series game—that's my big moment on the offensive side of it. I think it might have been Charlie Leibrandt that started the first game, so I got my hits off Leibrandt. . . .

There's really nothing like being involved in the playoffs and the World Series, let alone winning it. That's probably the biggest pinnacle of sports, is winning the world championship, and that overrides all the individual and personal things that you go through.

JERRY KOOSMAN

It was great pitching that led the "Miracle Mets" to their World Series victory over the Baltimore Orioles in 1969, and it was Jerry Koosman who was on the mound when they became world champions. But Koosman had a stellar career that lasted almost two decades and offered many highlights to choose from in selecting his greatest day.

I was lucky enough to play eighteen years, so there's more than one great day. As far as one of my greatest days, I suppose team-wise, it would be the last game of the '69 World Series. I was lucky enough to pitch nine innings and win the game 5–3, and everything worked out fine for us, and we were the World Series champs. I think that would probably be more of a team thing.

Individually, probably my greatest day was probably my first game in 1968 as a rookie, when I made the club as a starter. We were at spring training in Phoenix, and I pitched my last spring training innings . . . in Palm Springs, I take that back, it was in Palm Springs against the Giants.

Then we went from there to San Francisco to open up against the Giants. Seaver pitched the first game, and I was pitching the second game. That was when Martin Luther King was assassinated, and so the second game was canceled—all baseball was cancelled. Or maybe it was the third game, I don't remember.

So I got set back, and my next game was in L.A. So I got the first game in L.A.—I shut 'em out 4–0. We finished the road trip, and we go to New York, and now I'm pitching the home opener. The fifth day comes, or whatever it was, and I'm pitching the home opener at Shea Stadium against the Giants.

Standing room only—the first inning, the first guy gets on with a base hit. The next guy gets on on an error. The next guy is McCovey, and I walked him. So the bases are loaded and nobody out, and Mays is the hitter, and he's ready to eat my lunch—"Throw the ball, kid," that type of attitude. And so now I'm out there wondering, "What is a farm kid from Minnesota doing in a position like this?" I kind of wished I was still out on the tractor back home.

So anyway, I remembered what my pitching coach in '66 told me, "Whenever you're in trouble, throw your best." I struck Mays out on fastballs. I threw 'em as hard as I could. Then Jim Ray Hart was the next hitter. He popped a fastball up to Jerry Grote, the catcher, and I struck out Jack Hiatt to get out of the inning with the bases loaded. The crowd went nuts, and I went on to shut 'em out, 3–0.

That was probably my greatest day in baseball, because that first inning could have been do or die for me, really. I wasn't a proven player at that time, and had I got knocked out of the box at that stage of the ball game, I'd have had to prove myself for a long time. I went on to shut 'em out, so I started the season with two shutouts.

The next start was against Houston, and I beat them 3–1. Bob Aspromonte hit a low and away fastball for a double that scored a run all the way from first base. It was at Shea Stadium. So I could very easily have started the season with three shutouts.

The second one, that game against the Giants, was probably my biggest one, better than the first even. It was the first home opener the Mets had ever won, in front of our home crowd, a standing-room only type crowd—I mean, opening ceremonies, the media's there. So it was kind of establishing myself in my own town, really, and everything went well after that.

I just know that Gil Hodges deserves a lot of credit, because he was a guy that would stick with a young starting pitcher probably longer than someone else would. So he always gave me my chances, even in that last game of the World Series, I'm behind 3–0, and he stuck with me. . . . I told him in the dugout, "They won't get anymore." That was after the third—it was against Dave McNally.

Frank Robinson hit a home run off of me, and then Dave McNally hit a two-run homer off of me in a bunting situation. I threw him a high fastball. I wanted to pop him up—he went after it, and it didn't work out that way. I was so angry when I got them out, I said, "That's all they're gonna get. Let's catch 'em." So we scored five runs and won the game.

I know afterwards, it was—I, myself, personally, couldn't talk. You'd go to a teammate to talk about it, and you'd just swell up in your throat, and you couldn't talk. Tears come to your eyes, and you're so happy and just thankful, and most of the other players were the same way, sitting there hugging each other, tears rolling down their eyes.

And finally the moment wears off where you can talk. They had a party upstairs for us afterward and everybody and their families.

October 16, 1969

BALTIMORE (A.)	AB	R	H	RBI	NEW YORK (N.)	AB	R	H	RBI
Buford, lf	4	0	0	0	Agee, cf	3	0	1	0
Blair, cf	4	0	0	0	Harrelson, ss	4	0	0	0
F. Robinson, rf	3	1	1	1	Jones, lf	3	2	1	0
Powell, 1b	4	0	1	0	Clendenon, 1b	3	1	1	2
Salmon, pr	0	0	0	0	Swoboda, rf	4	1	2	1
B. Robinson, 3b	4	0	0	0	Charles, 3b	4	0	0	0
Johnson, 2b	4	0	1	0	Grote, c	4	0	0	0
Belanger, ss	3	1	1	0	Weis, 2b	4	1	1	1
Etchebarren, c	3	0	0	0	Koosman, p	3	0	1	0
McNally, p	2	1	1	2					
Motton, ph	1	0	0	0					
Watt, p	0	0	0	0					
Totals	32	3	5	3	Totals	32	5	7	4

Baltimore (A.)	003	000	000 — 3	
New York (N.)	000	002	12X — 5	

BALTIMORE	IP	H	R	ER	BB	SO
McNally	7	5	3	3	2	6
Watt (L, 0–1)	1	2	2	1	0	1
NEW YORK	IP	H	R	ER	BB	SO
Koosman (W, 2–0)	9	5	3	3	1	5

We went down later, onto the field, and it looked like a moonscape, all tore up—but it was a long winter.

The talent on that team was mainly pitching and defense, and it was all led by Gil Hodges. Gil Hodges made the team chemistry on that ball club work. He had one set of rules that applied to everyone, and he carried through with it. If you broke the rule, you did the punishment or were fined, or whatever it was. There was no, "Well, next time . . ." Everybody stayed in line, and everybody had one common goal, and that was to work as a winning ball club and do whatever it took.

So it was very simple—work hard, be ready to play, and give your best. The rules were simple—and don't be late. And it worked out well. I don't care if you were the star of the team or if you were the twenty-fifth guy on the team, the rules were applied the same way. That made the twenty-fifth guy feel as important as the first guy, because they all abided by the same rules.

I think that's something that's missing from today's game. But

I'm thankful that I had the opportunity to play under Gil Hodges, because he certainly made me a better ballplayer. I was raised that way, with those kind of rules. And when I went to whatever team it was the first time that didn't have those kind of rules, they were missed, and you noticed it—it was like black and white.

Individually, I think the first time I won twenty stands out. I should have won twenty in '68. I had won sixteen games by the first part of August, then I went, I think, seven games in a row without a decision. Then I ended up winning my nineteenth in my last start, so it was something like three games I won from the first of August in my rookie year. I had like a 2.08 ERA, but we just couldn't score any runs. . . .

Individually, it was when I finally won twenty, which wasn't until 1976, so that took a long time. I did it against St. Louis. I had a great curveball. I could throw a curve to a guy looking for a curveball and couldn't hit it. They'd just kind of bow their cap to you—that's rare that that happens.

BARRY LARKIN

Since the advent of free agency in baseball, few players remain with a single club for their entire career, and even fewer come to represent a city the way Barry Larkin's name is automatically connected with the Cincinnati Reds. This interview with Larkin was conducted during the final weekend of the 1996 season, when the Reds were in St. Louis for Ozzie Smith Weekend. Larkin spoke at the ceremony and then hit a pair of consecutive homers during the game that followed. In this interview he discussed his connection with Ozzie Smith, his Olympic and World Series experiences, and his individual achievements, which include a three home-run game and becoming the first short-stop in baseball history to join the 30/30 club.

My greatest days start with playing in the Olympics, that was when I was in college. I remember the opening ceremonies in L.A. Everybody in Dodger Stadium was rooting for us—and now when we go there they're rooting against us. The second one was the day

I hit three home runs in Cincinnati against Houston off of Jim Deshaies in '92, I believe, and the day after that I hit two more. And then I'd have to say another one of the greatest days I've had was the day I hit my thirtieth home run to join the 30/30 club, which was the first time in major league history a shortstop had done that. Then I'd have to say yesterday, being able to honor Ozzie, because he's meant so much to my career.

With Ozzie, when I first came up, he approached me. I was a rookie at the time, he was a ten-year or a nine-year veteran, very established. He was extremely popular. He came to me and asked me if I had any questions or if I needed any help—this was out at batting practice right here at Busch Stadium. I just thought that was special because he sought me out to ask me if I had any questions or problems or anything. I had never met him, but I'd idolized him my entire life for as long as I'd seen him play, and for him to come and do that was extremely special.

Today, up there [at the podium during the ceremony honoring Smith], with Jackie Joyner-Kersee, Bob Gibson, Stan Musial, Lou Brock, all these Hall of Fame guys, for me to be able to speak about Ozzie, who's going to the Hall of Fame, it was just an honor for me to be up there and be a part of that, to pay tribute to a guy who really helped me in my career.

I remember Ozzie's last at-bat in Cincinnati. He got sawed-off—he got jammed and hit a ground ball in between short and third, and I was the one who caught it, and I threw him out by about a step or two. Before he got up there for that at-bat he tipped his cap to the crowd—it was toward the end of the game, and it was probably his last at-bat in Cincinnati.

He chopped the ball, and I made the play, and I remember feeling kind of uneasy about making the play on him. I've seen him make so many plays, and he's such a good friend of mine that I kind of let personal feelings get involved, because he's just done so much for me and so much for the game. I was in college when I saw him make the play on Jeff Burroughs of Atlanta in San Diego, but to be a part of the finality of his capacity playing in Cincinnati, I just felt something different.

The night before 30/30, which happened during a double-header, we got rained out. I didn't get much sleep that night. I was tossing and turning a lot and really thinking about 30/30, that it was going to happen, that I needed to do it because I felt that was going to be my best chance. I've hit one home run since then, but I really felt like that next day in particular was when I really needed to do it.

My wife was telling me that I really needed to stop worrying about it. She said, "You're not gonna do it if you continue to worry about it." And my son, who's three years old, kept asking me, "Daddy, are you gonna hit a home run?" because he was coming to the game. They had come to Cincinnati to watch the game so that they could see me hit the home run and possibly do this. I remember that night getting absolutely no sleep.

And the next day I get to the ballpark, and my family came all the way up from Florida to be there for the game. My first at-bat I looked up in the stands, and they weren't there. My dad wasn't there either, and he was there for every single game. I swung at a pitch that was down and in—it was a change-up from Donovan Osborne of the Cardinals—and I hit a high fly ball to right field, and I thought it might go because the wind was blowing, and the guy caught it right in front of the wall on the track. So I was thinking that it was kinda good that I didn't hit it there, but I knew I might not get another pitch to hit out.

My next at-bat I looked up in the stands again, and my family wasn't there, but my dad was there, and I walked on four pitches. And then the at-bat after that when I hit it, my family was just sitting down in their seats, and I remember the count was 1–0—it was a change-up from Donovan Osborne. As soon as I hit it, I kinda went numb. I remember telling somebody after I got done running around the bases that I don't even remember running around the bases. I don't even remember touching first base. Someone said I almost missed first base when I threw my hands up in the air in celebration, but I don't remember doing it.

I don't remember almost missing first base, and I don't remember shaking the third base coach's hand when I was rounding third. I do remember that when I was coming around second base Ozzie was at shortstop, and I remember pointing at him and acknowledging him. That's about the only thing I do remember about the trot. And then when I got home my other best friend in baseball was there, Eric Davis, and he gave me a hug and congratulations. He told me I deserved it, that I'd worked hard to get to this point. From that point on I was just numb. I don't think I got a hit for the next three games. But it really didn't matter, because I'd done something no major league shortstop had ever done before.

I thought about Barry [Bonds]. He said something to me early in the season about 40/40. He still didn't have thirty bags when he told me about it, I think he had like twenty-something stolen bases the last time they were in Cincinnati. He told me that he was thinking about 40/40. He needed eight home runs and seventeen, eighteen, nineteen, however many bases in a month, month-and-a-half. I said to him, "Yeah, 40/40, that'd be something great." But I was thinking to myself, "Man, that's a long way for a man to go." I said to him, "I know you can get the home runs, but . . . well, maybe you can do it." That's what I said to him. Seeing him get it the other day, pick up the bag, that was great.

[Editor's note: Bonds stole his fortieth base during the last week of the 1996 season against the Colorado Rockies to become only the second major leaguer ever to hit forty home runs and steal forty bases, along with Jose Canseco.]

[The three homer game] was against Houston in Cincinnati. Jim Deshaies was pitching. This was in '92, I think. I hit twenty home runs that year—that was the first time I hit twenty home runs. That tied the shortstop's record for home runs in the Cincinnati organization. That particular day, I don't remember the ball carrying particularly well.

My first at-bat I hit a home run to left, I don't remember what the pitch was. My second at-bat I hit a ball to center, and I still can't believe it went out—it hit off the facing of the back of the wall in center field. It was one of the furthest home runs I've ever hit. I couldn't believe it at that time. And my next at-bat I hit a home run to right field. So I hit one to left, center, and right. When I hit the ball to right field I knew I hit it well, but I also knew it wasn't going out—but it did. I remember once again running the bases kind of like I was numb. It was like I couldn't believe this was happening.

My next at-bat I was facing some lefty from Houston, I think it was Osuna. I remember the crowd chanting when I came up to hit, "Barry, Barry, Barry," and it really made me nervous. I remember the pitcher didn't throw me a strike—he threw me four balls. I was thinking, "I'm gonna try and hit a home run this time," but I probably would have missed the ball.

The next day San Diego came in, and I hit two home runs that day. I couldn't believe it. I guess I was just in a groove.

My strongest memory of the Olympics was kind of a bittersweet thing. I was a sophomore in college at the time—I think I was nineteen years old—and I was from Michigan. We had all these players from the West Coast, all the coaching staff was from the West

Coast, and it seemed like the attitude was, "If you're not from the West Coast then you can't play very well, so we won't even give you a shot." So I didn't get a chance to play much at all. Gary Green was the shortstop, Flavio Alfara was the second baseman. I felt at the time that I was as good if not a better player, offensively and defensively, than both of those guys, but for some reason I couldn't seem to crack the starting line-up.

The thing that I got from that was humility, because that was the first time that I had been on a team and was not in the starting line-up. It was the first time I wasn't on a team when I wasn't one of the go-to guys, and that bothered me. But I stuck with it. There were plenty of times when I felt like, "Ah, I don't want to do this. I didn't get a chance to play, but I do want to represent the country." I remember when there were a lot of times when I said to myself, "I gotta use this to fuel my fire." So that's what I did. Every time I go out to the West Coast I seem to get hyped, because that's where people said I couldn't play.

My favorite memory from the Olympics was the opening ceremony in Dodger Stadium in '84. We had a separate ceremony from the entire Olympic entourage. We had a ceremony in Dodger Stadium for all the baseball teams. We marched in, and I just remember 60,000 people cheering for us, cheering, "USA, USA, USA." And then I remember next time going out there as a professional and people booing us when I was with the Cincinnati Reds. That was my favorite experience other than the medal ceremony, which I really don't remember too well. We won a silver medal—we got beat by Japan. But it was the opening ceremony that I remember quite well.

The World Series against Oakland was great, but there were different moments in each game. In Game 1 [in Cincinnati], when Eric Davis hit a home run, I think it was in the first inning or early in the game. There was a caption in the paper that said, "David Stuns Goliath"—it was the consummate underdog taking on the big dog and beating them up. With that home run, I had never seen the fans so hyped up in Cincinnati.

Game 2 in Cincinnati, Eckersley was on the mound, Billy Bates was on second base, and Joe Oliver hit a ground ball down the left field line in the ninth inning. It went right over the top of the bag, and the Oakland guys were yelling that it was a foul ball, but the umpire ruled it fair. Billy Bates came around to score, and I remember going up to the plate and going crazy. I remember that whole series we were really numb. I know I keep using that word, but it was so exciting that we just couldn't take it in.

September 22, 1996

ST. LOUIS	AB	R	H	RBI	CINCINNATI	AB	R	H	RBI
O. Smith, ss	4	0	0	0	Owens, lf	5	0	0	0
Lankford, cf	4	0	0	0	Goodwin, cf	0	0	0	0
Gant, lf	4	1	1	0	Morris, 1b	5	0	1	0
Jordan, rf	4	0	1	0	Larkin, ss	4	1	1	1
Gaetti, 3b	2	2	1	2	Davis, cf–lf	4	1	1	0
Mabry, 1b	3	0	1	0	Perez, 3b	3	1	1	0
Pagnozzi, c	3	0	0	1	Branson, ph–3b	0	1	0	0
Gallego, 2b	4	0	1	0	Boone, 2b	4	1	3	2
Osborne, p	2	0	0	0	Ki. Mitchell, rf	3	1	1	0
Petkovsek, p	0	0	0	0	Fordyce, c	2	0	2	1
Fossas, p	0	0	0	0	Portugal, p	1	0	0	0
Young, ph	0	0	0	0	Oliver, ph	0	0	0	1
Mathews, p	0	0	0	0	Salkeld, p	0	0	0	0
Ludwick, p	0	0	0	0	Remlinger, p	0	0	· 0	0
					L. Smith, p	0	0	0	0
					Greene, ph	0	0	0	0
					Mottola, ph	1	0	0	0
					Shaw, p	1	0	0	0
					Brantley, p	0	0	0	0
Totals	30	3	5	3	Totals	33	6	10	5

St. Louis	010	200	000 — 3	
Cincinnati	000	110	40X — 6	

Then we went to Oakland, and the first game in Oakland, I remember when we left Cincinnati some of the Oakland players made comments about how . . . the balls that we hit out in Cincinnati would not go out in Oakland, how when we got out on their turf they were gonna beat us up. The media played on that because the media believed that it was just a matter of time before the A's started beating up on us. Nobody expected this to be close.

We just crushed them the third game; it was 8–3 or something like that. I mean we beat the dog doo out of them. At that time I looked at the Oakland dugout and felt that maybe they could sense that this team was for real. And then the third game I remember Chris Sabo just going off, doing everything, hitting everything, catching everything, that was just an unbelievable experience.

The fourth game Jose Rijo just dominated. I remember Rickey Henderson taking a called third strike and then putting his bat over his head and trying to break it . . . because he was so frustrated. I got on base, and Herm Winningham bunted me over with a two-strike bunt. Then I scored somehow, and we tied the game. . . . I remember thinking, "Oh my God, we really are gonna win the World Series!". . .

In my trophy case I have the shoes I wore in the World Series. I put the number "30" on them because that's the year they released Ken Griffey, Sr. off that team to make room for some young guys, and I thought that was a bad deal. So I put "30" on my shoes and on my hat to pay tribute to Ken Griffey, because he had meant so much to our team.

In the celebration after [we won the World Series] game I remember getting my toes stepped on and feeling something on my toe. I looked down after we were all done celebrating, and my toe was bleeding. The top of my shoe was cut. Somebody stepped on my toe and ripped my shoe to shreds and spiked my toe. It was split open—and I didn't have to get stitches, thank goodness, I just had some strips put on it—I couldn't feel that, because I was just so hyped.

Afterwards I remember my parents came down, and my wife came down, and we were out on the field at shortstop afterwards, and I was talking to them, telling them about different plays in the game and how things happened at out at shortstop. We were out there until one-thirty or two o'clock in the morning. That was another "greatest time" in my baseball life.

I think about the All-Star games, the Gold Gloves, the Silver Slugger awards, I think about 30/30—those things happen because I go out and play with a team that's winning, and because I play with guys that I'm having a good time with, that's what I think about more. I think about enjoying myself when I'm going through what I'm going through, and then afterwards in the off-season I look at all the accolades and acknowledgments, and I'll assess the situation. But it's not something I think about consciously.

I just enjoy myself with these guys, that's what I think about. And I think about the time I've spent with Ozzie, the things he's done for me. Brian Jordan said yesterday [during the ceremony honoring Smith] that Ozzie's kept him sane in the game of baseball, and there's truth in that, because the guys in this room have kept me sane in baseball. Because it's a very frustrating game, and you need an outlet—you need some ways to vent your frustrations, and people to help you with that. The other stuff I really don't think about, the accolades and all, I just enjoy my time and that's about it.

TONY LARUSSA

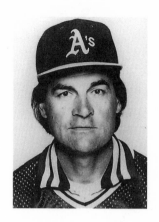

While he certainly wasn't the first manager to come into baseball equipped with a law degree, Tony LaRussa certainly seemed to use his calculating, shrewd knack for detail and strategy more than most skippers. LaRussa was renowned for being one of the first managers to rely a great deal on computers in formulating his strategies, and he also revolutionized the game to some extent in his definition of relief pitching roles and his selective one-inning use of the closer.

The toss-up for me is between two days. Everybody's goal is to be involved with a world championship team, so the day that we were able to win the fourth game in 1989 against the Giants, that's definitely one. . . .

There's another one. Because of the A's success, I was able to manage three consecutive All-Star games. And the first time I was ever involved in one was as a coach, which was the 1984 All-Star game. It just thrilled me to see all those great players from both leagues on one field. The workout the day before the game itself, I was totally captivated by that, and had always looked forward maybe to managing one myself.

I coached another one in '87, and it was the same thrill, so then I was able to manage the '89 and the '90 and the '91 games. I remember the impression that it made on me at the end of the '91 game. We had won—it was in Toronto—and as they were taking me to the interview area, somebody from the league or from the network or something said, "Congratulations." I said, "What for?" And he said, for the first time in history, a manager had won three consecutive All-Star games.

I tell you, that made such an impression. Because number one, I really enjoyed the All-Star game. To be fortunate enough to do that, I think, and to come back over and be able to be on the winning club, especially early on, because the National League was dominating at that time. Also, we started coming back, and we had a real good run. That third win was, you know, Cal [Ripken] hit the big home run—he was the MVP—Eck saved it. It was just real special.

So that's it, either the '89 World Championship or that third All-Star win. The biggest memory in '89 was to actually get it done, because the year before we had gotten to the World Series and gotten beat in five games by the Dodgers, so the club was on a mission. I think as a coach your goal is to have your athlete or your team peak at the magic moment. And that '89 club, when it got to the end of the season and then in against Toronto and then the World Series, it was peaking.

And it was really a talented group of guys, to see them peaking, it was a real force going into the World Series. We win the first two games by something like 5–0, 5–1, and then—earthquake. So we had to sit around for eleven days. We thought we would play; there was some talk about canceling it. Then when you come back out you wonder, did we lose our edge? There's a lot of concern.

In Game 3, we were just real sharp again. So then in Game 4, you realize that it's possible, your boyhood dream. You know everybody that plays baseball—your boyhood dream is mostly to be a player on a World Series club—but to participate, to be a coach or manager . . . I remember the game. We got off to a big lead, and they made a comeback at the end, and Eckersley closed it out.

The celebration afterwards, if I had any understanding of the significance it came when I saw Bill Rigney, who was Sandy Alderson's advisor, consultant . . . you know, a superscout. And he gave me a hug, and I said, "Now I know how you feel," and he said I didn't. Fifty-two years and this was the first World Championship I've been involved in. And boy, he'd had a great career. He was in that magical '51 game with the Giants with Thomson. And you realize, man, this is it—if you're involved in one, you're real lucky.

There was some talk about how with the loss of life we shouldn't be playing, and if you're playing, you ought to really mute your enjoyment. I mean, there was a lot of people that died. But I knew we should play, because the Saturday or maybe even the Sunday after it happened they played college football and pro football, so why shouldn't we play ours?

But I know we didn't pop champagne because we were trying to be respectful of what had happened in the area. Mayor Walter Haas would always talk about how he felt that we had missed the parade. He wanted to have the parade, and we tried to get it for him, but we couldn't do it. That took something away from it. But all I know is that all winter long, you're the world champions, and

October 28, 1989

OAKLAND	AB	R	H	RBI	S. FRANCISCO	AB	R	H	RBI
R. Henderson, lf	6	2	3	2	Butler, cf	5	1	3	1
Lansford, 3b	4	1	2	1	Oberkfell, 3b	3	0	0	0
Canseco, rf	4	1	2	0	Thompson, 2b	1	0	1	1
McGwire, 1b	5	0	1	0	Bedrosian, p	0	0	0	0
D. Henderson, cf	3	2	1	0	Clark, 1b	4	1	1	0
Steinbach, c	4	1	1	3	Mitchell, lf	4	1	1	2
Phillips, 2b	5	0	1	1	Williams, ss	4	0	1	0
Weiss, ss	3	1	0	0	Kennedy, c	3	1	0	0
Moore, p	3	1	1	2	Litton, 2b	4	1	1	2
Phelps, ph	1	0	0	0	Nixon, rf	3	0	0	0
Nelson, p	0	0	0	0	Robinson, p	0	0	0	0
Honeycutt, p	0	0	0	0	LaCoss, p	1	0	0	0
Burns, p	0	0	0	0	Batha, ph	1	0	0	0
Parker, ph	1	0	0	0	Brantley, p	0	0	0	0
Eckersley, p	0	0	0	0	Downs, p	0	0	0	0
					Riles, ph	0	0	0	0
					Maldonado, ph	1	1	1	0
					Lefferts, p	0	0	0	0
					Uribe, ss	1	0	0	0
Totals	39	9	12	9	Totals	39	6	9	6

```
Oakland        130   031   010 — 9
San Francisco  000   002   400 — 6
```

OAKLAND	IP	H	R	ER	BB	SO
Moore, W	6	5	2	2	1	3
Nelson	0.1	1	2	2	1	0
Honeycutt	0.1	3	2	2	0	0
Burns	1.1	0	0	0	0	0
Eckersley, S	1	0	0	0	0	0
SAN FRANCISCO	IP	H	R	ER	BB	SO
Robinson, L	1.2	4	4	4	1	0
LaCoss	3.1	4	3	3	3	1
Brantley	0.1	3	1	1	0	0
Downs	1.2	0	0	0	0	1
Lefferts	0.1	1	1	1	1	0
Bedrosian	1.2	0	0	0	2	0

Opening Day they give you a ring, and you've still got it.

We had the two similar situations which don't always happen. We clinched the league championship early, so we had, in one case six days and in the other case five days to get ready. The year before, when we tried to get serious in our workouts—you know, nobody likes to hit against their own pitchers, and the pitchers didn't want to pitch against their own hitters, so everybody was real reluctant.

The interesting part of that was that I don't believe that I've ever been with a club that had fewer down moments. That club had one eight- or nine-day sluggish period—it was unbelievable. It coincided with us losing both of our catchers, Steinbach and Hassey. One got hit in a collision with a guy and hurt his knee, and we had Matt Sinatro come up and catch or something. Except for that period, the club was relentless. . . .

We didn't go to Arizona prior to starting the series, we went to Arizona during the earthquake break. But prior to starting the World Series we did these intense workouts that got us ready for Game 1 and Game 2, and then we went to Arizona. And the Giants laughed at us, they said, "Hey, why are you going to Arizona?"

I remember I read Riley's book, *Showtime*, and he talked about how when they were trying to repeat he would take the club away from L.A. to some place else, San Luis Obispo or someplace else where they were all by themselves. They ate by themselves. We wanted to get away. We just didn't want to be distracted in the last couple of days.

And I remember there was a little reluctance from the club when we were flying in. The pilot said that we were going right from the airport to the ballpark. And the pilot said that we were gonna have to wait for a minute on the ground, because they had to clear the bus coming through because there was so much traffic. We got to the ballpark and had like a 3 o'clock workout in the middle of the week, and we had about a thousand people there watching us work out.

Guys just went crazy—all of a sudden they were showing off. We worked out, did a little intersquad game, did that for two days, and I'm sure that the people . . . It was a great story—fathers took their kids out of school, we had guys in ties with their kids—over 8,000 people in two days. We got back, and it was no contest. The Giants just—there was no way they were gonna be that ready. It was incredible, our club was just not giving up.

As far as comparing that with the awards, I don't really think you should give awards to anybody but the players. Somebody gives you an award, you don't say, "I'm not gonna accept it," but they should just give 'em to the players, that's all they'd have to do. Did you read *Men at Work* [LaRussa's book], about what Dave Duncan does with our pitching staff? Why didn't he get the pitching coach award? It should be a stack award or an organizational award. I think the managers awards are really overrated.

Longevity—now if you're around long enough and you have any kind of success you're gonna pile up some wins. So I think you look at the individual games and the accomplishments by players, and that's the way it should be done.

TOMMY LASORDA

© JOHN SOOHOO

No one personifies the modern legacy and history of the Dodgers better than former manager Tommy Lasorda, whose debut with the club as a pitcher hails back to its origins in Brooklyn. The feisty, combative Lasorda steered the Dodgers to two world titles before finally stepping down after twenty years at the helm following the 1996 season.

I don't know about great days, but I've been involved in five achievements in my career that I never thought I'd see, and I'm gonna tell you what they are and then I'm not gonna answer any questions. The first was making my debut with the Brooklyn Dodgers in 1954 after I pitched with the Montreal Royals, and the second was being named the manager of the Dodgers in 1977.

The third was becoming the champions of baseball for the first time, with Steve Garvey and Ron Cey and those guys back in 1981. Then in 1988, Orel Hershiser broke Don Drysdale's record for consecutive innings, which was something I never thought I'd see anyone do in my lifetime. And that same year we beat the Oakland A's in five games to win the championship—that was just an incredible feat.

[Editor's note: This interview was conducted during the 1996 season after Lasorda's retirement. The following year he was elected to the Hall of Fame. The above photo was taken as Lasorda got the emotional call notifying him of his Hall of Fame status.]

VERN LAW

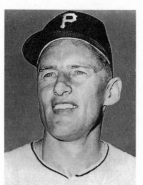

Vern Law was an outstanding pitcher during his career for the Pittsburgh Pirates, but he'll always be remembered for his eighteen-inning stint against the Milwaukee Braves, a game in which he didn't even get a decision. Perhaps just as amazing was the fact that four days later, Law pitched another thirteen innings against the Cincinnati Reds.

Of course the greatest day was the year that we won the World Series [1960]. But individually speaking, the best game that I was involved in was one that I wasn't even supposed to be in, when I pitched eighteen innings against the Milwaukee Braves. I wasn't even—I was pitching on two days' rest. I think it was in '56, somewhere around there, '56, '57.

I remember everything about it. I'm out in the outfield running—I'm not scheduled to pitch, but our starting pitcher comes in ill. . . .

[Danny] Murtaugh hollers at me, he says, "Can you pitch?" And I said, "Yeah, I can pitch." He said, "Yeah, come and get ready." So I come in and change, and then we go out and warm up, and we start the ball game. Both teams scored early—the score was tied 2–2 going into the fifth inning. I shut 'em out the rest of the way through nine, and so Murtaugh asked me how I felt, and I said, "I'm fine." And he said, "OK, stay in there."

So we go out there and shut 'em out through twelve, and he says, "I better take you out." And I said, "Skip, I'm fine. I got 'em out one, two, three." And he said, "Well, you know. Are you sure?" And I said, "Yeah, I'm OK," and he said, "All right." So we go through fifteen and nobody scores.

So finally he says, "I gotta take you out," and I said, "Skip, after pitching this long, jeez, let me stay in to either win or lose it." I said, "I'm OK. I'm gettin' 'em out one, two, three. . . ." He let me stay in.

Well, we go through eighteen, and nobody can score again. And so he says, "That's it, good job, you're done. Because if you hurt your arm they're gonna run me out of town, so you're finished. Go take a shower."

So anyway, I said, "You're calling the shots, so . . . whatever."
I went out, and Bob Friend comes in and relieves me, gives up a run.
So now we're getting beat 3–2. So we come back and score two, and
he gets credit for the victory.

I pitched eighteen innings, and in those eighteen innings I give
up nine hits, struck out twelve, and gave up two runs. That was the
best game I remember being involved in.

And ironically, four days later, I had to pitch thirteen before I
won against Cincinnati. I had a 1–0 lead in the ninth inning, and I
had two outs, and Frank Robinson was the hitter. I get two quick
strikes, waste a couple pitches, keep jammin' him inside, inside.
Everything has been hard—hard sliders, hard fastball—and I said,
"Now's a good time to take a little bit off the breaking ball and get
him out in front, get a nice little ground ball." I guess he was right
with me on it, because the last time I saw the ball it went over the
center field fence. And in Crosley, too—you know that center field
fence was pretty close in, but he hit it good, and he deserved the
home run.

But like I said, I had to go thirteen before we finally scored one
then. I did not have too much luck having somebody relieve me or
trying to save a game for me. All during my career, if I didn't win it,
I usually didn't win it—nobody saved it for me.

I just went ahead and pitched like I normally do against guys.
I was the kind of pitcher—I was a control pitcher, you know—
pitch to their weaknesses if they had one, and change speeds. I
used my infielders, outfielders, probably as good as any pitcher. I
didn't strike out an awful lot. I probably averaged five, six strikeouts a game. I made 'em hit the ball. I got a lot of ground balls—
keep the ball down and change-up on 'em enough to take a little
off, make 'em hit the ball on the ground. That's basically the way
I pitched. . . .

There hasn't been anyone pitched that long, particularly now,
with the emphasis on the bullpen. You're not gonna see—that year I
had eighteen complete games. If you see a pitcher today have maybe
five or six at the most, that's pretty good, because so much emphasis
is on the bullpen.

Those are the things that I remember during my career. Like I
said, the greatest day was the day we won the World Series, because
we were predicted to lose four straight. Of course, we went up
against the great Yankee ball club—they didn't know that we had
twenty-five guys that wanted to win.

KENNY LOFTON

One of the great young base stealers and defensive outfielders in the game, Kenny Lofton got his first taste of World Series action playing for the Cleveland Indians in 1995 against the Atlanta Braves. Ironically, two years later, Lofton was traded to the Braves, and once again he played a pivotal role in Atlanta's drive to the Fall Classic in 1997. A native of Arizona and a two-sport athlete who once played point guard for the Arizona Wildcats, Lofton returned to the Tribe after his stint in Atlanta, signing with Cleveland again as a free agent in 1998.

First game of the World Series in 1995, that's the greatest day.

I don't know what stands out about it, just the excitement, I guess. I don't look at things too much and make it too big, anyway. I guess I could just say that was just a game where you've got millions of people watching you, and you're out there, and you get in

October 21, 1995

CLEVELAND	AB	R	H	RBI	ATLANTA	AB	R	H	RBI
Lofton, cf	4	2	1	0	Grissom, cf	4	0	1	0
Vizquel, ss	4	0	0	0	Lemke, 2b	3	0	1	0
Baerga, 2b	4	0	0	1	Jones, 3b	4	0	0	0
Belle, lf	3	0	0	0	McGriff, 1b	3	2	1	1
Murray, 1b	3	0	0	0	Justice, rf	1	1	0	0
Tavarez, p	0	0	0	0	Klesko, lf	2	0	0	0
Embree, p	0	0	0	0	Devereaux, ph–lf	0	0	0	0
Thome, 3b	3	0	1	0	O'Brien, c	2	0	0	0
Ramirez, rf	3	0	0	0	Polonia, ph	1	0	0	1
Alomar, c	3	0	0	0	Lopez, c	0	0	0	0
Hershiser, p	2	0	0	0	Belliard, ss	2	0	0	1
Assenmacher, p	0	0	0	0	Maddux, p	3	0	0	0
Sorrento, 1b	1	0	0	0					
Totals	30	2	2	1	Totals	25	3	3	3

Cleveland	100	000	001 — 2
Atlanta	010	000	20X — 3

the World Series. I mean, what other day could be greater than being in the World Series?

I just looked at it as any other game, but the excitement through the media made it more exciting than what it really is . . . it's just another game, but it's considered the World Series.

Just being on the field is what stands out about it. . . .

Nothing in particular . . . just being in the World Series stands out.

People in the media didn't make a big deal out of the other things . . . All-Star game, first day, those kinds of things. The media can make or break a situation, and that's what happened—the media made the World Series bigger than life at the time. The All-Star game is just a game where guys have fun, and my first day in the big leagues was fun, but none of that was as exciting as the World Series.

The hype is there, but the game is all the same. You have a bat, and the pitcher has a ball, and there's three bases out there and home plate—it's just the same as any other game.

GREG MADDUX

Despite the fact that he owns a shelf full of Cy Young Awards and a World Series ring and has made a plethora of All-Star appearances, Greg Maddux was one of those players who chose his major league debut as his greatest day.

I don't know if it's my first day or the World Series or what. I think it would have to be my first day. My first day was pretty special. It's one I remember better than the others.

I got called up in September in Chicago, and of course I don't know where anything is. I flew in at night, it was dark. And I'm staying in a hotel, and they say it's about ten or fifteen minutes to the ballpark. So they say, "If you get there by 10:00, you'll be fine." So I go to leave the hotel at 9:00, to get there at 9:30 at the latest, and I'm going down Lake Shore Drive, and the drawbridge opens.

So now it's—by the time all the boats went under it and all that, we were there for like forty-five minutes. So now of course I'm panicking, because I'm just late, first day, and all that. I get to the park, and Sutcliffe was the first guy I met—my locker was right next to his. He greeted me and said, "Congratulations," or whatever.

My first game it was Nolan Ryan against Jamie Moyer. I was excited, because I got to see one of the greatest pitchers ever on my first day. It was just something I've always remembered. I knew Jamie Moyer from the minor leagues, and I grew up watching Nolan Ryan, and to get to see him in person and be in uniform was a big thrill.

I knew I was gonna get called up a couple of days before that. I really didn't know what my chances of pitching were—they told me I was gonna start in about seven days. I didn't think I'd be used out of the pen, but sure enough it was one of those games that gets suspended because of darkness—it went into extra innings. I kind of decided, well, I'm in the big leagues, I finally got here, and all that. And I wake up the next morning and read the paper, and we had used six or seven pitchers in that game. So now I'm kind of thinking that there's not a whole lot of pitchers left, when we resume this game tomorrow, I could be in there. Sure enough, as soon as it started up, they asked me to go down to the pen and start throwing. It was against the Astros, and I went down there and started warming up, and there was one out, and Jody Davis hits a double.

And they asked me if I'm ready to go in, and I'm thinking, well, there's one out, there's no double play, I've got at least two hitters, so I said, "Yeah," and they said, "Go in, you're running at second." So I went in, and I pinch ran for Jody Davis. The next two guys make outs, so I kinda figure—I didn't really know what was going on, it's just kind of funny that they warm me up and put me in and I go in to pinch run, and now I'm done.

So I'm sittin' on the bench, and one of the coaches, John Vukovich, says, "Hey, you're in the game!"—hey, I didn't know what a double switch was!

I went out there, and I got my first taste of Wrigley. I gave up my first wind-blown home run. Billy Hatcher hit it—it ended up in the basket, it was a fastball. I tried to throw it away, threw it in a little bit, jammed him just a little bit. But he hit it up in the air, the wind blew it out, it ended up in the basket, and I looked up in the stands. I threw one inning, got a loss. I think I threw about ten or eleven pitches.

I would say my second year was when I finally got my feet on the ground. My first year, counting September, I was 8–18. And I had gotten sent down twice that year, so I was still trying to just . . . forget about arriving or belonging. I was just trying to stay on the team. And then after that year I went to winter ball and started off real good—had a real strong beginning in the second year, and that was when I finally felt like, hey, I got a chance to get guys out here, and hopefully for a long time—I would say by the All-Star break of my second year.

My change-up was probably the biggest thing that turned it around for me. I didn't throw a very good change-up my first year. I had had a good one in the minor leagues, but once I got to the big leagues I forgot how to throw it, if that makes any sense. It was mechanics, not nerves. I've never really been too nervous. I'll get jittery at times, and I'll get anxiety a lot of times, but I've never been nervous to the point where it affected me.

At least I had an idea of what I was trying to do, I just wasn't any good at doing it. So I learned how to throw a change-up. I was holding it wrong, and my stride was a little bit mixed up. My arm angle was a little bad on it, too—there was a couple of things wrong. I fixed that. Dick Pole worked with me in the minors, and he got me straightened out. Before that I was a one-pitch pitcher, and now at least I had two pitches. I could pitch hard and soft.

You know, the longer you pitch, usually the better your location gets. Very few of the pitchers that have been around for awhile are as wild as they were when they first came up—their control always seems to get better.

Making it to the big leagues, that's what you wanted all your life, that's what you worked for—it becomes an obsession. Winning a Cy Young was never an obsession. Winning a World Series was never an obsession—it's the reason why you play the game, but it was more of an obsession just to be able to play the game first.

Being in high school and wanting to play, and then being in the minors and wanting to play, and getting closer to the big leagues—it was something that just built up for four or five years. And when it finally arrived, it's a big accomplishment. The World Series is something that starts off in spring training, then drifts away, and then it comes back at the end of the year once you're in a position to get there.

It just seems like once the season starts your focus isn't on the World Series—it's on your next start, it's on that game tonight, until you get there. Whereas that first day, that was every day—that was something that you thought about every day in the minor leagues, getting there, what do you have to do to get there.

Once I felt like I belonged—you kind of change your goals a little bit. My goal was never to win a Cy Young, it was to win twenty games. When I first came up it was to win twenty games, I never considered or thought about that. You've got people like Mike Scott when I'm coming up, Dwight Gooden, Orel Hershiser, David Cone, and others, guys like that, Doug Drabek, you know? You know you're not as good as them—and I knew that, I definitely knew that.

I didn't try to be as good as them. I tried to learn from 'em and be as good as I can be, drop the Army motto on 'em. I always just tried to be as good as I could be. My goal was to win twenty games, and when I finally accomplished that, it's like I backed into a Cy Young. I think Glavine had twenty wins and I had fourteen or fifteen at the time, so the Cy Young was never an attainable goal to begin with. Your goals have to be attainable. It was never really attainable. I just backed into one, it just kind of happened.

He had gotten hurt, missed a couple starts. He was pitching with a broken rib. I was thrilled to death to win twenty games that year. They told me I won the Cy Young—it was more icing on the cake. Really, that's all it was, from an individual standpoint.

I don't really have any achievements in the postseason, other than last year. I did pretty well last year. The game I won in the World Series I would say was easily one of the best games I've ever thrown. The last out stands out the most—throwing to Carlos Baerga, that last change-up that he popped up—knowing that it was a one-run game, knowing Albert Belle's on deck.

I don't want to face Albert Belle in that situation, so I know I have to get this guy out. I have to keep myself out of the position where I have to face Albert Belle. That was something I knew going into the eighth inning. I knew he was hitting eighth as of the eighth inning, so I knew I had to get six outs in that situation.

I've had maybe two or three games in my career where I've thrown as well as I did that night, but never under those circumstances. So that's why I feel that if I had to pick games that I'm gonna remember, probably for a long time, it would be my first day and the game in that World Series.

DENNIS MARTINEZ

Few players have had a career with more resurrections than Dennis Martinez. A dominant starter for the Orioles in the late '70s and early '80s, Martinez battled injuries and alcoholism before resurfacing in the National League with the Montreal Expos, for whom he pitched a perfect game. In Montreal, the man from Nicaragua who became known as "El Presidente" also established himself as the first pitcher to win 100 games in both leagues. Then Martinez once again resurfaced to lead the Cleveland Indians to their first pennant in forty-one years, as well as to a World Series appearance against the Atlanta Braves.

The most exciting day that I had in the big leagues was the first day that I got brought up into the big leagues. I got a chance to pitch, and we were losing 7–0, and I got a chance to get into the game in the third inning. I struck out the first three guys, and we came back and won 8–7. So that was my first big thrill in the big leagues. That was something that will always stay in my mind.

That was in 1976. I was playing for the Baltimore Orioles—we were playing the Detroit Tigers. I remember that it was Willie Horton, Mickey Stanley, and—I can't quite remember the last guy I struck out, that's a little difficult for me.

There's been a bunch of other good ones. To be able to be in my first All-Star game, the perfect game, Game 6 of the Championship Series. There's a lot of different games I remember. It's a little bit different for every team I've played for. I guess it's hard for me to pick one.

The one for the Orioles was the most important for me from that team, that was the one that allowed me to break in to the big leagues, to establish myself in the big leagues. I pitched a lot of good ones for the Orioles.

The perfect game is the one that stands out from the Expos. It was really great to be able to give that kind of performance—that's another game that will stay in my mind also.

When I was with Montreal, I was with a different team in a

different country—that was the second team I was with, and I was able to establish myself as a pitcher again.

The game has been something that—it's beautiful to play this game, baseball. The people that don't understand that don't realize that it's a game that's been played for a long, long time—so to me, that's all I know, and it's been my life. I don't know what I'll do when retire, but I think I'll try and think of a way to stay in baseball, some way, somehow.

It's a bond that I've been able to share with people from all over the world, different countries, different cities, people who speak different languages. Being able to get along with them, to get the challenge to produce on a consistent basis, year in and year out. That was something that I'll always remember, that this game has been so great and that it's been so good to me.

With the Indians, it started with the Opening Day in the new ballpark—that was something that really meant a lot. In the sixth game of the Championship Series against Seattle that put us into the World Series—that was something that these people have been waiting for for forty-one years. And it was something that made me feel so proud and so good that I was able to contribute in this stadium for these people that have been waiting this long. For me, too, I was able to win in the postseason and help get this team into the World Series.

It was a challenge just to be able to face the Seattle Mariners in their stadium, in the Kingdome. We were able to face Randy Johnson. Everybody was talking about the Big Unit facing the old man who was forty-one years old. It's something that I took as a challenge to myself, and I was able to perform as well as I could. It was a great achievement to beat them, and it was something that I was looking forward to. I was happy just to be able to contribute something to this organization.

So I guess that was my ultimate goal when I signed with this ball club—they went after me to sign me to achieve something that they hadn't achieved, and I was happy to be able to help them do that.

I don't think about the personal things, because those always come around if you stay long enough in this game. But as I get closer now and I achieve these things, you start to be able to feel when you're getting closer to each one of them. I remember when I was coming up on 100 wins in the National League, and that made me the seventh pitcher to win 100 in each league.

So that kind of thing is important, and now I'm starting to think about Juan Marichal's record, which is the most wins in the big leagues for any Latin pitcher. That's in my mind now. If I'm healthy I will be able to give my best shot to overcome that record. But the main thing for me has always been to be able to be consistent, to be able to give my team a lot of innings, to go out every five days and take the mound.

[Editor's note: The following season after this interview was conducted, Dennis Martinez retired just short of reaching Marichal's record after a brief stint with the Seattle Mariners.]

TIM McCARVER

Behind the plate, Tim McCarver had a reputation for being an excellent defensive catcher who could call a great game and come up with a big hit at just the right time. The bright, witty, and analytical receiver also went on to have an outstanding career as a broadcaster with the New York Mets and for the national networks.

I don't have one greatest day, there are just too many to mention. I can give you a great day—I wouldn't say that it's the greatest day. I think one of the great things about a team sport like baseball is that you can vicariously reap benefits from other people's performances, as well as your own. And I would have to say that a great day in my young life at the time was back in 1964, the fifth game of the World Series, when I hit the three-run homer against the Yankees in the tenth inning off Pete Mikkelsen.

But it was what preceded that that stands out in my mind as much as anything. Bob Gibson's performance during that game—he was to win his first World Series game and then win his second one, the first of seven in a row, I might add. That, of course, is a record.

Not only his performance for nine innings but his performance in the ninth inning, when a ground ball by Joe Pepitone came back through the box. He knocked it down, and the ball rolled halfway between the mound and third base. Bob went over and barehanded it, and, jumping in the air, he made a real Harlem Globetrotter move, as only Gibson could do. Nobody else could make a play like that.

He threw to first and had Pepitone by the width of a shoelace. It was the most remarkable play that I'd ever seen, not only in World Series history, but by a pitcher. Pitchers were not really known as great athletes—and, of course, Gibson was one of the great athletes, not only of our generation, but maybe in the game's history.

So that day, there were so many things—I've got a picture, that I still have and cherish, of me hugging Gibson and Gibson hugging me. After the game, of course, in Yankee Stadium, in the old Yankee Stadium, with the monuments—a lot of people forget what that stadium looked like.

So with everything surrounding that—and ultimately we won the World Series, and Gibson was the winning pitcher—that has to stand out, certainly, as among the top ten days.

I do remember [in the tenth inning of Game 5] that with nobody out, and with Bill White on second base—I think Dick Groat was the batter, but I could be wrong—Elston Howard threw behind Bill White at second base, and Bill White went to third on a close play, a bang-bang play. And then Groat walked. I know that set it

October 12, 1964

ST. LOUIS	AB	R	H	RBI	NEW YORK (A.)	AB	R	H	RBI
Flood, cf	4	1	1	0	Linz, ss	5	0	0	0
Brock, lf	5	0	2	1	B. Richardson, 2b	5	0	3	0
White, 1b	4	1	0	1	Maris, cf	5	0	0	0
K. Boyer, 3b	4	0	1	0	Mantle, rf	3	1	0	0
Groat, ss	4	1	1	0	Howard, c	3	0	0	0
McCarver, c	5	1	3	3	Pepitone, 1b	4	0	1	0
Shannon, rf	5	0	0	0	Tresh, lf	3	1	1	2
Maxvill, 2b	5	0	1	0	C. Boyer, 3b	2	0	0	0
Gibson, p	4	1	1	0	Blanchard, ph	1	0	0	0
					Gonzalez, 3b	1	0	0	0
					Stottlemyre, p	2	0	1	0
					Lopez, ph	1	0	0	0
					Reniff, p	0	0	0	0
					Mikkelsen, p	0	0	0	0
					Hegan, ph	1	0	0	0
Totals	40	5	10	5	Totals	36	2	6	2

St. Louis	000	020	000	3 — 5
New York	000	000	002	0 — 2

up—one out and runners on first and third, and I was trying to hit the fly ball. So that inning was very vivid.

The count was 3–2, and on the previous pitch before I hit the home run I hit a ball that was just foul down the third base line. I played against Mikkelsen in the minor leagues. I knew what he threw, but he was a good pitcher. Usually you don't get that many good pitches to hit against a sinkerballer. He's trying to get a ground ball, and I'm trying to hit it hard. I did hit it hard, and had this ball been fair nobody was gonna catch it. But it was just foul, and I was disappointed. I had to gather myself back up and attend to the task at hand.

And then I hit the home run, and Mantle was playing right field. I remember seeing number "7" running away from me. When I initially hit it, I thought it was deep enough for a fly ball to score a run. I didn't realize, not playing in Yankee Stadium, that a ball hit 360 feet to right-center field would be out—it was about four rows back or something.

I think what makes it stand out in my mind is the fact that Mantle was the right fielder. He had such a tremendous series—that was his last World Series. All of those things—Gibson's performance and the greatness in that game; playing against Maris for the first time and then three years later being a teammate of his in '67; Howard; and Berra was the manager; and Whitey Ford, that was his last series—he hurt his arm and was in a lot of pain and never pitched after that first game.

You put all of those guys together, and that's a pretty exciting time for a guy who had just turned twenty-three years old a couple days earlier.

After the game I remember the picture of Gibson and me, primarily. I had been there before. I had no idea, growing up in St. Louis, of the power of the New York press. And the next day, you know, we came home at night, and there were about 10,000 people at the airport—which in those days was a staggering number of people—with signs, "Gibson for President" and "McCarver for President."

You would have thought the Series was over, really, but I remember the very impressive impact that the New York press made on me. And I remember taking the flight home, and my girlfriend, who's now my wife, was there, and it was just a very exciting moment. But the one thing about baseball, I was fully aware that you only have a few hours to celebrate because you only have a few other things to do to win, with the realization that you haven't won anything.

As a broadcaster, I think the sixth game of the 1986 playoffs against Houston is probably among the greatest games I've ever seen or participated in. Dykstra leading off with a pinch triple—and usually, with the score 3–0 against a guy who's held a team to two or three hits for eight innings, Bob Knepper, you don't think of that as a big hit, because he was leading the inning off, but it was a real eye-opener.

The Mets tied it—Hatcher hits the home run to tie it in the fourteenth. And then the Mets go on to win it with three in the top of the sixteenth, and Kevin Bass was the last hitter, and he struck out against Jessie Orosco.

I'll never forget that game, because everybody was so emotionally drained going into that game. There was a rainout. Both teams had played the night before—you get in about three or four in the morning, there's a three o'clock starting time in Houston—everybody was just emotionally drained. But there's something about the game that can pick you up and make you forget your fatigue, and that's what happened to the Mets. In my mind, there was no way the Mets could come back and beat Mike Scott. I didn't think anybody could have beaten Mike Scott that year, as hot as he was.

Working with Keith Jackson—that's what stands out. That was the only time I ever worked with Keith in a postseason series. I'd worked with him that season, and it was just a joy to work with him. I've gotta believe that even though Keith's not a baseball announcer that if you talk to him, he would probably list that in his top twenty-five moments, even though he doesn't have a lot to compare it with, but it was an exceptional game.

I remember trying to get . . . a funny story, we were trying to get Kevin Bass to do an impression of Sammy Davis, Jr.—he did a great impression of Sammy Davis, Jr. And I was trying to get him to go on, and he said, "No, man, I can't do that." And then he said—I didn't know him prior to that, we became good friends after this happened—he said, "OK, if you give me $200, I'll do it." I said, "No, I'm not giving you anything. The network's not giving you any money. This is a freebie."

And he said, "I like those shoes you have on." And I said, "I'll tell you what, you do the interview," I said, "What size shoe do you wear?" "10½." I wear 10½. I had just broken these shoes in, they were about a month old. I loved these things, the loafers that

I had on. I said, "If you do the Sammy Davis impression, I'll give you the shoes."

This was during the series—I don't think it was before Game 6, I think it was before Game 5. He did the impression, and I gave him my shoes. And I thought he'd give 'em back—he kept him. I've never seen those shoes since. And Kevin Bass ultimately made the last out in the series.

MARK McGWIRE

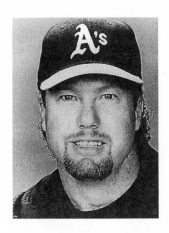

Before Mark McGwire became one of the most feared sluggers in the game, he was also one of baseball's most amazing rookie phenoms, hitting forty-nine home runs in his rookie year. McGwire's meteoric rise was an integral part of the success of the great Oakland A's clubs of the late '80s, and in his second season he went to the World Series. His greatest moment took place in Game 3 against the Los Angeles Dodgers in 1988, but it became a bittersweet triumph when the A's lost the Series, 4–1.

In the midst of a fifty-home run season in 1996, McGwire compared that moment with the achievements of his rookie year and the A's World Series victory over the San Francisco Giants in the earthquake-tarnished 1989 Series.

You know, right now I would have to say that it would have to be the game-winning home run in the bottom of the ninth inning against the Dodgers. Only because when you're a kid and you're out playing in the street, and you're playing with a tennis ball or a nerf ball or whatever it is, you always mimic, "Bottom of the ninth, World Series, facing so-and-so . . . "

And I just distinctly remember running around the bases, thinking, "You know, this is a childhood dream come true." There are a lot of players who get an opportunity to play this game, but not many players get to have dreams like that come true. It happened to me at an early age, in 1988 in my second year in the big leagues, and I've had a lot of things happen to me, but that's just the one thing that sticks out in my mind.

We had just gotten beat by Kirk Gibson—he hit his dramatic home run to win the first game. The second game we didn't play very well, we got beat again. So we're down 2–0, and we play a tight game, and, basically, we were supposed to be the team to win everything. The Dodgers had a good year, and people were saying, "They're not gonna match up to the A's," and they're ahead 2–0.

And here we come in and it turns out it was my only hit. So I was more nervous than expected, because I hadn't gotten any hits the first couple of games until the ninth inning of the third game. I was at such a young age, and I think that everybody knows what pressure is, but I didn't really accept the pressure at that young an age. Today I think the pressure would be a lot greater, because I know what it's all about.

We hoped that the home run I hit would get us over the hump, so that we could at least win the next game and get it tied up and get it back to 2–2. But they ended up winning two straight and beating us 4–1. The Gibson home run probably did deflate our sails, but it was just one of those things. That's just the greatest thing about baseball—you can have the greatest team, the highest-paid team, but you're not going to win every game.

It's like a pitcher—every time out he has a chance to pitch a no-hitter. Every time a hitter gets into the box, he has a chance of getting a hit. But it doesn't happen. That's why it's so great to play this game, because of the fluctuation of things that can happen. It's almost like being a cop. Every day's a different day, and you might be going on the same calls as a policeman—we go to the same ballparks every year—but there's always something different you can look at.

I don't know what I was thinking when I hit the home run. I'm such a different player now than I was back then. I don't even know if I had preparation—I think I just showed up at the park and played. And the media crush was so bad during the Series. Playoff and World Series is pretty bad—there's not much room to maneuver and get ready for the game. There's always something that somebody wants to ask you that might offset you from really concentrating during the game.

I just remember saying, "I just want to get a hit. If I get a hit and do something . . ." I remember hitting the ball, and I remember running down the line and putting my arms up, and I remember seeing the ball, because it was night, and at night in Oakland the ball doesn't carry very well. And I just remember saying, "Oh, my God.

The ball's got topspin on it, that might not get out," so I put my hands down and started running faster. But it ended up getting out. It was just one of those thrills, like a childhood dream.

I don't even remember the count. It might have been a 2–1 count, if I remember. I just remember seeing a fastball and taking a whack at it—that's all I remember. I think it was middle, maybe middle-in a little bit.

I was numb after I hit it. That was when we started the bash, was in '88, so I remember bashing everybody. And I remember a lot of guys were sore the next day because I was doing it so hard, and when your adrenaline is flowing so much you don't realize how strong you are.

I see highlights of that, and I look at myself now. I had longer hair, a goatee back then. Now I'm clean-cut. I was skinnier. And it's like, "God, did I really look like that?" That's like eight years ago, and people change.

I think anytime you lose something like that and you work so hard—we didn't play well in '88, we didn't play well in '90. We played well in '89, and we won the World Series. And in '89 we won it, and then we had the earthquake. We didn't really get to celebrate, because we had to give all due respect to what happened to the people.

I really haven't had the true taste of what it's like to win a

October 19, 1988

LOS ANGELES	AB	R	H	RBI	OAKLAND	AB	R	H	RBI
Sax, 2b	5	0	1	0	Phillips, lf	1	0	0	0
Stubbs, 1b	4	0	1	1	Polonia, lf	3	0	0	0
Woodson, 1b	1	0	0	0	Henderson, cf	4	0	0	0
Hatcher, lf	4	0	1	0	Canseco, rf	4	0	0	0
Marshall, rf	1	0	0	0	McGwire, 1b	4	1	1	1
Heep, lf	3	0	1	0	Steinbach, c	3	0	2	0
Shelby, cf	3	0	2	0	Lansford, 3b	3	0	0	0
M. Davis, dh	2	0	0	0	Hubbard, 2b	3	1	1	0
Anderson, dh	1	0	0	0	Hassey, c	1	0	1	1
Scioscia, c	4	0	1	0	Weiss, ss	3	0	0	0
Hamilton, 3b	3	1	1	0					
Griffin, ss	3	0	0	0					
Totals	34	1	8	1	Totals	29	2	5	2

Los Angeles	000	010	000 — 1
Oakland	001	000	001 — 2

championship. I haven't had a taste of doing the champagne, having the parade down in downtown Oakland. We had a little rally. There's always going to be a little asterisk next to that World Series, and there's always going to be an asterisk next to '88 and '90—"A's should have won. Didn't play well." So even though I'm lucky enough to say that I've been to three World Series and four playoffs, I still don't think I've felt what you see when you see the Braves or what Minnesota's done or what Toronto's done—the real true feeling of what it's like.

That home run definitely ranks there at the top in terms of what I've done. I've always said that it would be neat to write down all the accomplishments that I've done, because sometimes I don't even remember. The one thing I'd really like to do is to write down all the really great players that I've played with. But I'd have to say there's the World Series home run, the forty-nine home runs as a rookie, seeing Nolan Ryan's 5,000th strikeout.

The Series home run ranks above forty-nine home runs because that's just something you dream about when you're a kid. You don't dream about hitting forty-nine home runs when you're a kid. You just dream about hitting the ball, you don't dream about numbers. That's why I think I'm the player I am today, because I don't think about numbers that much. Of course I'm aware of home runs and RBIs, but all the other stuff, I don't think about it or look at it.

JACK MORRIS

Jack Morris won almost 200 games during his lengthy career with the Detroit Tigers, Minnesota Twins, and Toronto Blue Jays in the 1980s and early '90s, but the pitcher's calling card was his ability to rise to the occasion in big games. In Morris's biggest game, he delivered one of the great postseason pitching performances of the post-war era against the Atlanta Braves in the 1991 World Series.

Well, I think it's pretty obvious that my greatest day was Game 7 of the 1991 World Series. All the writers predicted that the two teams, the Atlanta Braves and the Minnesota Twins, would finish last in their division when the season began. So it just showed the determination of both ball clubs.

I don't know what the stats are; you'd have to look it up: four extra inning games, five one-run games. It was just a Series that was a dogfight. It was almost appropriate the way it ended (ten innings, 1–0) because of how balanced both ball clubs were and how hard we fought to try and win it.

I guess one thing that I don't quite understand . . . I've been in different mindsets before. Prior to the Series I was quite confident we could be there—we had beaten Toronto in the playoffs and played quite well against Toronto. I had been in the World Series before with Detroit, and I kind of realized what it was all about.

To me, what it was all about was blocking out the media hype and the fan hype about what it meant . . . it's just another ball game, you've just got to take it almost that simple. I think that as the Series progressed, everybody was quite aware of what a unique Series it was.

What set the tone for my greatest day was an incident prior to Game 6 during batting practice. I went up to Tom Kelly, our manager, and almost begged him to let me pitch. Kelly didn't know if Scott Erickson was gonna be able to pitch because he was a little tender with his arm.

TK was pretty impressive. He said, "No." He said, "This guy deserves his day. I believe he's gonna pitch well. He'll be OK. And besides, if we don't win today, without today there is no tomorrow, and if we win today we're gonna need you tomorrow." The whole thing made me feel real good because he showed confidence in both of us.

But what really set the tone was the extra inning home run by Kirby Puckett. When that ball went out of the ballpark, it was almost like everything I'd ever played the game for came over my being. There was a calmness that came over me. I knew right then that the next day was meant for me.

It's crazy, I can't explain why—it's almost like it had been planned or that I had dreamed it so many times as a little boy. You know, you play the game in the sandlots, you dream about the seventh game, World Series, and you throw this pitch, and it was crazy because I'd almost planned it my whole life.

I got total rest that night. The next morning I woke up and had breakfast with my family, and my kids were with me, and I never was nervous, I never had butterflies, all I had was confidence and a little anxiety because I couldn't wait for the game to start. I think as I progressed as a veteran player, people always asked me, "Did you ever get butterflies?" and I always said, "No." I was never nervous, I was just bored, and I couldn't wait for the game to start. Typically in baseball it's a hurry-up-and-wait situation, and I just wanted to get it going.

The game itself was just what happened. I was really aware of what the game meant. I remember so much, but one memory stands out. I don't remember whether it was the sixth or the seventh inning, but I kept looking at the opposing pitcher, a young John Smoltz. He wasn't as recognized or as famous as he is today, but he turned in one of the greatest games a pitcher has thrown in modern baseball. Here he was, pitching his ass off, too, doing everything he could to help his ball club, and I just cherished the battle that was going on. I almost wanted to have it all go forever, because for me, that's what this damn game was all about. It wasn't about too many other things.

I remember looking up in the stands, and as a kid growing up in Minnesota, I had been a Minnesota Twin fan and a Minnesota Viking fan, and I remembered how the Minnesota Vikings had been to three straight Super Bowls and lost all three. And I just looked at the people, literally looked at the people, how drained they were. They'd almost all lost their voices, they were waving their hankies, they were just physically exhausted in support of their club.

And I remember, and I shouldn't do this, because the man I'm gonna talk about was a fantastic athlete, but I remember Fran Tarkenton, and I remember three straight Super Bowl losses, of course Joe Kapp was one of 'em, and I said to myself, "We aren't gonna do that today. We're gonna win this thing." And I didn't mean me, and I didn't necessarily mean the team. I meant everybody that was at that ball game. . . . We're gonna go home, and we're gonna celebrate.

Again, it's almost like another calmness came over me. At that point, I really truly believed that if the thing went twenty innings I would still be out there, and I was still gonna be pitching, and we were still gonna win. That was my mindset, and it was amazing.

I did not feel fatigue at all, it was a case where neither team had a game the next day . . . or the next day, or the next day. This was it, it was the last game of the year. Whatever strength and endurance I had left was going to be exhibited that day. I truly was not tired. In fact, I think I was getting stronger as the seventh, eighth, ninth, tenth innings came along.

And TK, there's a great story about all that, it was basically nothing, but a lot of people thought there was more to it. He looked at me after the ninth inning, and he said, "That's it, you did

October 27, 1991

ATLANTA	AB	R	H	RBI	BB	SO	MINNESOTA	AB	R	H	RBI	BB	SO
Smith, dh	4	0	2	0	I	I	Gladden, lf	5	I	3	0	0	I
Pendleton, 3b	5	0	I	0	0	0	Knoblauch, 2b	4	0	I	0	0	0
Gant, cf	4	0	0	0	0	2	Puckett, cf	2	0	0	0	3	I
Justice, rf	3	0	I	0	I	I	Hrbek, 1b	3	0	0	0	I	0
Bream, 1b	4	0	0	0	0	0	Davis, dh	4	0	I	0	0	I
Hunter, lf	4	0	I	0	0	I	Brown, pr–ph	0	0	0	0	0	0
Olson, c	4	0	0	0	0	I	Larkin, ph	I	0	I	I	0	0
Lemke, 2b	4	0	I	0	0	I	Harper, c	4	0	2	0	0	0
Belliard, ss	2	0	I	0	0	I	Mack, rf	4	0	I	0	0	0
Blauser, ph–ss	I	0	0	0	0	0	Pagliarulo, 3b	3	0	0	0	I	0
							Gagne, ss	2	0	0	0	0	I
							Bush, ph	I	0	I	0	0	0
							Newman, pr–ss	0	0	0	0	0	0
							Sorrento, ph	I	0	0	0	0	I
							Leius, ss	0	0	0	0	0	0
Totals	35	0	7	0	2	8	Totals	34	I	10	I	5	5

Atlanta	000	000	000	0 — 0	
Minnesota	000	000	000	I — I	

ATLANTA	IP	H	R	ER	BB	SO
Smoltz	7.I	6	0	0	I	4
Stanton	.2	2	0	0	I	0
Pena, L	1.I	2	I	I	3	I
MINNESOTA	IP	H	R	ER	BB	SO
Morris, W	10	7	0	0	2	8

a hell of a job. I couldn't ask for anything more." And I looked him right in the eye, and I said, "I'm not going anywhere." He looked back at me, then he looked at Dick Such, the pitching coach, and then he looked back at me again, and he said, "What the hell, it's just a game."

Well, I interpreted that as TK wanting to give me an out. He was giving me an opportunity to take myself out of the game in a way that I could have been very proud and dignified, and the truth is, he didn't want me to take myself out, he wanted me to say what I said. Because I knew I still had my stuff. We all knew that, and in that situation he didn't want to bring anybody else in, because everything means everything at that point, and I was on a roll. He truly wanted to hear what I told him. I had no intent of ever having a reliever come into my game at that point.

It was absolute ecstasy and chaos when we scored. It was just such a relief. I can hardly remember the exact thoughts, but I remember looking up at the stands, trying to find my kids.

My dad had brought 'em down to the railing, along the first base line, and as the team was kind of circling the field in a victory lap I saw my kids, and I just went over to them, and they came down on the field, and my youngest son was crying, and I was really worried that somebody had pushed him or shoved him or he was hurt or something happened. And I asked him what's wrong, and he said, "Dad, I'm just so happy." That was probably the best part of the whole thing.

I never got to sleep that night. We stayed around the ballpark for a long time, because it was a close-knit team, it really was. Also, I remember there was an adjoining room, a laundry room, between the locker rooms in Minnesota in which Mark Lemke, and David Justice, and a couple of the guys kind of sneaking through there, it was Chili Davis, myself, and two or three other guys, and we sat there and had a drink together after the thing was over. We were enemies but we were reminiscing about how great the whole thing was. It was kind of amazing, because I didn't know Mark Lemke from Adam, and I really didn't know David Justice. I never did talk to Smoltz, in fact I've never talked to John about it. It's crazy. I know that at one time when he was growing up in Detroit, I was kind of one of his idols, so it's ironic that a game like that would turn out the way it did.

The reason I put Game 7 in 1991 as my greatest day is because there was never a game in my whole life that had more importance. To pitch in any World Series is wonderful. I feel like I was lucky: in '92 I pitched in the World Series and got my butt beat twice by the same Atlanta Braves, and I remember the reporters looking at me as though I were supposed to be invincible, saying to themselves, "You've done this in Detroit, you've done this in Minnesota." I said to myself, "Hey, I'm the luckiest guy in the world. I'm here, and all the other guys in baseball are sitting at home wondering and wishing they were here." I didn't do as well, but I was still pitching in the World Series, and I felt great about that.

It's hard to compare the different World Series, because each one is special. It's like comparing three different kids—you love 'em all. The first one was in Detroit, and that one was wonderful because it was the first one. Minnesota was great, Toronto was great as well. I won two in Toronto . . . they're all great. I think Game 7 was the biggest day because it was the only Game 7 I ever pitched in.

I guess I took pride in the fact that I had a reputation as a big-game pitcher. It all started in high school, playing basketball, to be honest with you. I had a coach who took me aside and flat-out told me, he said, "You're a screwup in practice. You only play when you have to play." And he said, "It's a shame that you only turn it on when you have to."

I guess there's a part of me that, even at a young age like that, I always . . . in the minor leagues and all through my baseball career, I kind of got beat up by guys that I took for granted. Some of the greatest no-names in the world have hit home runs off me. I put a lot of guys on the map. I guess it's just concentration more than anything else; it's not that I consciously wanted to do that, but I probably mentally let myself down, and all the sudden I got myself in trouble. But in the big games I was able to focus a hell of a lot better.

I really don't have many regrets about my whole career, to be honest with you, because I might be talking here of one at-bat in one entire game, and that at-bat, most of the time, didn't have an effect on the game. I might have given up. . . . I remember one year, I forget what year it was, I gave up like thirty-six home runs. That was unbelievable. I think Bert Blyleven set an American League record that year with fifty home runs.

And what's so crazy about those thirty-six home runs is that I gave up thirty home runs that were solos, and very few of them had any significance in the game, because I was still able to kick it into gear when I needed to shut the door and win that game.

As far as my chances for the Hall of Fame, I've talked about this with some of my good friends in baseball, and teammates, for example Alan Trammell is still one of my best friends. And we've talked about it for years, about certain guys we felt were absolute slam dunks into the Hall of Fame who aren't there, and we realize that there's a problem with the way it's all . . . the committee, and the voting, and all that.

And we just both decided that, hey, we don't ever have to worry about whether we make it or whether we don't. The fact is that for the period of time that we played we were as good as anybody else, and our teammates and our peers recognized that, that's all we can hope for and thank God for, because whether or not we get into the Hall of Fame or not is irrelevant. We know that's all that matters.

DON NEWCOMBE

A dominant pitcher for the Dodgers during the late '40s and '50s, Don Newcombe won the MVP as well as the Cy Young Award in 1956, and in his rookie year he became the youngest pitcher ever to start a World Series game. So Newcombe had plenty to choose from in selecting his greatest day, including his major league debut with the Dodgers in 1949 and the help and guidance he received from Jackie Robinson and Roy Campanella.

How about not just a great day, the greatest day, but the greatest time maybe? My going to join the Dodgers would probably be my greatest day, but then the game that I pitched against the Yankees, for instance, when I lost in the World Series might be another great day. Even though I lost the game it was a great day for me, because of the way the game went.

I remember being called into the Dodger office or the Montreal Royal office in 1949 on the 15th of May by Buzzy Bavasi, who told me that I was gonna join the Dodgers, and for me to go home and pack my car and get my wife and drive her home to New Jersey, and to meet Branch Rickey in Roosevelt Field in New York to fly to Chicago to join the Dodgers.

What a thrill that was. I rushed home from Montreal in that car, repacked my bags and everything, and got over to New York and got into Mr. Rickey's little puddle-jumper Beechcraft airplane. He said, "You've finally arrived, young man. And we're going, and I'm taking you, and I promised you before that you'd make it, and now I'm taking you to prove it to you."

And we got on the plane and stopped in Harrisburg, Pennsylvania, and picked up another great Dodger who was gonna join us, Billy Cox. And the four of us flew out, Mr. Rickey and myself and the pilot and Billy Cox, to Chicago to join the Dodgers. When I entered that Hilton Hotel on Michigan Avenue in Chicago, I walked into the room where Jackie Robinson and Roy Campanella were having dinner, and they had the room service waiter waiting on them.

I said, "God, is this the way we live at the major league level?" And Mr. Rickey said, "Yes, that's the way we live if . . ." and I said, "If what?" And he said, "If you stay here." And that opened my eyes, because it wasn't going to be just because my name was Don Newcombe that I was going to stay with the Dodgers. I had to perform.

Chicago was fine, but the next city we went to was St. Louis, and there I found very quickly that we could not stay with our team-mates in the Chase Hotel in St. Louis. They got in the air-conditioned bus in St. Louis and drove out to the Chase Hotel in comfort, while the black players . . . Robinson, Campanella, Newcombe . . . had to get a taxi cab and go to a hotel that was . . . it couldn't have been third class, it must have been fourth class, for us to stay in. No air conditioning, no restaurant . . . yes, it was a fleabag.

And then about two or three months later on a trip to St. Louis, a friend of ours . . . or maybe it even happened the next year. Probably the next year, 1950, a friend of ours in St. Louis, Charlie Abernathy, a real estate man, bought a hotel called the Adams Hotel from a white group and he turned it into a black hotel. It was much nicer than the hotel we were staying at.

The Adams Hotel, though, didn't have air conditioning, Charlie couldn't afford it, nor a restaurant, so if we wanted to eat anything we had to walk or get a cab to a restaurant. And we soaked our sheets in cold water many times and put 'em on the bed and tried to sleep. The trolley car would come clanging by until 2 o'clock in the morning, then it would start again at 6 o'clock in the morning, and the only way you could sleep in that hotel was for the windows to be open . . . and then the mosquitos would come in, so you had to sleep with your head under the sheets if you were going to keep these mos-quitoes from buzzing in your ear. Charlie did the best he could, God bless him. He tried to make us comfortable, because that was the only hotel. We stayed there for seven years in St. Louis.

I joined the Dodgers in Chicago, but I didn't pitch in Chicago, but I did get a chance to relieve in a game in St. Louis. The first hit-ter I struck out with three fastballs, but the next four hitters in the Cardinal line-up got base hits and I think they scored four runs off those four base hits. The first hitter was Chuck Geary. I had pitched against him at the Triple AAA level. He was with Rochester, I was with Montreal. The next four hitters were Red Schoendienst, Stan Musial, Eddie Kazak, and Enos Slaughter, and they got four runs off me. And I thought after they took me out of the ball game that I was going back to Montreal.

I felt very sad about that, and I got in the corner of the dugout and I started crying. So the manager came over to me, his name was Bert Shotton, he said, "What are you crying about?" I said, "Well I didn't do very well tonight, Mr. Shotton, I guess I'm going back to Montreal." He said, "When did you join this ball club?" I said, "The other day in Chicago." He said, "You're managing already?" And I said, "No, sir, I don't mean to manage but I didn't do very well."

And he said, "Well, that's not the way we run things at the major league level. What's tonight?" And I said "Wednesday night," and he said, "Where we gonna be this weekend?" I said, "In Cincinnati." And he said, "What are we gonna do on Sunday afternoon?" and I said, "We're gonna play a doubleheader, Mr. Shotton." He said, "You got the second game, so go get yourself ready. Go in the clubhouse, and take that sweatshirt off, come back out here on this bench, and cut out that goddamn crying, and you might learn something."

Well, I got to Cincinnati and I started that second game, and I pitched a five-hit shutout, and that started a career for Don Newcombe. A lot of it was based on '49, because I was lucky enough to make the All-Star team that year, and I became the second rookie in the history of baseball to start in the World Series. Paul Derringer was the other one when he was with Cincinnati, I think.

I started against the New York Yankees, and got beat 1–0 by Allie Reynolds. He gave up two hits and struck out nine, and I gave up five hits, including a home run in the ninth inning, and struck out eleven. And even though I lost that game, I often consider that game one of the better games that Don Newcombe had ever pitched.

I remember striking out Jerry Coleman and striking out Joe DiMaggio and Yogi Berra even. But Tommy Henrich hit the home run off me leading off the ninth inning. I was thinking about going as far as I could, and so was Allie Reynolds, the way he was pitching. We would have been still trying here in 1997 to get a run off Allie Reynolds. So I just hoped that I could survive, but I didn't. I didn't survive the first hitter in the ninth inning, because Tommy Henrich, he led off, on an 0–2 pitch he hit a home run. We only had two hits, and they were singles, I think. Like I said, he struck out nine, we didn't get too many men on base. I don't know how many walked, probably one or two. Allie didn't walk too many, but this is one of his great games, and one of my great games.

The World Series, that stands out in your mind, and being a rookie, and being the second rookie in the history of baseball, I wasn't supposed to start the game, Preacher Roe was. He come up with a stiff arm, but he pitched the next day, a shutout, or won the game 2–1 or something like that, I don't know what the score was. But the fact is, I got that distinction, to be a rookie and to start that World Series, and that stands out in my mind.

I was 0–4 against the Yankees in World Series play with the Dodgers. But Bob Feller never won a World Series game either, and he was a pretty good pitcher.

Other games that you pitch during the season, I really don't remember too many of 'em that I really worried about. I know I pitched a one-hitter against the Cubs in Chicago. I never pitched a no-hitter in the major leagues, so there aren't any games that stand out in my mind, in my memory, just because I won them. They don't stand out the way that loss did, because it was such a great game, and there were so many people in the stadium that day, and a lot of them were black people, and they were cheering for me. . . . God, I was just hoping I could get a run or two and win that game, but it didn't work out that way. But it stands out in my memory as one of the greatest games I've ever pitched.

I was a rookie back in Cincinnati, and I wasn't going to let that game go to my head, because one game does not a season make. So I had to keep my feet on the ground, and playing with Jackie Robinson and Roy Campanella and all those other great Dodgers, but most certainly Jackie Robinson and Roy Campanella, who were more experienced than me. I was only twenty-two years old.

They were more mature men, and they knew what the purpose of our being there was, and they were not going to let a twenty-two-year-old rookie get a swelled head and think that he was God's gift to the Dodgers and baseball and forget what we were there to do. Not just to play and win baseball games and do well. We had more things to do that carried beyond what we did on the baseball field as individuals.

They made me win. . . . They made me keep my feet on the ground. I remember Jackie Robinson coming to the mound one day in Pittsburgh when I had an 11–0 lead in the third inning. I had started goofing around, experimenting with a change-up here and a little slow curveball there, when I walked three men and got the bases loaded with Ralph Kiner coming up with nobody out.

Jackie said, "You big, dumb son-of-a-bitch, why don't you go in and take that uniform off and go home, for chrissake?" So I said, "What's the matter with you, Robinson?" He said, "You're out here screwing around, with an eleven-run lead. You got the bases loaded and no outs and Kiner at bat, and you're gonna get taken out of this ball game, you dumb son-of-a-bitch. You're gonna lose the game, at least you're not gonna get credit for the win, somebody else is on the Dodger team, so why don't you just take the uniform off, because you're not pitching."

I struck Kiner out, retired the side, and won the game—I think about 11–1. I'll always remember that. He knew from then on what he had to do to make Don Newcombe keep his feet on the ground. Jackie didn't mind, because he was not afraid. He feared no man. He was not afraid to come in and get on me and let me know that I was not performing to the 110 or 115 percent of my ability. He didn't mind, and he could back himself up. I wasn't about to challenge him about what he was saying and what he was helping to make me do.

Campy was more of a fatherly type. He was more . . . of course, we were in Nashua, New Hampshire, in Class B together. Campy was more of a fatherly type—he would come out, he would talk, but he wouldn't curse at me the way Jackie would. He wouldn't use the forcefulness that Jackie did; he was more civilized.

But they were both there to help the Dodgers win, but they also wanted me to win, and they didn't want me to be a failure. I really don't think they would have given a damn if I was sent out and

October 5, 1949

BROOKLYN	AB	R	H	RBI	NEW YORK	AB	R	H	RBI
Reese, ss	4	0	1	0	Rizzuto, ss	4	0	0	0
Jorgensen, 3b	3	0	1	0	Henrich, 1b	4	1	1	1
Snider, cf	4	0	0	0	Berra, c	3	0	0	0
Robinson, 2b	4	0	0	0	DiMaggio, cf	3	0	0	0
Hermanski, lf	3	0	0	0	Lindell, lf	3	0	1	0
Furillo, rf	3	0	0	0	Johnson, 3b	3	0	0	0
Hodges, 1b	2	0	0	0	Mapes, rf	3	0	0	0
Campanella, c	2	0	0	0	Coleman, 2b	3	0	1	0
Newcombe, p	3	0	0	0	Reynolds, p	3	0	2	0
Totals	28	0	2	0	Totals	29	1	5	1

Brooklyn	000	000	000 — 0	
New York	000	000	001 — 1	

BROOKLYN	IP	H	R	ER	BB	SO
Newcombe, L	8	5	1	1	0	11
NEW YORK	IP	H	R	ER	BB	SO
Reynolds, W	9	2	0	0	4	9

released, but they knew what my ability was, and they knew I could pitch, and they knew I could win, and they weren't gonna let me do anything else but use my, not only 100 percent ability, but 110 or 115 percent of my ability. He wasn't going to take anything less . . . Jackie never did.

The days when I got awards were great days, but not the great days like I talked about. They were given to you, those awards, for your success after you had that success. You had to have that success before you could be the recipient of those awards. Well, the Rookie of the Year, yes, I was 17–8 after joining the team on May 17th, 1949, and won Rookie of the Year. Now that was an accomplishment, and I was entitled to that first award. I wish it was named the Jackie Robinson Award at that time but it wasn't

But the fact is that I was given that award for that year. Then my accomplishments in 1956, when I was given the Cy Young Award, the first ever in baseball, and the MVP award. That meant that I was the best player in the National League for that year. Now that is for accomplishments, that's for winning twenty-seven ball games, and the ironic part about that 1956 season was that I didn't make the All-Star team despite being 9–5.

I was 18–2 after the All-Star game. But I don't remember any of those games I won. I don't even remember how I won the twenty-seventh game. I had a big lead and I was taken out of the ball game in the seventh inning and a guy saved the ball game for me after I had the big lead.

I remember the voting, or of being apprised of the voting by Buzzie Bavasi, about how it was going down. I had already won the MVP in the National League.

But there was talk among some of the writers about giving the Cy Young award to Sal Maglie. I said to Buzzie, "Buzzie, what the hell's going on? Here I am 27–7, Sal 13–5, and they're talking about giving the award to Sal Maglie." Buzzie said, "Don't you worry about a goddamn thing. Go home, go to sleep, and don't worry about it. There's no way that they can not give you the Cy Young Award." And Buzzie was so right.

But that shows you, I think, a racist level. Had I been a white guy, there would have been no question, no question at all, by any writer, about the fact that because Don Newcombe won the MVP award, he automatically, without even writing about it, should win the Cy Young Award.

Later, because I was a black man doing well, they began to write things about me, about my lack of intestinal fortitude, about choking, about being gutless. And I listened to it—and allowed it to break me. Because after 1956 my record was just so-so, and my departure from the major leagues at only thirty-two in 1960 was hastened by my drinking of alcohol. I became an alcoholic.

I bounced back when I stopped drinking—in 1966 and 1967. When I stopped drinking I began to think rationally about my life. I stopped complaining, I stopped feeling sorry for myself, I stopped bitching and moaning about how I should have had a longer career.

Now I was on the same level with Warren Spahn and with Robin Roberts and all those other pitchers who stayed until they were thirty-eight, thirty-nine. I never hurt my arm in baseball, but because of the press I changed my approach to conditioning, and to taking care of myself and paying attention to what went on in the major leagues.

In fact, as I think about it, the greatest day in baseball in Don Newcombe's life has yet to occur. It will come when a national holiday is established in honor of Jackie Roosevelt Robinson. It will be a day that will teach people, especially young black kids, who Jackie Robinson was and the contribution he made to American society, and yes, even the world.

I hope that I'm alive to see it, and I hope that it happens, because there won't be a black man in the next century who will ever be allowed to do enough to warrant the thrill and honor of being given this kind of day, this kind of honor, in his memory, for his family, especially for his widow, Rachel, and for the guys who played with Jackie and stood by him like myself and Joe Black. It would be a great thing.

Whatever way they do it, it would be a great honor for my friend, Mr. Jack Robinson.

HAL NEWHOUSER

In addition to pitching the Detroit Tigers to victory over the Chicago Cubs in Wrigley Field in the seventh game of the 1945 World Series, Hal Newhouser won over 200 games in his major league career. Newhouser also accomplished a rare feat for a pitcher, winning the MVP twice in consecutive seasons during the World War II years. Unfairly branded a "wartime" pitcher in subsequent decades, he

was finally voted into the Hall of Fame by the Veteran's Committee in 1991.

I've had a number of great days in my career, but I would have to say that the day that stands out the most for me is pitching in the last game of the World Series in 1945 and winning against the Cubs. We were on their home turf in Wrigley Field, which made it that much tougher and that much more special.

It was a nice day, a little cool. I remember being a little nervous as we took the train to Chicago, not sleeping well the night before. Some fans had come down from Detroit, and they came up to me in town and wished me good luck, but I just wanted to hide someplace. So I got something to eat and went out to the ballpark . . . that was my sanctuary.

When I got to the park, the players had to take batting practice, so I did a little bit of bunting. I noticed that, because it was warm, most of the fans in the center field bleachers had taken their jackets off, creating a wall of white shirts.

So I went up to my catcher, Paul Richards, and I said, "Paul, I've got 20/20 vision, but I'm really having trouble seeing the ball. With all those white shirts, it seems to me that if I come right over the top their hitters are going to have some problems. It's going to be very hard to pick up the ball." The angle of the sun at that time of year made it very tough to see the ball, especially against all the white shirts.

So Paul said to me, "What do you have in mind?" Now I give Paul a lot of credit for helping me in my career. He helped make me a winning pitcher, he'd caught Carl Hubbell, and he knew a lot about hitters and about pitching. He was a quiet man who really knew baseball.

I asked him to stand up a bit (so he'd be roughly at the batter's eye level) while I threw some to him to see if he had the same problem. I came straight over the top, and sure enough, he had trouble picking up the ball.

Now I was basically a high-ball, fastball pitcher, and in those days we had the strike zone extended from just beneath the armpits down to the knees, just the way it was written in the rule book. I believe I might have a lot of trouble pitching today, the way they're calling the strike zone. I stayed up high almost all the time, because to me all hitters are basically low-ball hitters. Just look at their swings and the motion of their arms.

I'd had a little bit of arm trouble right before this game, and my normal motion was somewhere between three-quarters and over the top. Coming over the top wasn't something I usually did, so I was a bit worried that I might get hurt. But it was the last game of the World Series, and we decided it might be worth a try, so we did it

Well, I got lucky, because we scored five runs in the top of the first inning. Hank Borowy was pitching for the Cubs, and he didn't throw over the top. He had more of a three-quarter motion. That's why our hitters were able to pick up the ball and theirs weren't and we were able to score those runs. I was sitting on the bench during the first inning, and I stiffened up a little bit and got kind of nervous because it was a long inning, but it did take some of the pressure off me.

So I went out and started throwing high fastballs, and when I didn't throw a fastball I threw a curveball that broke down from those shirts into the ivy, which of course was the normal background at Wrigley Field, and the curveball was pretty tough to pick up as well. Well, I didn't have exceptional velocity, because I'd already been knocked out in the third inning against Borowy in Game 1, but I had ten strikeouts that day. I believe I broke the strikeout record, and we won the game, 9–3.

The next day that comes to mind is the match that I had with Bob Feller in 1948 on the last day of the season. He had just come back from the war, in fact he'd beaten me the day he got back from the service. He and I had some great duels. We used to draw crowds of fifty, sixty thousand whenever we pitched against each other. But that last game was a very important game, and he didn't get the upper hand against me that day.

It was the last day of the season, and the Red Sox and the Cleveland Indians were battling for the pennant. I'm not sure exactly what the standings were, you'll have to look that one up. But I do know that if the Indians won that game they would have clinched the pennant.

Well, we were playing a three-game series against Cleveland, and it was in Cleveland, and I'd already pitched the day before that series started. So our manager, Steve O'Neill, said, "What the heck, you don't have to make the trip down to Cleveland, your season's over." And I said, "No, that just wouldn't look right to the rest of the guys," so I made the trip. But I knew I wasn't going to pitch and I had nothing to do, so I was gonna just loaf around.

And then right before the last game one of our pitchers, Freddie Hutchinson, got sick, and Steve asked me if I could go out there and pitch. I was kind of reluctant, because I hadn't done any running. I hadn't had a chance to do any of my normal training, and that was at the point in my career where I was just beginning to have arm trouble. But Steve said that it wouldn't look right if we didn't put our best pitcher out there—the pennant was on the line, and Boston would look down on us if we put another pitcher out there. So I decided to go out and give it a shot.

Well, we got to Feller in the third inning, and I ended up throwing one of the best games of my life. We beat the Indians 7–1, and that put 'em in a tie with the Red Sox. Those Cleveland fans, they weren't real happy about that, so we just got on the train and got the heck out of there real fast.

There are several other games that stand out. One is the first time I won my twentieth game, which I did after having four losing seasons. After that I won twenty-nine games, and then twenty-five, twenty-six, eighteen, and twenty-one. I won my 200th game against the St. Louis Browns on September 9th in 1953, the last game I ever won for Detroit.

Winning the World Series was a team effort, and in fact all of these things are team efforts, because you're not gonna win the games without your teammates catching the ball and hitting for you. But winning 200 games or winning twenty games, those are personal records, so from that they stand out in a different way.

The other thing that I did that was a personal record was to win the MVP twice. The first time I did it was in 1944 when I won twenty-nine games, and then I won it again the next year when I won twenty-five. That was something that no pitcher had ever done before, and it's a record that I don't think will ever be broken. People talk about DiMaggio's hitting streak and Ted Williams hitting .406, but for a pitcher to win the MVP and then do it again, that just isn't going to happen.

Now you probably want to know why I didn't get a shot at winning thirty during the year I won twenty-nine. As it happened, I won my twenty-ninth early in the last series of the season.

It's true that if we'd have been in third or fourth place I would have got my shot in the final game of the season, and if there'd been trouble I would have been the first one out of the bullpen. But we were in a pennant race against the Senators and that was an important game, so it wouldn't have been right for me to be out there just to get a chance at a record.

Now I struggled quite a bit early in my career, and I formed my personal philosophy after the year I had in 1943, when I lost seventeen games for the Detroit Tigers. It's a philosophy that's stayed with me ever since. I had a tough time up until that point, but I got married that winter, and my wife and I, we had a youngster, so that kind of settled things down for me.

I remember there was this fan, an old-timer, he must have been about seventy-five, and he came up to me in spring training down in Lakeland, Florida, it must have been in 1944. I had been struggling, and he asked me what the easiest thing to do was, and I said that I really didn't know. And he said that if you didn't do anything, that if you just gave in, that you were a loser.

I got to think about what he meant by that. For me, it meant

October 10, 1945

DETROIT	AB	R	H	RBI	CHICAGO	AB	R	H	RBI
Webb, ss	4	2	1	0	Hack, 3b	5	0	0	0
Mayo, 2b	5	2	2	1	Johnson, 2b	5	1	1	0
Cramer, cf	5	2	3	1	Lowrey, lf	4	1	2	0
Greenberg, lf	2	0	0	1	Cavarretta, 1b	4	1	3	1
Mierkowicz, lf	0	0	0	0	Pafko, cf	4	0	1	1
Cullenbine, rf	2	2	0	0	Nicholson, rf	4	0	1	1
York, 1b	4	0	0	1	Livingston, c	4	0	1	0
Outlaw, 3b	4	1	1	1	Hughes, ss	3	0	1	0
Richards, c	4	0	2	4	Borowy, p	0	0	0	0
Swift, c	1	0	0	0	Derringer, p	0	0	0	0
Newhouser, p	4	0	0	0	Vandenberg, p	1	0	0	0
					Sauer, ph	1	0	0	0
					Erickson, p	0	0	0	0
					Secory, ph	1	0	0	0
					Passeau, p	0	0	0	0
					Wyse, p	0	0	0	0
					McCullough, ph	1	0	0	0
Totals	35	9	9	9	Totals	37	3	10	3

Detroit	510	000	120 — 9
Chicago	100	100	010 — 3

DETROIT	IP	H	R	ER	BB	SO
Newhouser, W	9	10	3	3	1	10
CHICAGO	IP	H	R	ER	BB	SO
Borowy, L	0	3	3	3	0	0
Derringer	1.2	2	3	3	5	0
Vandenberg	3.1	1	0	0	1	3
Erickson	2	2	1	1	1	2
Passeau	1	1	2	2	1	0
Wyse	1	0	0	0	0	0

that if you didn't train, if you didn't listen to your manager and your teammates, if you didn't listen and think and then apply the things you were learning so that you could get the best out of your ability, then you were a loser.

And then he asked me what the hardest thing to do was, and I said, well I think I can answer that one. That was when I formed my personal philosophy, which was: never give up, and never give in. Sometimes I talk to these young players today when they're struggling, and I tell them that story, and I think it's one of the most important things you can do, is to convey that to young people today. If you do all those things, if you work hard and never give up and never give in. Well, if it worked for me, then it can work for anybody.

I remember one game when I pitched in Yankee Stadium and gave up five runs in the first inning. It would have been easy to quit, but I shut 'em out the rest of the way and we came back and won the game. When you're going bad, you just have to stick with it and find out what's going wrong and how to fix it, that's what I wish I could instill in these kids today.

I signed with the Detroit Tigers when I was fifteen years old, and really I could have signed with any team. But I grew up in Detroit, and I remembered the World Series in 1935, when Goose Goslin won it for the Tigers that year, and I just thought that would be the greatest thing in the world to play for the Detroit Tigers.

So after I turned things around mentally, I won twenty games, which was one of my personal goals, and then I just started setting my other goals. I wanted to win the World Series, and we did that in 1945, and I wanted to make the All-Star game, and Joe McCarthy of the Yankees selected me for the All-Star game in 1943. In 1944 I won the MVP, and I said to myself, "OK, where do I go from here?" And I decided to keep plugging away, to just try to keep on winning.

It took me over thirty years after my career was over to make the Hall of Fame. Of course that was the culmination of everything you work for. The reason for that was that a new generation of writers came along in the '50s who hadn't seen me play, and they gave me the label of a wartime pitcher.

I never thought that was fair, because I had a long career, and I had a lot of good years, and it didn't seem right that people only considered those two years in 1944 and 1945, even though I kept winning during the years after that when everyone who made it back from the war was playing again. All they had to do was look it up in the record book. I had fans who came up to me for a long time, and said, "Why aren't you in the Hall of Fame?" and what could I tell them? That frustrated me for a long time. There was nothing I could do about it.

But the best thing about getting into the Hall of Fame is that once you're there, everybody's the same. It's not "Joe DiMaggio, who hit in fifty-six consecutive games," or "Ted Williams, who hit .406," or "Hal Newhouser, who won two MVPs," it's "Hi, Joe," or "Hi, Ted," or "How you doin', Hal?" Because everybody that's in the Hall of Fame is the same whenever you go back to Cooperstown.

In February of 1997 the Tigers called me, they wanted to take me out to lunch. I was talking with my wife, and we were trying to figure out what they might want. I said that maybe they might want me to come down to Florida and help with some of their young pitchers, they're struggling a bit right now. But then I thought, that's not right, because if I talk to one of those pitchers and he makes an adjustment that I told him about and I'm not there during the season, what are they gonna do then?

So we went to lunch, and we sat there talking, and it got to be quite a while and nobody said anything about what they wanted or why they invited me. I was starting to think that they'd spent a lot of time with me not to come away with anything, I still didn't have any idea what it was all about. And then they said that the Detroit Tigers were going to retire my number on July 27 at 1:00, to go along with Hank Greenberg's, Charlie Gehringer's, and Al Kaline's.

I got a lot of awards and accomplished quite a bit, but if it wasn't for my teammates, without them to hit and field and throw behind me, I would have been just average. So that's the last paragraph and the last chapter and the last sentence in my part in the history of baseball, and if there's one final thing that I'd like to leave behind and to say, it's . . . never give up, and never give in.

TONY OLIVA

The Minnesota Twins had some great hitters on the halcyon clubs of the 1960s, but the one hitter pitchers hated to face the most was Tony Oliva. The former batting champ could beat you with power, speed, and then later in his career when he became a Gold Glove outfielder, his glove.

My greatest day in baseball . . . the first one would have to be in 1962. The

October 7, 1965

LOS ANGELES	AB	R	H	RBI	MINNESOTA	AB	R	H	RBI
Wills, ss	4	0	1	0	Versalles, ss	5	2	1	0
Gilliam, 3b	4	0	0	0	Nessek, cf	3	0	1	0
W. Davis, cf	4	0	0	0	Oliva, rf	4	1	1	1
Johnson, lf	4	0	0	0	Killebrew, 3b	3	0	2	1
Fairly, rf	4	1	2	0	Battey, c	4	0	1	0
Lefebvre, 2b	4	0	2	0	Allison, lf	4	1	1	0
Parker, 1b	1	0	1	0	Mincher, 1b	4	1	1	0
Roseboro, c	4	0	1	1	Quilici, 2b	2	0	0	0
Koufax, p	2	0	0	0	Kaat, p	4	0	1	2
Drysdale, ph	1	0	0	0					
Perranoski, p	0	0	0	0					
Miller, p	0	0	0	0					
Tracewski, ph	1	0	0	0					
Totals	33	1	7	1	Totals	33	5	9	4

Los Angeles	000	000	100 — 1
Minnesota	000	002	12X — 5

Minnesota Twins called me up from the minor leagues to be in the big leagues. Being in uniform next to Zoilo Versalles, Harmon Killebrew, Jim Kaat, Camilo Pascual, Pete Ramos, next to all those great players, that was a dream come true.

And in 1965, the year we won the pennant, I think that that was the highlight of my career, because the dream of each ballplayer is to be able to play in the World Series. We won the American League pennant in 1965, we played the Dodgers and we lost in seven, but at least we finished second. We didn't finish first because we didn't win the World Series, but we were there. That counts, and it was a great time in baseball for me.

It's hard to pick a greatest day from that season or that World Series, because there was so many exciting days that year. I would say in the World Series it was in the first or second game, when I hit a double off of Sandy Koufax, the best pitcher in baseball. We won the game, that was the more important thing, but to be able to get a big hit like that, that meant a lot. After that, there's too many to remember one.

I remember one game that year against Baltimore. I was on second, and there was a ground ball and I scored from second on a double play ball. I just kept on going, I never stopped, and that was the winning run, that was very exciting. I surprised everybody, and we won the game. That was another day that was very important to me.

Baltimore was only about two or three games out of first place, so it was a very important game for us to win. I scored the winning run, it was in Minnesota, and from that day on we kept winning, and Baltimore got behind and they never caught us. It was in September. I think that was the big game that turned things around.

It's hard to say about the individual awards, because I have a lot of good individual stuff. In '64 I won the batting championship, and then I won it again in '65. But you have to win, because you remember more of that stuff when you win, whether it's the batting title or being Rookie of the Year or winning the Gold Glove, which I did in 1967. I came from being one of the worst fielders in baseball to being the best, so that meant a lot to me. But what you really remember is what you do to win ball games.

STEVE PALERMO

BILL FRAKES/ALLSPORT

I've interviewed dozens of All-Stars and Hall of Famers, but only once in my life have I asked anyone in baseball for an autograph, and that person was umpire Steve Palermo. My father was a high school umpire who literally taught me the game from behind the plate, and Palermo was one of my few sports heroes, both for his integrity and excellence as an umpire, and because of his effort to track down a mugger who robbed a woman outside the Texas restaurant where Palermo was eating, a rescue attempt that may have cost him his umpiring career when he was shot and disabled by her attacker.

Palermo has since walked with the aid of a cane since suffering spinal cord damage from the bullet, but no one who knows him and his love for the game would ever rule out a possible comeback.

When I first interviewed Palermo in 1994, my father had just recovered from a heart attack, and Steve Palermo personally autographed a baseball for my father and gave it to me to give to him. It was an honor to interview him for this collection as well, and there was a certain wonderful irony to the fact that two of his three greatest days took place at Fenway Park in Boston, the city I've called home for fifteen years, and that the third involved the Red Sox as well.

I could give you about two or three, but at the top would be the time my dad first saw me umpire a big league game, at Fenway Park in September of '76. I was working with a legend in that game, Nestor Chylack, and Joe Brinkman, Greg Kosc, and Jimmy Evans. I was umpiring in the minors at the time, but Nestor suggested I join his crew for this late season series.

It was a Boston and Baltimore series, a pretty good one in those days. Yes, that was my introduction to Earl Weaver, it sure was. As a matter of fact, we had a play that he felt a balk should have been called on, where Reggie Cleveland stepped off and picked Reggie Jackson off of first base when Jackson started to break toward second. And Reggie Cleveland stepped off and they got him in a rundown, and Weaver thought it was a balk. He didn't realize that Cleveland had stepped off and faked to second to kind of freeze Jackson between first and second.

So he came out yelling at the second base umpire. He came over to me at third and said, "You're new, you know what's goin' on, show these guys, teach these guys something." So that was my first introduction to Weaver.

In Fenway we dress on the second tier. The umpire's room is above and kind of off to the side from where the Red Sox locker room is. So we go up a flight of stairs, and my dad's standing at the top of the stairs, and he's going down, and I said, "Come on, Pop, you can't stand up here all game." He just kind of froze, enjoying the moment, looking at the four of us as we were walking down the stairs, me going out to work my first game in the big leagues. It was kind of an exciting day for him, as well as for me.

He was just excited. There really wasn't any conversation, because I don't think he knew what to expect and I didn't know what to expect. We couldn't really tell each other what to look for. It was more listening than talking, because the more you listen the more you'll learn, and that's what I tried to do in the locker room before the game, listen as much as possible about how they worked, and what they were going to do. Of course I had worked with Nestor in '75 and '76 in spring training, and then I got to work with him in '77.

I was working in Connecticut, and they had called me and said, "Are you going to be home this weekend?"—they being Nestor and Joe Brinkman. And I said, "Yeah, I think my season's over in the minor leagues, I should be here. I was thinking of coming up to watch you guys work anyway." I enjoyed going to a big league ballpark to watch umpires work.

I knew that they were in town for the last couple of games, and that would have been nice to see them work, and have something impressed in your mind, because there was a possibility that I might have a chance to get to the big leagues in '77. And they said, "Hang loose, we're gonna let you know in a day or two. How'd you like to work in Boston if we can set it up?" and I said, "Great."

I think the only thing I said was, "I'm gonna take my plate stuff, right?" because I thought most definitely I'd probably work the plate, because those guys had probably had enough after a long season. That was a time when they didn't have vacations or anything, and they said, "Nah, I don't think you need to . . . just take everything, and we'll see what you need."

That was basically it, there wasn't too much conversation, it was just the anticipation of thinking about whether I was gonna work those two games or not. And Dick Butler, he was the supervisor of umpires at the time, said, yeah it's OK. It's a good idea to bring him up and just let him have a little taste and keep him hungry for next year.

I was at third base to start for that game, and then my second game I worked at second base on Sunday, it was Saturday and Sunday. I just remembered that Sunday's game was really more memorable, because Nestor worked the plate, and of course you've got this legend behind the plate. Here it is the last game of the season, and there's a bang-bang play at home plate in like the ninth inning to end the game, and Nestor calls the guy out, and we go into extra innings.

Boston was going to score, and that would have ended the game, and he called the guy out, you know, home team, everybody wanted to get out of there, it was the last game of the season, neither team was involved in the playoffs that year. Nestor called out a runner at home plate—I don't even remember who the runner was. We don't even look at the uniforms, it's just somebody in a uniform, they're all faceless.

We went fifteen innings. I think it was thirteen or fifteen innings. I think it was either in the twelfth or the thirteenth inning, and Nestor just looked overhead, and he saw this plane taking off, and he just kind of waved to it as if that was his plane that was going back to Pennsylvania that would have taken him home for the offseason.

Just the thrill of that game, and being in the big leagues, and how much you wanted that feeling again, to be out on the big league field, that was what I took with me into the offseason. Because that was the first time I ever walked out on the field at Fenway.

My dad was really excited coming into the locker room after the game, and now everybody's talking. Everybody's hollering— yeah, it figures, we're gonna stay one extra day, you know, you can't get enough baseball. And Nestor said, "Well, I figured you needed the little bit of work, so I just figured I'd keep you out there five or six innings extra and get you a little extra work."

He kind of made a joke out of it. It just goes to show you what a professional he was . . . hey, the last game of the season, it didn't mean anything to either club, didn't have any effect on the standings or anything else, and the players really wanted him to call the guy safe at home, and he just went about his business as he always did. He got the plays right, and no we're gonna play this game. You guys are gonna decide it, I'm not gonna decide it.

Afterward my dad just said, "What do you think?" I just said, "I don't know. I'm a little numb." I understand the joy of somebody getting called up to the big leagues as a player, because it's the same thing for an umpire. This is what you strive for, to get to the big leagues.

It was really an exciting time, and the conversation with my dad later . . . he couldn't wait. I know those guys wanted to go home and have the offseason and everything else, and I'm saying, I wish spring training would start tomorrow, because I couldn't wait to get out there and start working this stuff again.

I don't know if there was ever really a comfort zone that you get in, especially your first year, and especially working with Nestor, because you're learning three years worth of experience in one year when you work with him. You never felt comfortable, because you say, alright, this is just gonna be another routine game, or whatever.

He told me, don't ever play the game before it starts because you'll sit in the lobby or whatever and worry about interference or obstruction or spectator interference or suicide squeeze or somebody stealing third base and it'll never happen in that game. This is a game of action and reaction, they're gonna create the action and your job is to react to it. That's one of the philosophies that he had that I still take with me.

He was kind of a mentor as far as temperament goes, as were Frank Pulli, Richie Garcia, Bill Haller, Davie Phillips after I started working with Davie, and that was from '78 on, I worked with him quite a bit. Those are the guys who really taught me a lot about how to conduct yourself on the field. They said, you still have to be your own person.

Mr. Butler taught me a lot, too, and Mr. Butler was a person who never wore an umpire's uniform, but he understood, he was self-taught, and he understood a lot about the game because he listened to a lot of umpires and talked to them. And he said, "You can't do what Nestor does, or what Richie Garcia does, you do what you do best and you'll be just like them. It'll take a couple of years for the players to understand who you are because you won't get to see every team for a few years, so they won't understand how competent you are. It's gonna take some time. So don't try and rush the process."

That wall's a whole lot closer than you think it is. That was one of the things that Nestor told me. He said, "Don't run yourself out of this ballpark, Steve. You're a lot faster than most people, and you turn around and start running down that third base line, you'll bang you're head on the wall as quick as you are, going out on a fly ball or whatever."

I remember him telling me that, and then I worked second base, and he mentioned it the next day. It's not that you didn't listen to him, it's just that that was the reminder of the day. Depending on where you worked, he always had these reminders. It was great, he taught you so much, and I wish he was still around so that we could teach these people a lot of what he taught me. Sometimes you'd think, "Oh God, I've heard this before, I know, I know," but it doesn't hurt to be reminded. He's not doing it to embarrass you or to belittle you, what he's doing it for is to make you a better umpire, and to keep concentration level high.

You know, spring training or the regular season, I don't care if it was March, April, August, or the last three days of the season in the pennant race; Nestor always approached the game in the same way. Every pitch was important, every play was important, that's what I took from him. It may be a 10–1 game in spring training without any regulars, but you still had to work hard, because you didn't want to let anybody think that it was less important in March than it was in August.

The playoff game between the Yankees and the Red Sox stands out, what was that, October 2nd, 1978, or October 3rd I think . . . the Bucky "Bleepin'" Dent game, to use the terminology they use in New England. That was an unbelievable game.

The excitement, the aura, there hadn't been a playoff game of that magnitude in thirty years, since 1948, and now in '78 here you've got . . . and this is my second year in the big leagues and I'm working this type of game, which was unheard of. I figured, they're just gonna get me out of the league right now, if I make a mistake, that's it, I'm done, my career's finished before it ever gets a chance to get started.

It was an action-packed game, a very exciting playoff game, and with those two great teams, the history, the tradition, the rivalry, there was an electricity in the stadium.

They took Don Denkinger and myself from one crew, Al Clark from another crew, and Jimmy Evans from another crew, because other people were gonna be working the playoffs and all these other different things during the postseason. And they said, OK, these are the people we have available who can get here and can work who we feel comfortable with. And they had Don Denkinger working the plate, Jimmy Evans at first, Al Clark at second, and me at third. Mr. Butler made the selection.

Naturally, Bucky's home run stands out, Reggie's home run to deep center field, the sun in right field when Piniella made a heck of a stop to prevent Burleson from going from first to third. And I'm saying, no . . . please, Lou, catch this ball, stop this, no close plays, no close plays at third.

There was a bang-bang play early in the game on a steal play with Al Clark. And I walked over to him after the half-inning and I said, "No pressure in this game, huh, Al?" And he looked at me and he went, "Whew, good thing it wasn't any closer, that was close enough as it was."

You knew that it was action-packed, it was very, very tense, like I said, very electric, and you knew that every single pitch, every throw, every play, every out was a big out. And what prepared you for it was, again, Nestor's thinking that you approach the game like this in March so therefore it became just your regular work habit. I mean, two teams tied after 162 games, that's incredible, it really is. And now it's all gonna be decided in this one game in a very historic ballpark . . . I mean, either one of the ballparks would have been terrific with the history of both of them, and with the teams. It was very exciting.

And Nettles turns to me at third base, and he just says, "This is fun, isn't it?" And I'm thinking, "I'll let you know after the game's over."

Then it was those two teams again, back in '83, Dave Righetti's no-hitter that I worked behind the plate. July 4th, Monday, because in 1983 that was the fiftieth year of the All-Star game, it was gonna be played in Comiskey Park, where the first All-Star game was played, and it was on a Monday because the All-Star game was gonna be on the exact same date, fifty years later, on a Wednesday.

I worked the plate for Righetti's no-hitter, I believe the score was 4–0, and I think he walked four people in that game. And I didn't know he had a no-hitter until the ninth inning. They had a good-size crowd, 45,000, 50,000 or so, something like that at the stadium, and when he comes walking out for the ninth inning, they give him a standing ovation. Prior to that, in the eighth inning, Lou Piniella had popped the ball up over to first base near the on-deck circle.

And Jeff Newman was the catcher for the Red Sox, and I went over toward the wall with Newman, and we kept going toward the Yankee's on-deck circle, and Don Baylor was on-deck. Newman dived into the stands to catch the ball, and I could see this blue crash pad coming at me, and my leg had blown out, my left knee, and I went crashing into the pads and never really saw the play, whether Newman caught the ball or not, and I had to ask Rick Reed, the first base umpire, whether he caught the ball or not.

And I said, "Ricky, I'll take the heat for this, you just tell me whether he caught it or not." I crashed into the wall, and the first

October 2, 1976

BALTIMORE	AB	R	H	RBI	BOSTON	AB	R	H	RBI
Bumbry, cf	3	0	0	0	Burleson, ss	4	0	3	0
Dauer, 2b	4	0	0	0	Doyle, 2b	3	0	0	0
Muser, 1b	4	0	0	0	Ri. Miller, cf	2	1	1	0
Re. Jackson, dh	3	0	2	0	Rice, lf	3	0	2	1
Singleton, rf	4	0	1	0	Cooper, dh	3	0	0	0
Shopay, pr	0	0	0	0	D. Evans, rf	3	0	0	0
Mora, lf	3	0	0	0	J. Baker, 1b	3	0	0	0
Bailor, pr	0	0	0	0	Whitt, c	3	0	0	0
B. Robinson, 3b	4	0	0	0	Hobson, 3b	3	0	0	0
A. Garcia, ss	3	0	2	0	Cleveland, p	0	0	0	0
Dempsey, c	2	0	0	0	House, p	0	0	0	0
D. Martinez, p	0	0	0	0	Willoughby, p	0	0	0	0
Totals	30	0	5	0	Totals	27	1	6	1

```
Baltimore   000   000   000 — 0
Boston      100   000   00X — 1
```

person to me was Don Baylor, and the second person was Gene Monahan, and the third person was Billy Martin. And they're all hovering over me, and they're saying, "Don't move, Stevie, we don't know what's wrong with you. Is your neck OK? You all right, where does it hurt?"

They're asking me all these things, and I just look down at my pants, and I said, "God, I just had these dry cleaned." And Bill looked at me like I was about half-crazy. "What are you worrying about your pants for? Big deal. Just get up slow. Why don't we get you up and take a look at it." And I said, "Nah, I'm OK, I'm OK." I did not know that Righetti had a no-hitter at the time, and this is the bottom of the eighth inning.

Sometimes umpires are aware of it, sometimes not. In this case I just wasn't. There was so much going on in that game. It's July 4th, I believe it's Righetti's mom's birthday, it's Steinbrenner's birthday, I guess he was an independence baby also, they were giving away all this stuff, they were giving away a car, and all these things at Yankee Stadium, all these giveaways. There was a lot of excitement, I just thought they were gonna give away a car to somebody. I thought, ah, that's kind of nice.

It was kind of fun. I started to get up, and Piniella says, "Don't move, Stevie, you might be hurt, just take your time and take it easy . . . and just remember when you do get up and we start this game again. . . . Newman didn't catch the ball. He did not make the catch in the stands."

The four of us, me, Billy, Don Baylor, and Gene, we all looked at Piniella and said, "Are you crazy?"

So now I had to call Piniella out on that, and he went real crazy, but not at me, and Baylor says, "Lou, he did catch the ball," and Lou went down in the runway and broke about four or five bats. He was really upset and everything.

Then Righetti came out in the ninth inning and everybody's cheering and giving him a standing ovation, and this is really great, it's good stuff, and I said, this is nice, he's had a good first half, it's a nice sendoff going into the second half of the season and all this stuff. And here I look up at the board, I was standing about thirty feet behind home plate, there's about that much distance between home plate and the screen, and I saw "Boston: 0, 0 . . ." and I think they might have had an error.

And I said, "Is that scoreboard broken?"

Butch Wynegar was the catcher, and I walked up to Butch as he was taking Righetti's last few warmup pitches, and I said, "Butch, I gotta talk to you at the end of this game and tell you something." He says, "Stevie, you better tell me now, because I might be jumpin' up and down at the end of this game."

And I said, "Why didn't you say something about this guy havin' a no-hitter?" Of course you're never supposed to mention a no-hitter in progress. And he says, "You've gotta be kiddin', Stevie?" and I said, "No, I'm serious, I didn't know he had a no-hitter." He said, "That's why you're the best, you just work pitch-to-pitch, don't you?" It was kind of funny the way that all broke down.

People think, oh, that was an easy call, or that was a tough call. They're all tough, some are just tougher than others. And there are so many that I could think of or bring up, just a freak thing that happened the way things played out in a particular ballpark, too many to mention maybe.

A great day for an umpire is to be perfect, to get every play right, to get every pitch right. And guys have told me, "You were flawless out there today," and I say, "I don't know, that 1–1 pitch on a corner I might have been able to call a strike, maybe not." Again, I replay it over in my mind, whether I could or couldn't have called it a strike, and I weigh the merits both ways. It was my way, and a way of self-improvement. People have told me, "Now I've gotta go back and try and do what you did? Are you crazy?" And I'd say, "Well, I hope you're better than me," and they'd say, "Yeah, right."

Not to sound immodest or cocky about it, but it just felt like you had this perfection. I know I'm a perfectionist with respect to getting every pitch right, and every play. And all four of the guys expected that same thing, a perfect game. But you walk off the field, and there's nothing said, just "Goodbye, we'll see you tomorrow."

I felt like that working with Nestor an awful lot. Of course he had that respect where very few people were gonna say anything to him, because they knew that they were gonna get a great day's work, and they knew that his crew would be ready. Richie Garcia was very much that way, he prepares everybody to be ready mentally, and he's in the sixth inning when the game is in the fourth inning. He's two innings ahead of everything.

I made a statement one day as we were walking on the field, I said, "Well, boys and girls, today I'm not missing a pitch." And I went out there, and I came back in, and my crewmates said, "What are you, makin' predictions now? You always do what you say?" You just challenge yourself. It was a very tense series going into that as I remember. I don't remember the exact series, but there were a lot of things that had been happening. Not like we had riots going on, but to aim for a quiet game with no complaints and to let them decide the game, created a lot of pressure. But that's what happened.

I don't know if I did work a perfect game or not, but to let everybody know that they weren't gonna holler at us . . . you guys duke it out on the field, because we're gonna get it all right. It kind of sets the tempo for everybody, your crewmates as well as both teams.

JIM PALMER

Several players in this collection chose their first major league game as their greatest day in baseball, but Jim Palmer's choice had a particularly personal slant. Palmer's greatest day came during his rookie year, when he already had his first appearance and first victory but was still struggling to stay with the club. Palmer's performance against the Yankees in a meaningless September doubleheader against New York may have slipped past most observers, but it was noteworthy to his manager, Hank Bauer, and it brought Palmer back to his New York upbringing as an adopted child.

When I think of my greatest day in baseball, it happened right here in Yankee Stadium. I grew up in New York, and I was adopted, and the first baseball game I ever went to kind of reminds me of the story in the movie *City Slickers* where they're riding on the horses and he says, "Tell me about your best day ever." And Billy Crystal says, "It was the day my dad took me to Yankee Stadium . . . I never realized, we didn't even have a color TV, I never really knew how green the field was."

That's the way I felt when my dad took me here when I was about eight years old. I walked through the tunnel, I think the Yankees were playing Cleveland, and Allie Reynolds was pitching against Mike Garcia, and Irv Noren hit a home run to beat him.

So then you've got to fast-forward to 1965, my rookie year. I'd come up, and I was happy to be on the ball club, more or less. You only protected one guy in your whole minor league system; instead of having a forty-man roster you only had a twenty-five-man roster. I was the one guy they wanted to protect, so they kept me on the big league team. I was nineteen, and I pitched in relief a couple of times and I got a couple of starts.

The only thing they told me was "try to get the ball over" (I was throwing ninety-seven miles an hour). Sit there and learn a lot. I was rooming with Robin Roberts, he was my first roommate, and then he was gone to Houston. He had a clause in his contract, and he was trying to win 300 games and he had an option to go somewhere. He started out 4–0, but then he lost some tough games, and they took him out of the rotation, so he was gone.

So I'm here, and I hurt my elbow a little bit, I had a little tendonitis in my elbow that I got when I warmed up a little too quickly. I was real raw. I had no idea what I was doing. But I did come in, in a Labor Day doubleheader, and Frank Bertaina, a left-hander, started the second game. Phil Linz hit a line drive back up the middle, we were down 2–0, having given up two runs in the first inning, that hits Bertaina in the pitching hand and he can't even pick the ball up.

And here I come from the bullpen. I think I threw about a fifty-eight-foot curveball, and it bounced. I threw another one up off the screen. It wasn't a pressure game, but there was pressure because I'd grown up in New York and I idolized the Yankees, and even my first year in baseball when I was in Aberdeen, South Dakota, playing for Cal Ripken, Sr., I rooted for the Yankees, because I didn't know any of the Orioles. I'd grown up rooting for Mantle, and Maris, and Berra and all these guys.

I'd already earlier in the year in Baltimore won my first game, and in it I hit a home run off of Jim Bouton. I had also come in in relief in that game. So here I am on Labor Day, runners are at first and second, and Horace Clarke is the first hitter, and he hits a little ball off the end of the bat, and Aparicio catches it, but he has no play so the bases are loaded.

So I strike out Mantle, Maris, and Elston Howard on about ten high fastballs. Andy Etchebarren hits a three-run, inside-the-park home run off of Bill Stafford. Stafford throws at me, I'm the next hitter, I'm in the shadows and all of that because it's late September, and he buzzed one all the way back to the screen. And then Curt Blefary hits a two-run home run, and I strike out eight in four innings.

You know you don't strike out Mantle, Maris, and Elston

Howard with the bases loaded, and Hank Bauer, who of course was a former Yankee, says "Nice going, kid," which was one of the few times he talked to me during the second half of the year.

I think a lot of people might think that my World Series shutout against Koufax might have been my greatest day ever, and that's certainly one of them. But I think when you consider my background growing up in New York and being adopted, I mean I was one of these kids who'd run down the driveway to get the *Daily Mirror* and see the headline, "Yanks Sweep Two." My most traumatic year as a kid was 1954 because the Yankees played great but the Indians played even better and lost four to the Giants, which kind of ruined my year, actually it really did ruin my year. I think my whole youth was very impressionable according to how the Yankees played.

To come here at nineteen and get to face Mantle and Maris and so on and end up striking out the side, then to have your manager congratulate you, not to mention getting a win, was something special. I was a fastball/curveball pitcher and I had no idea really how to pitch. My stuff was good enough that when I got those pitches over it was very effective, so I was just trying to throw strikes, and they couldn't hit the high hard stuff.

Mantle had the bad left knee and the bad knees in general, but in general he wasn't the same hitter he was from the right side. He was hitting left-handed, and he couldn't hit that pitch. Maris was the guy who broke Babe Ruth's home run record, I was just throwing high fastballs, and they were swinging at it, and they couldn't hit it. I was pretty pumped.

It's funny, your feelings at nineteen are so different. I hadn't had a bad year, I think I was 5–4 with a 3.90 ERA, but I didn't know what I was doing. I was just trying to survive, and at that point in my career you don't know if it's going to be a Hall of Fame career, you don't know if you're gonna win twenty games, you don't know if you're gonna be with the ball club the following year, because you're nineteen, and you had to be there, and you're trying to make some impression.

I thought that maybe they would think about this when they thought about formulating the ball club for next year, that I hadn't really had as good a year as I would have liked, but if you strike out Mantle and Maris and Elston Howard in Yankee Stadium when you're only nineteen then maybe they're going to give you a chance to make the team the next year.

The turning point for me was that a lot of people got hurt in spring training the next year and I made the ball club. I had fifteen or sixteen scoreless innings in spring training, even though I was walking guys and leaving the bases loaded and all of that. Really we had a number of arm injuries, and I pitched against the Yankees, against Al Downing, and I had a five inning no-hitter, then I pitched against Jim Maloney, who pitched with the Cincinnati Reds, and I beat him. I think Frank Robinson hit a home run off of Maloney to beat him 2–0. Then the next game I was ahead 2–1 when I finished my five or six innings, and then I started and ended up winning fifteen games and had a World Series shutout.

I think back and maybe the Yankees game was the springboard performance, so that when guys got hurt the following spring the Orioles said, "Well, he was destined probably for Triple AAA, but let's give him a chance." Maybe, just maybe, that had some influence on them keeping me the next year.

September 6, 1965

BALTIMORE	AB	R	H	RBI	NEW YORK	AB	R	H	RBI
Aparicio, ss	5	0	1	0	Clarke, 2b	4	1	2	0
Snyder, lf	4	0	0	0	Tresh, cf	5	1	2	0
Powell, 1b	4	1	1	0	Mantle, lf	4	0	0	0
Robinson, 3b	4	0	2	0	Howard, c	3	0	1	0
Blefary, rf	4	1	1	2	Boyer, 3b	3	0	0	1
Adair, 2b	3	2	1	0	H. Lopez, rf	4	0	4	1
Blair, cf	3	1	1	0	Pepitone, 1b	4	0	0	0
Etchebarren, c	3	1	1	3	Linz, ss	3	0	1	0
Brown, c	1	0	0	0	Richardson, ph	1	0	0	0
Bertaina, p	0	0	0	0	Kubek, ss	0	0	0	0
Palmer, p	3	0	0	0	Stafford, p	1	0	0	0
S. Miller, p	1	0	1	1	Barker, ph	1	0	0	0
					A. Lopez, ph	1	0	0	0
Totals	35	6	9	6	Totals	34	2	10	2

```
Baltimore    000   032   001 — 6
New York     200   000   000 — 2
```

BALTIMORE	IP	H	R	ER	BB	SO
Bertaina	1	3	2	2	2	0
Palmer, W	5	4	0	0	0	7
S. Miller	3	3	0	0	0	2
NEW YORK	IP	H	R	ER	BB	SO
Stafford, L	7	7	5	5	0	5
Reniff	2	2	1	1	0	1

I think that day is very close to the top if not right at the top, if only because when I was doing those other things I was a much different pitcher, I was much more seasoned, I had much more experience, and the bottom line is that I think that I didn't know what I was doing, I was really just fighting for survival. I was really just trying to make some kind of impression.

It was kind of like when I hurt my shoulder a couple of years later [1968]. You can only look good running in the outfield so often. I think at this point I was just trying to let Hank know that I had some chance of fitting into their plans at some point in the future, whether it be next year or whatever.

To beat the Yankees and pitch well against the Yankees when your manager's a former Yankee and he's been on five straight world championship teams as Hank Bauer had, it made a big difference.

Going into the Hall of Fame and the induction ceremony is obviously very special, there's no doubt about that, but to me it's just totally different because you're not as emotionally involved as you were at nineteen. The Hall of Fame is when you get back and reflect on twenty years of things, you think about your first start, when you ended, and all the great things you got to be a part of, and so on and so on.

I happen to be the only one who was ever rained out, Joe Morgan and I, so it was little bit unusual. I don't think emotionally I would have gotten through it. The ceremony was on a Sunday, because after they said they were gonna call it off it was just pouring, and we said we have to go out and acknowledge all the people who came up here. And they said, "No, there's no security," and I said, "What, you think there's snipers out there?"

So Joe and I went out there to wave to everybody, and it was just pouring. I think there must have been 10,000 people, and 4,000 of them had orange-and-white umbrellas, Orioles stuff, and I got goose bumps and all that. I didn't write my speech, I just wrote down some notes and I just winged it.

I think if you read something it can be very emotional, but you can get through it because it's there in black-and-white, but when you're trying to talk and your emotions . . . you know, your first home run off of Bouton, the ball Mantle hit off the football spotting box in '66. I saw Maris on deck and I had a 2–0 lead and Mickey was up and I'd struck him out the first two times and he comes up choking up, and Andy Etchebarren says, "Hey, Mick, you're choking up," and he says, "Yeah, how else am I gonna hit the inside fastball?"

Well, all those memories come back to you, and that's what the Hall of Fame's all about, you've got the World Series games, and it's just a culmination, a total collection of all your thoughts, so it becomes very emotional. Whereas, this game, it's like, "I've got the bases loaded, I've got Mantle and Maris and Elston Howard coming up, what do I have to do?" You try to get Mantle out, and I did, and you try to get Maris out, and I did, and you try to get Howard out, and I did.

It just happened, and I think your instincts dig in. You're nineteen years old, whereas now I'm forty-five, or whatever I was when I went in the Hall of Fame, and you've traveled a lot of miles.

DAVE PARKER

When Babe Ruth called his shot in Chicago against Charlie Root, one of baseball's greatest legends was born. Dave Parker was one of the game's great sluggers from 1975 to 1980 for the Pittsburgh Pirates, a stretch during which he predicted his back-to-back batting titles, a feat that may lack the dramatics of Ruth's call but nonetheless requires a certain amount of confidence and chutzpah.

I predicted my first two batting titles. I predicted a batting title before the season in '77, came back the next season and predicted I'd win it in '78. To me those are my two greatest feats. I think that's pretty tough. It puts a lot on the line, to come up and say at the beginning of the season, "I'm gonna win a batting title." And then to come back and pick me to win it again, I look at that as two great individual achievements.

I would say predicting them is the highlight. It's tough enough when you come out to put yourself on the line when you say you're going to do something, so just the idea of putting myself on the line and going through what it takes to achieve it, to predict it, that takes a lot. A whole lot.

I was under contract, a contract that was less than the contract they gave a player that had less numbers, and I was going through a thing where I said I want this contract modified to put me in the category with top players in the league. And it was something where they said, "You're under contract, and we're not gonna do it."

And after winning the batting title they did do it, you know, so that was why I came out and predicted it, because it was more or less a contract dispute, and I just wanted to show 'em and take all doubt away. At that time I was the best player in the game, from '75 until about '80.

During my second batting title, I broke my jaw at home plate. I missed about six weeks. And I came back, and this was after predicting I was gonna win it, I came back after missing six weeks and the first ten at-bats when I came back I had great success and then I went about zero for twenty. And then every month after that, for the last four months of the season, I didn't hit under .375. I had a couple of .400 months, and I batted around .375 for the last four months.

I beat out Bill Buckner one year, and it might have been Rose another year. I was consistent, I was getting two or three hits a day, it seemed like, for the last four months of the '78 season. Not only did I come back and win the title, I had 217 hits that year, and that was after missing about six weeks.

I didn't believe in changing my approach to do that. I knew myself, and I was fundamentally aware of what I was doing when I was going good, and any time I had a tailspin I could just get in the mirror and correct it myself. I think knowing yourself mentally prevents you from going into prolonged slumps, and I knew myself mentally pretty well.

The best hitting day . . . I can't pick out one from that stretch. I think I had a host of four-hit days. I think the best hitting day I ever had was with Cincinnati in '85, where I had eight RBIs. I hit two doubles and two home runs and drove in eight. That's the hitting day that stands out in my mind over my career.

I remember just having a sense of pride when I won it, basically this was something I said I was gonna do, and I did. I was nicknamed the Ali of baseball for doing it, for predicting the titles. That was just a great feeling of accomplishment, most people kind of ease their way back into batting titles. I actually told people that I was going to do it. So I take a lot of pride into being able to predict that and back it up, so it was definitely my greatest achievement that brought an enormous feeling of pride.

The thing that I enjoy most about this game . . . the individual achievements are great, but the things that you can rejoice in collectively as a team are the most outstanding things that stick out. The '79 world championship Pirates went through all kinds of problems: we battled through injuries, we lost key pitchers, we maintained while they were gone, and we just pulled together as a unit.

We had the name of "We Are Family," and that's basically what it was. The things that we do collectively as a team are the things that I really look back on and treasure, because everybody played a role in making it happen, and everybody rejoiced in that achievement.

MIKE PIAZZA

In his brief career, Dodger catcher Mike Piazza has been an All-Star game MVP, won the Rookie of the Year award, and hit countless clutch homers. But his greatest day came during his first season and his initial exposure to the intensity of the timeless rivalry between the Giants and the Dodgers.

Well, I'd have to say my greatest day was probably in my first year on the last day of the season when we were playing the Giants. They had to sweep four games in the last series of the season to get a playoff berth. They won the first three. I guess I had already done enough to be Rookie of the Year going into that last day, but I hit two home runs. I broke the Dodger record, which was held by Steve Garvey and Pedro Guerrero at thirty-three.

I had thirty-three going into the game—I hit thirty-four off of Dave Burba, and then I hit a home run off of Dave Righetti. It was really exciting, the last time was really neat because it was my last at-bat, and I got a standing ovation coming to the plate, and then to hit a home run was just that much more exciting.

The Giants had a great team that year. They won 103 games, and they had "murderer's row"—Clark and Williams and Bonds. . . . It was a pretty good team. The series was in L.A., and the last day of the year was Fan Appreciation Day. It was really exciting for me, I think that day we were just trying to save face, they won three out of four. We were out of it by about ten games or so.

The season series with them had been a very exciting series. It was very intense, going into San Francisco for the first time that year. We played three games there, and every game was a sellout. It was just an incredible rivalry, probably the most exciting baseball I've played, as far as intensity goes.

I remember Orel Hershiser and the guys who had lost to the

Giants the previous year, and there was also two years ago, I think '91 when the Giants beat them on the last day of the year in the last series to knock them out of the playoffs. So there was just a lot of bitterness and acrimony and a lot of history that came into play. Again, it wasn't the kind of thing where we were in the playoffs or anything, but it was still kind of exciting because of the tremendous rivalry.

They had to start Salomon Torres, because they didn't have anybody left to start, I guess. He was pretty young, I think he was nineteen at that point, I'd seen him a couple of times in the minor leagues. My first at-bat I flied out, and then we started scoring some runs against him, it was 4–0, and then they scored one, so it was 4–1.

I think I came up again in the fourth or fifth against Dave Burba, and I hit the first pitch over the wall. I hit a fastball, up and away, to right field, and then I think I hit a single. My last time up was when I walked up and hit a home run off of Dave Righetti. The game was already out of hand at that point, but it was still kind of exciting because I got a standing ovation and the fans gave me another curtain call. I hit a fastball away off of Righetti, pretty much in the

October 4, 1993

SAN FRANCISCO	AB	R	H	RBI	LOS ANGELES	AB	R	H	RBI
Lewis, cf	4	0	0	1	Butler, cf	3	0	1	0
Thompson, 2b	4	0	0	0	Offerman, ss	2	2	1	1
W. Clark, 1b	3	0	1	0	Hansen, 3b	2	1	1	1
Williams, 3b	4	0	1	0	Wallach, 3b	2	1	1	0
Bonds, lf	4	0	0	0	Harris, 3b	0	0	0	0
Da. Martinez, rf	4	0	1	0	Piazza, c	4	2	2	4
Clayton, ss	3	1	2	0	C. Hernandez, c	0	0	0	0
Manwaring,c	3	0	1	0	Karros, 1b	4	2	3	2
Torres, p	1	0	0	0	H. Rodriguez, lf	2	0	0	0
T. Wilson, p	0	0	0	0	Mondesi, lf	2	1	1	2
Burba, p	0	0	0	0	Snyder, rf	4	1	2	2
M. Jackson, p	0	0	0	0	Reed, 2b	3	1	0	0
Sanderson, p	0	0	0	0	Bournigal, 2b	1	0	1	0
Righetti, p	0	0	0	0	K. Gross, p	4	1	1	0
Deshaies, p	0	0	0	0					
	—	—	—	—		—	—	—	—
Totals	31	1	6	1	Totals	33	12	14	12

San Francisco 000 010 000 — 1
Los Angeles   002 131 05X — 12

same spot. I was in a groove that day and I was seeing that pitch pretty well.

Kevin Gross pitched for us, and he pitched a great game. We shut them down pretty much; they scored only a couple of runs. It was an exciting game for the fans, because the Giants had knocked the Dodgers out so many times before, you could even go back to Joe Morgan's home run, which was in '82. The history just made it that much more exciting.

Everything else was pretty much just icing on the cake. It was nice for a while that year, just knowing that I'd established myself, but then the way I've always looked at things is to think about how much more work I have to do to stay at that level.

That year was just a dream year for me. The whole year was kind of like my greatest moment. I was on adrenaline the whole year. I made the All-Star game. The All-Star games are always fun, but it just seemed that there was just that much more emotion involved in that game with the Dodgers.

It's really tough to put one specific moment ahead of all the rest, and I hope one day to win the World Series, and that will be my greatest moment. Postseason last year was cool, we weren't there too long. I hit a home run in the postseason last year, that was kind of neat, and looking back at winning the division last year was exciting. That was really pretty special too.

Every moment is very emotional, but they all have different degrees of excitement for me. I'm the type of guy, I like to sit back and take everything in. I can't really bring it down to specifics. For me the memories just keep coming and coming.

It was a little bit of a disappointment, not winning the batting title last year, but some things are out of my control, and you can only do so much. I'm proud of my accomplishments, and it's something where I'd be lying if I said I didn't want to win one, but it's not a priority with me. I know I'm not going to come to the ballpark thinking about winning a batting title. Maybe if we win the division and then the playoffs and then there's a couple of days left, then maybe it's something I'll think about.

I don't really think about longevity and records. I'm just trying to play to the best of my ability, I'm trying to stay healthy, I'm trying to work as hard as I possibly can. I keep things simple and try not to change too many things. Records are nice to talk about, and obviously people are very nostalgic; they like to talk about records. This is a records sport and I don't deny that, there's no question about it.

But as a player, I think you do yourself real harm if you dwell on those things and keep thinking about it. I'm just going out there, and if the records come there's something nice about that, to think about it, but really you're just trying to do your job and win a world championship. Everything else is secondary.

KIRBY PUCKETT

© MIKE RUCKI

The baseball gods definitely broke the mold when they put together Kirby Puckett, who is without a doubt one of the most remarkable players ever to play the game. The stocky center fielder opened his career as a great leadoff hitter, then developed into a stellar power man with a knack for getting it done in the clutch. Puckett had several greatest days, culminating with his amazing performance in Game 6 of the 1991 World Series.

I guess I've probably had about four greatest days, maybe. Actually I think the first thing I remember is my first big league game, when I got called up to the big leagues in Anaheim. In my first at-bat I hit a ball in the hole, and Dick Schofield just threw me out on a bang-bang play. And I looked back and I said, "Wow, that's a hit in Triple AAA."

The next four times at bat I hit line-drive base hits, got to steal a couple of bases and scored three runs, and caught everything in center field and we won. That's what I remember about my first game, that was a big moment for me. I don't remember the score, all I remember was that we won.

Jim Slaton was the pitcher that day. I noticed from that day on that major league guys were around the plate. I'm a wild swinger as it is, and so for them to be close, which is anywhere near my area code, was a blessing for me, and I noticed that all big league pitchers were around the plate. So for me, I thought that that was pretty exciting. They were right where I wanted it to be, and I was swinging at it and puttin' the bat on it and getting hits. So for me that was real, real, real exciting.

I was a different player back then than I was a couple of years ago. When I first came up to the big leagues with the Twins I was a number one hitter, I was a leadoff batter, and my job was to get on base and set the table for the likes of Hrbek, Gaetti, Brunansky . . . that was my job. And I thought that I did a great job at it. I think my rookie year I had like twenty-nine bunt hits, something like that. I bunted even up until the time that I got out of the game.

So bunting was always part of my arsenal, and I always broke it out when I needed it. There were other times when I could have done that, but I broke it out when we needed it the most and was very successful at it, believe it or not. But as far as expectations go, my job was to get on base and set the table for the big guys to knock me in, and they did a great job of doing that over the years.

I got my first three hits off Jim Slaton, and then they brought in a guy named Sanchez. He had the crooked arm, sinker/slider guy for the Angels, and I got a base hit off of him. Got to steal another base. I got three off Slaton and one off of Sanchez, I do remember that much.

The first one was the one I remember the most, because some guys go for a lot of at-bats without getting a hit when they start out. I was thinking, I hope I get this hit, to kind of take the pressure off me . . . I hit the first ball hard, and Schofield threw me out, bang-bang, and then I remember I hit the next one right up the middle, and it was a base hit. I hit the next one in right-center, and the next one up the middle again, and I hit the next one to left-center field, so I used the whole field, there was no doubt.

I was the nineteenth player in major league history, I think, to get four hits in his first big-league game. As long as there's been the history of baseball, there's only been nineteen guys to do that, so I'm in very elite company.

My next greatest day would probably have to be in 1987 against the Milwaukee Brewers, actually it was two days. I went ten for eleven against Milwaukee—four for five, and then I went six for six. Saturday I went four for five—made out on my first at-bat, hit a line drive, pulled it hard, hit a bullet at somebody. I always swung good in Milwaukee, I always did, and you know, people just like Milwaukee, it was a good hitting park for me, I always had good success there.

Then the next four times I got hits. And then I came back the next day, and I went five for five, and then in our last at-bat Greg Gagne was hitting in front of me with two outs and there was a trapped strike three that was caught but then rolled back to the cage, and Gags beat it out, he was safe. It gave me a chance to come up in the shadows against Dan Plesac, back in those times he threw about ninety-eight miles an hour, and I told myself, "The first fastball I see, I'm swinging."

And I hit it, and it was a line drive, and it went out to right field, and I'm going six for six, and I have to give Gags credit for hustling down the first base line. If he hadn't got on, I wouldn't have had the chance to go six for six. So I went ten for eleven in two days. I set a major league record.

Actually, before the game started, I told Tony Oliva, who was the hitting instructor at the time, "I feel like I'm swinging the bat so good that I can pretty much do whatever I want right now, but I'm hitting balls right at people, you know, and nothing's happening." And Tony said to me, "Puck, you're a good hitter," and he gave me the speech, and we sat there, and we talked our way through it, and before you know it I hit a line drive on Saturday, and then I got four consecutive hits. I think I got a home run and two doubles and a base hit.

And then the next day I hit two home runs and two doubles and two base hits. Milwaukee is our biggest rivalry here in Minnesota, since we're so close, and it was a packed house in Milwaukee, and it was in August. All I remember was that I felt like I was unconscious. I just knew that every time up at bat I was gonna get a hit. And I've done that lots of times in my career. I just knew that no matter what, I was gonna get a hit. And I went through that again, and I was just locked in, and it kind of went from there.

Everybody was just shaking their heads, thinking this is unbelievable, because I hit every ball hard the whole series. I didn't hit anything soft, every ball I hit was hard, and they were just scratching their heads and shaking their heads and going, man, this is unbelievable. I think after the game TK [Tom Kelly] said something like, "Kirby Puckett, he can get ten hits faster than anybody I've ever seen." And I didn't realize what I had just done, all I knew was that I'd gone six for six and we'd won both ball games. I think we swept Milwaukee that weekend.

So for me it was pretty exciting, and I had no idea what I had done, but now that I reflect on it, I had an awesome weekend, it was unbelievable, I was unconscious. I think I hit something like .356 that year, so it really didn't effect my average that much, not at all.

Of course my third greatest day, everybody's gonna say . . . Game 6. I happened to do it at a time when things are magnified, totally magnified. I just went up there, and . . . I was gonna bunt, that's the honest to God truth. They brought in Charlie Leibrandt, and when Chili Davis was on deck we were talking, and I said, "How about if I bunt off of Charlie Leibrandt? He can't field that good. I can bunt right here. If I get it down right, Pendleton's playing back, I can get this down, and I can get on base, and you can knock me in."

And Chili Davis looked me right in the face and said, "What'd you say? Bunt?" He said, "Bunt my ass. If you get a good pitch, hit it out." That's exactly what he said.

So I went up there, and I did something I never do—I said I'm gonna take it until I get a good pitch. Anybody who knows me knows that I always go up there swinging at the first good thing that they throw, you know? But I get a hit off of it most of the time. So I told him I'm gonna take this time, and I remember taking the first two pitches for balls, and then he threw the next pitch and it was a strike, and I think the count was 2–1.

He threw a change-up, and he hung it, and I hit it. I didn't know if it was out when I hit it. I didn't know if it was high enough. I thought it was gonna hit off the Plexiglas. But it just kept going, and it went out about eight or nine rows up. And I heard that Jack Buck, the national TV announcer, said that old saying, "We'll see you tomorrow night."

I remember running around the bases. It was unbelievable. Because I've come up in my career lots of times and got the base hit or whatever to win—the base hit or the double or whatever, the sacrifice. . . . I've done that. But in order to win a game with a home run, I had never done that. So I guess I picked a hell of a time to do it. . . .

All I was screamin' was, "Yeah, yeah," because we needed to win because we were down 3–2 at the time. We needed to win Game 6 or there wasn't gonna be a Game 7. So for us, we needed that game bad. And for me to come up big, and earlier in the day I had told my teammates, jump on my back, I'm gonna carry us today. And not only did I talk the talk, but I walked the walk also, and believe me, that made it more special, to see my teammates look at me like, man, that's unbelievable, he said what he was gonna do, and he did it. They were, like, in awe.

I used to say that all the time. I said that every day in my career, jump on guys, I'm gonna carry us today. I just knew that I was gonna hopefully be the deciding factor in that game. I wanted to be the guy who was up when the game was on the line. I wanna be that guy, because I know that I'm not afraid to fail. I've never been afraid to fail, and I always want to be that guy, because in baseball, you're either gonna be the goat, or you're gonna be the hero . . . it's that simple.

Most of the time I did it . . . like if I tell a guy in a certain situation, extra innings or something, and I see a certain guy warming up, and I tell my teammates, if they bring in this guy to face me, the game is over. And sure enough, that guy comes in, I get my pitch, I get a base hit, and the game is over. I did that lots of times in my career.

It was so hectic, I remember people calling me out for a standing ovation, so I came out a couple of times. And then I went upstairs and my teammates had champagne waiting for me, and we were all drinking champagne and toasting the big hit, toasting me saying what I was gonna do, to get us to Game 7. I remember them pouring champagne all over me, and just giving me hugs, everybody was just so elated, that's what I remember, everybody was so . . . like this big burden had been lifted off their shoulders for some reason. And for me it was like, wow, finally, I did something like this. It took a long time to do, but I got it done.

When I said that we were gonna do it, it all started from the first inning on. Dan Gladden got a base hit or something, and I hit a ball down the third base line which was fair, and I ended up getting a triple out of it. So that was the first thing I did. The next at-bat I hit a sacrifice fly, and then I don't know if I got walked, whatever I did, made an out, and then they walked me intentionally another time.

And then I came up against Charlie Leibrandt, and I did it. So for me, it was a tremendous day, because I said what I was gonna do, and I did it. And believe me, that made me feel great.

The catch happened the same night, in Game 6. Ronnie Gant hit it off Scott Erickson. He hit it high. And I always told myself, playing the outfield, that if it's high enough so that it's gonna stay in the park I can catch it. That was my thinking as an outfielder, that if this stays in the park I should be able to catch it. If I get close to it I should catch it.

And it went up, and I said, "This ain't goin' out." So I was going back, and I heard Dan Gladden yelling, "You're all right, you're all right, feel for it, feel for it, feel for the fence." And I remember looking back for the fence just for one second, and I said, "I've gotta time this jump just right, I can catch this."

And I timed it just right, man . . . caught the ball, came down with it, and made a nice one-hop throw which was off-line. It cut on me at the last minute otherwise I would have doubled Pendleton off first base, he was all the way around on third base. And I remember just taking it and throwing it as far as I could.

It was unbelievable that it happened in the same game . . . not only did I save us a couple of runs, I ended up saving us the game. So that was great.

That was my job—to play good defense, and I took a lot of pride in my defense. A lot of guys don't really care, I don't think. Everybody wants to hit, but nobody wants to take that extra step or that extra mile to be a good defensive player also. And I really worked on my defense, I took a lot of pride in throwing people out from the outfield. I had the respect of my peers, the third base coaches, and the other guys.

It was special for me, and my terminology in the outfield was that if it stayed in the park, and I get close to it, I should catch it. So that's what I thought.

As far as the Hall of Fame goes, I really don't think about all that. I think that I got to play for twelve years, and I got 2,300 hits, so I think if you add that up that averages out to about 200 hits a year. So all I can say is that from the time that I started to play until the time that I finished, I averaged about 200 hits a year, and I think in anybody's book, those are pretty good numbers.

I never thought about it when I was playing. People asked me, and I had it figured out that I had . . . if I was able to play again, I would only have to average 150 hits for the last four years, and I could have got those easy. But I averaged between 190 and 200 hits a year, so it would have taken me approximately anywhere from two to three, maybe even four years on a longer scale.

There's no doubt in my mind I would have gotten 3,000 hits . . . there's no doubt.

Actually, I don't even think about the Hall. I think more people talk about it than I do. I never mention it. Because I've been the kind of person . . . I never worry about things I can't control, and I know I can't control getting into the Hall of Fame, because the guy who was my guru, who I feel should be in the Hall of Fame and isn't, Tony Oliva . . . I know Tony was a great hitter and a great player in his time, and he's not in the Hall of Fame. So I don't worry about things I can't control.

If it was in my control, of course I'd say, "Oh, yeah, no doubt."

But for me, I don't know, and things I don't know about, I don't like to say anything about. So for me, it's up to the writers to vote, and it's up to them whether they vote me in, and if they vote me in, that's great. If they don't vote me in, that's great too, because I know that I had a great career.

In a twelve-year period, I was one of the best players that played on this planet. And that right there says a lot.

I'd just like to be known as a player who came to the park every day and played the game the way it's supposed to be played. That's the bottom line. I never, not even one time in my career, you know, I

October 26, 1991

ATLANTA	AB	R	H	RBI	BB	SO
Smith, dh	3	1	0	0	1	0
Pendleton, 3b	5	1	4	2	0	0
Gant, cf	5	0	0	1	0	0
Justice, rf	4	0	0	0	1	1
Bream, 1b	4	0	1	0	1	0
Mitchell, pr–lf	0	0	0	0	0	0
Hunter, lf–1b	5	0	0	0	0	0
Olson, c	5	0	0	0	0	1
Lemke, 2b	4	1	2	0	0	0
Belliard, ss	2	0	1	0	0	1
Gregg, ph	0	0	0	0	0	0
Blauser, ph–ss	2	0	1	0	0	1
Totals	38	3	9	3	3	4

MINNESOTA	AB	R	H	RBI	BB	SO
Gladden, lf	4	1	0	0	1	0
Knoblauch, 2b	5	1	1	0	0	0
Puckett, cf	4	2	3	3	0	1
Davis, dh	4	0	0	0	0	1
Mack, rf	4	0	2	1	0	0
Laius, 3b	3	0	2	0	0	0
Pagliarulo, ph–3b	1	0	0	0	0	1
Hrbek, 1b	4	0	0	0	0	1
Ortiz, c	2	0	0	0	0	1
Harper, ph–c	2	0	0	0	0	1
Gagne, ss	4	0	1	0	0	0
Totals	37	4	9	4	1	6

Atlanta	000	020	100	00 — 3
Minnesota	200	010	000	01 — 4

might have been dragging, you know how one day is different than the next day, I'd be tired, but when that bell rang for the game to be played, for the game to start, I'd get this certain burst of energy inside of me, and I'd just think, well, I wanted to win.

I wanted to win every day, and I tried to be a winner every day, even though we know that that's not possible, to win every single day. But I can honestly and truly tell you that every step I took on the field, I never went through the motions, ever. I never did, no matter how bad I was going.

You can hit a ball back to the pitcher, and people laugh about it now, but I'd hit a ball back to the pitcher, and I'd sprint to first base. My teammates used to laugh at me. But I remember I won a game once against Roger Clemens. I hit a chopper, and he jumped up and kind of took his time and ultimately ended up throwing it high, and Mo Vaughn had to jump, and by the time he jumped up and came down, I was safe. And somebody ended up hitting a double in the gap, and I ended up scoring, and we ended up beating Roger Clemens.

So they laugh, and it doesn't happen that often, but I was always a guy that said, "Hey, I'm gonna bust my butt. I'm only out here for three or four hours anyway. If I can't bust my butt for three or four hours, then I don't deserve to be out here." And the fans came to see me play, and I wanted to show them the way to play the game. I took a lot of pride in giving everything I had. It might not always have looked pretty, it might not always have been good, but I know in my heart that I gave it everything I had, and that's the bottom line.

JIM RICE

Red Sox fans will forever wonder what the outcome of the 1975 World Series against the Cincinnati Reds might have been if Jim Rice had been healthy in the line-up. A dominant slugger during the '70s and '80s who hit for both average and power, Rice chose a pair of multiple home-run games as his greatest days.

My greatest day . . . I can't remember that far back. I remember hitting three home runs, in a game in Oakland, and I also hit three home runs against Kansas City, I think there was maybe ten years, or five years difference there between the two games. But as far as memories, there's not too many.

I remember who I got my first hit off of, but I don't remember where the ball went or anything like that. It was Wilbur Wood. I didn't play in the '75 Series, I remember seeing the ball go through Buckner's legs, I remember Bernie Carbo hitting the home run. I remember seeing Carlton Fisk hit the home run in '75, because they show it all the time, but I didn't play in those games because I had a broken hand. So those are the memories that you think about, because they're more advertised in the history of the Red Sox.

Those two three home-run games are probably my greatest days. I know that I maybe had a chance to hit four home runs against Oakland. I don't know what I did in that last at-bat. I don't go back and look at my history or analyze myself. I think if you go back and look at some of the highlights that the Red Sox have accumulated in your career you probably remember certain days, but I don't.

When I played baseball, I just played baseball from day-to-day. I didn't go back and look at what I did five years or six years [ago], I didn't do that. I just played ball and went home, and became a dad and a husband. I didn't take my work home, I didn't take it as something to be proud of. It was a job, a way for me to earn a living for me and my family, and I did enjoy every bit of it. That's the most that I remember.

The MVP is the thing I remember most in terms of awards, but it was a toss-up between me and Ron Guidry. I can't understand why it was a toss-up, because Guidry was a pitcher, and I was a guy that played every day.

A pitcher can win MVP, but a player can't win Cy Young, so there's something wrong there. I remember that, I think maybe I beat him by three or four points, but I don't see how it could have been that close. I played 163 games that year; I missed one at-bat. But that's the way it goes.

It didn't phase me as far as milestones, going back to look at it, I didn't do that. Some guys could probably tell you day-to-day . . . I didn't do that. I probably could go back and look at the books and tell you something, but I think I could find something better to read. You've got to be very frustrated or very boring to read something about yourself, you know what I mean?

I think you had more fun in the minor leagues trying to get to the big leagues, because of all the things you had to do. You didn't have the resources that you have in the big leagues that you had in the minor leagues. I think a guy should remember the things he did in the minor leagues to get to the big leagues. When you get to the big leagues the only thing you have to worry about is to play every day and staying.

Back in the minor leagues, that was tough, the busses . . . ten, eleven, twelve, sometimes fifteen hours. When you get up you don't have to worry about taking your bags, you've got people picking up your bags, everything's cake right now . . . these guys got it made. In the minor leagues it was tough, that was the thing you should remember, you don't remember the big leagues.

My biggest memory from the minor leagues is that mainly you're more together. Everybody's the same age, everybody's making approximately the same money, everybody goes to the ballpark early, just trying to get more at-bats, more BP, because you didn't have the variety that you have right now. You didn't have five or six dozen bats. You had two or three bats, and you had to make the best of it. Now in the big leagues you get a dozen or so bats every other week.

In the majors you've got guys throwing gloves at you, throwing batting gloves at you, shoes. Man, when you play in the minors you have two pairs of shoes and one glove. Now you have to have a contract, you say, "Hey, man, I need a glove," and all of a sudden you get five different gloves—Wilson, Rawlings, whoever makes 'em.

The only major league All-Star game that stands out was playing in Chicago. Freddie hit a grand slam, and then I came up and hit a home run right behind Freddie. Freddie was playing for the Angels at the time, and even at that time I wasn't chosen to play left field, Reggie Jackson was. I was leading the American and the National League in RBIs, home runs. I don't think I was leading in batting average, but I wasn't a starter.

Reggie said he wasn't coming. He said "It's not right. A man leading both leagues in home runs and RBIs, he's not starting," but that's the way the voting was. I remember that. So he didn't show up. He said, "I'm not going, that's it." And so I started that day . . . if I'm not mistaken I think Freddie was in center, I was in left, and I think Yaz was playing right, or something like that.

I didn't keep any of that history stuff. I've got my All-Star rings, but I don't have . . . when you come to my house, my wife's got pictures of Fenway Park, she's got pictures of me sitting on the bench when a guy was just doing a photograph session. Everything else in my house—you see books, it's all golf, no baseball. Baseball was more of a team thing. Even the things that I accomplished are because of the team getting me in certain situations. But if you come to my house you'll see all golf books.

CAL RIPKEN, JR.

Think of Cal Ripken, Jr., and you automatically think of 2,131. But Ripken's greatest day took place early in his career, during the great shortstop's second season with the Baltimore Orioles. Ripken talked about that day early in the 1997 season, fresh off a playoff appearance the year before and with a bit of a perspective on the magnitude of "the streak."

I don't know if I can think of one particular one . . . you know, obviously the celebration of 2,131 on September 6th was a personal high. You have to say that that's one of the greatest days, I think mainly because it encompassed more than just what you did on the field, with the appreciation for going out and playing all those games in a row.

I think the first greatest day that still lasts in my memory was something that was not really a great game for me personally, but for what it meant overall. I caught the last out of the World Series. When I caught it . . . I can't remember, I don't think I got any hits in that game. I think I walked once or twice. Eddie [Murray] hit two home runs in the game, we clinched it in Philadelphia.

Just being a part of the team and catching the last out, putting a punctuation mark on the season and bringing it to closure, that was one of the best feelings that you can have. The finality of that last catch, it leaves a mark on your memory.

To me, the '82 Series at the end of the year really put a stamp on the next season all the way around. We came from way back to try and catch Milwaukee, and we tied them up the next to the last day of the season. The last day of the season we lost to Milwaukee, and the next season I think everyone on that team was on a mission. I remember that curtain call the last day, I remember that well. . . .

PF SPORTS IMAGES

Having that experience the year before, and then going into the season and pushing to win the division, we took it one step further and had a tough series with the Chicago White Sox. We got through them, and then we go to the World Series, which almost seems anti-climactic at first, but once you're there, only one team can walk away being the world champions.

Once we were in that series, we lost the first game, and then we battled back and it just seemed like we took control in Philadelphia, and we pitched really well, and we scored runs. I think it was a really uneventful game. Scottie MacGregor shut 'em down, shut 'em out, and Eddie Murray hit two home runs.

So to me, it wasn't a big leadup for a personal achievement or anything, it was just, to me, the World Series stood out in my mind because that's everyone's goal, and you really understand that very deeply when you're that close to it and that involved in it. So the last out, to me, probably has to be my best day in baseball. I've had a lot of 'em, but that has to be considered the best.

The celebration began right after the out. Everyone ran to the mound, a lot of people came from the stands, to grab a hat, or to grab something. They contained everybody well, but the celebration,

October 16, 1983

BALTIMORE	AB	R	H	RBI	PHILADELPHIA	AB	R	H	RBI
Bumbry, cf	2	0	0	1	Morgan, 2b	3	0	1	0
Shelby, cf	1	0	0	0	Rose, rf	4	0	2	0
Ford, rf	4	0	0	0	Schmidt, 3b	4	0	0	0
Landrum, rf	0	0	0	0	Matthews, lf	4	0	0	0
Ripken, ss	3	1	0	0	Perez, 1b	4	0	0	0
Murray, 1b	4	2	3	3	Maddox, cf	4	0	2	0
Lowenstein, lf	2	0	0	0	Diaz, c	2	0	0	0
Roenicke, lf	2	0	0	0	DeJesus, ss	3	0	0	0
Dauer, 2b	4	0	0	0	Hudson, p	1	0	0	0
Cruz, 3b	4	0	0	0	Bystrom, p	0	0	0	0
Dempsey, c	3	2	2	1	Samuel, ph	1	0	0	0
McGregor, p	3	0	0	0	Hernandez, p	0	0	0	0
					Lezcano, p	1	0	0	0
					Reed, p	0	0	0	0
Totals	32	5	5	5	Totals	31	0	5	0

Baltimore	011	210	000 — 5	
Philadelphia	000	000	000 — 0	

the unity of the team took over when we were in the clubhouse. That was the fun celebration.

Just being able to spend the offseason knowing that you were the champions. I had a chance to live that life. Making the last catch had a lot bigger meaning—it had a lot of meaning from the year before, it had a lot of meaning for the offseason afterwards. Until baseball started again, you were the world champions, and you got to feel proud about that.

I established myself in the first year as an everyday player. I had some ups and downs in the beginning. Once I got on track, Earl moved me to shortstop, I guess in July, and I felt good in establishing myself coming into the next season. Everyone was talking about the sophomore jinx, and now the league knows you, so we'll see if you can do it again. So it was a big personal challenge to get off to a good start.

Just like the team took off, I really took off in my second year, and I think that really identified me as a player. I was able to play all the games. I was able to contribute a lot of home runs. I was able to drive in a hundred runs hitting in the middle of the Oriole line-up. So I knew that was the time when I was learning, and I was trying to establish myself as a player in the middle of the line-up with the Orioles. That year couldn't have been any better.

You really don't realize the significance of breaking in with a veteran club when you go through it, but it's a situation where if circumstances had been different it could have put more pressure on me or given me less of an opportunity. It is a big help to come in with a veteran club, a club that had won, knew how to win. There's a lot that can be taught, and there's a lot that can be learned.

And I was in a good situation, because the pressure was on everyone else. I was able to go out there and play and establish myself in a good atmosphere. I don't know if your career path would have been the same if the conditions in which you come up had been different.

When you hear people say that the name of the game is to win . . . I mean, it's true. Sometimes you forget if you haven't experienced it, then maybe you tend not to think that way. You tend to put more emphasis or significance on your individual accomplishments.

I realize that because we won the World Series in '83 and then last year was the first year we went back to the playoffs as a wild-card team. Being in the playoffs, and seeing the excitement, and seeing how the team really pulled together and went down the stretch when we had our success, it really brings it right back to the forefront.

This is what it's all about, playing in Yankee Stadium in that kind of atmosphere and in those kind of circumstances. This is why you play. You can't derive any more satisfaction than that, and that includes going five for five, that includes being the MVP of the All-Star game, or being the MVP of the league.

When you've been through it and you realize the significance of winning and the importance of winning and how it makes you feel, that's why you want to do it.

I can't say that winning again now would be a bigger thrill, but you're in a position to appreciate it that much more, to take it in from all different sides. Whereas in the beginning, you don't know about certain things, it's new, and it's exciting for that reason.

Once you know about it, and then you have the opportunity to go back and win again, it's got to be a little bit . . . I'm not going to say sweeter, but it's gotta be a little bit different experience, maybe one that could be a little bit more gratifying because you know about it, you can absorb all the good things that happen to you and take it all in whereas you might miss a few things along the way the first time.

I haven't even thought about the possibility of going into the Hall of Fame. To me, very simply put, you only have a small window in your life to play this game, and you should play it and give everything you have for as long as you can.

That really is what my approach has been all about, that's what the consecutive game streak is all about, knowing that you have so much time to play, trying not to waste your opportunity, coming to the ballpark all the time, wanting to play, willing to play, and hoping that the manager wants me in the line-up.

ROBIN ROBERTS

Like his teammate and fellow Philadelphia Hall of Famer Richie Ashburn, Robin Roberts's greatest day was the Phillies victory against the Brooklyn Dodgers in the final day of the season in 1950 in Ebbets Field. Roberts pitched that game, his fourth game in eight days, in an heroic performance that will always be remembered as one of the greatest days in Phillies history.

Well, that was the day we won the pennant in Ebbetts Field, October 1, 1950. It was a ten-inning ball game. We had blown a

seven-and-a-half-game lead, we were one game ahead with one game to go. There had been a lot of injuries and everything, a lot of different things had happened.

It was very exciting: Richie threw the guy out at home, which kept us from getting beat, and Sisler hit a three-run homer. I pitched the whole ball game, and I'd done a lot of pitching the last week because we'd had a lot of injuries and everything, but it was a remarkable game for us.

Without winning that game, of course, we wouldn't have won the pennant. I don't know what the reaction would have been to the club in the organization, maybe it would have worked out better, I don't know, that was the only one we won, you know. They might have traded some people, and made some moves that weren't made otherwise.

It was just the most exciting sports event I was ever involved with, and for us to win was just an unbelievable thrill and a great moment.

Number one, we had had so many injuries at the end, we weren't even sure who was gonna pitch it. Curt Simmons had been called into the service, and Bubba Church had been hit in the eye, and Bob Miller had hurt his back. I had started, and this was the fourth game, and if I was to pitch that game it would be the fourth start I had in eight days.

So as I go to the ballpark I assume I was pitching, but nobody had told me definitely that I was pitching. I was sitting in the clubhouse, and it was a very solemn clubhouse, because we had been a very outstanding club until we had Simmons go in the army and all the injuries; we really had a lot of problems the last month. I was sitting in the clubhouse, and Sawyer walked over, our manager, Eddie Sawyer, and he gave me a baseball, and he said, "Good luck." . . . Well, that's the first time I definitely knew I was pitching.

I walk out to the mound to warm up, and I was tired, you know, nervous. I had pitched a lot, and I didn't know how I was gonna react. But fortunately for me, Newcombe was pitching for the Dodgers, and he had been on pretty much the same schedule in a reverse way. They were fighting to get to win the pennant, and he had been doing an awful lot of pitching the last week like I had.

So as I saw him warming up I was able to get over my feeling of tiredness, because Newc was in the same situation. And that thought in itself—I just looked at him, and I thought, "My God, he's in the same position I'm in, so we're even." And I never gave one more thought to being tired or having pitched a lot. Obviously he didn't, either, because he pitched quite a ball game, the way it turned out.

I just cranked it up, and when they asked me to get out there, I did. I wasn't a big thinking pitcher. I had a good arm, and I stayed ahead of people, and I stuck it in there pretty good, below areas, you know, places where normally it was pretty hard to hit. I just tried to stay ahead of batters and keep working. I just enjoyed the competition and worked at it. I didn't change anything for all ball games. Some ball games you're keyed up more than others, and of course for that game, you couldn't get more keyed up than we were for that one.

The things that were specific: I remember our first run; Puddinhead Jones drove it in. I was surprised as I looked at the box score—Eddie Waitkus had eighteen putouts at first base, and I was mostly a fastball/flyball pitcher. And to have eighteen putouts at first, I had six assists myself, but I only recalled this as I looked at the box score. I didn't realize it at the time.

When Snider was hitting in the ninth, I thought he was gonna bunt, and he ripped the ball that Richie fielded and threw Abrams out at home. And I remember after that hit there were runners at second and third, and we walked Jackie on purpose, and Furillo popped up, he just flew out to right.

I remember Sawyer leaving me in to hit in the top of the tenth. I got a base hit up the middle, which was a big part of it when you think about it, starting the inning off. The ninth inning, the last inning after we got the three runs, I remember throwing better that inning than I'd thrown for a long time.

I think those three runs really charged us up and charged me up, particularly. I really had good stuff the last inning, and after pitching all that way, it was great for me to have that good feeling, but I do remember being able to throw the ball as good or better that last inning than at any other time.

Afterwards I was tired, I really didn't . . . I do remember the train ride, I remember specifically Jackie Robinson coming over and congratulating us. I thought that was a remarkable thing to have him over there. He was a tremendous gentleman and competitor, and I'll never forget that, because I was just sitting by my locker, completely tired, and I feel the guy tugging on my shoulder, and I looked up and he said, "Congratulations, Robin."

And I was tired as could be, but I thought more later on what a tremendous thing . . . he wasn't the only one. The clubhouses in Ebbets Field were close together, and there were a number of the Dodgers who came over to congratulate us, which I thought was . . . it's very seldom that the clubhouses are so close.

In other ballparks, you've gotta walk all the way around, and I don't imagine a lot of that goes on other than managers, who tend to pay their respects to each other after the series is over. But the players, to have the Dodgers in there, and particularly Jackie, was something I remember.

I was really whipped. I was emotionally drained, I was physically tired, I had done an awful lot of pitching, and I was really relieved, and I just sat by my locker. I didn't do much hollering or anything. . . . There was a lot of noise and a lot of screaming and hollering, but I don't remember being a big part of that.

Now on the train ride home to Philly, I remember eating a nice meal. I remember that celebration. When we got to Philadelphia, we went to the Warwick Hotel. My wife was eight months pregnant with our first child, who was born on October the 20th, so we stayed around for the celebration at the Warwick, but we did leave early, because she was tired, naturally, and I was whipped, so the celebrating was not something that I was that involved in. I was happy that we were celebrating, but I also was happy to get home and get to bed, because I really was tired.

The pennant game . . . nothing even came close to that. I think the Hall of Fame selection was nice, also, but it didn't have nearly the effect that that game had. You cannot imagine how almost blowing that pennant, how that effected us. To finally pull it together, and the World Series was a beautiful thing to be involved in, and we played well for the first three games particularly, all one-run games, but the pennant thing . . . I played college basketball and I played all the sports in high school, football, basketball, and baseball in high school, and I played baseball in college along with basketball, and as exciting as all that was nothing was quite like the pennant. That was an unbelievable situation.

I think the 200th win also stands out, probably, because that was . . . when I was a boy in Springfield, Illinois, Grover Cleveland Alexander had . . . They had a guy who was kind of taking care of him, because he was kind of down in his luck. We had a sports night when I was in the eighth grade in grade school, and he came out to speak. I remember the little thing he said, "Boys, sports is great and everything, but don't drink. Look what it did to me," and then he sat down. And I remember that speech.

He had won more games than anybody in Philly history, and I went up . . . I won the game that went ahead of him, and I kind of reflected on that, because when I met the guy I had no idea I was even gonna be a ballplayer. To pass his total was great, it was kind of nice for me.

Going into the Hall was an interesting thing, because I reflected back on all the people that had helped me, my parents and my wife and my teammates and coaches. I was more grateful that day than anything else, because although I had worked hard at baseball, it had been a cooperative effort from a lot of people's standpoints, and I realized that. I was never particularly caught up in my own performance, really, other than the fact that I always felt that I should do well. I had the ability to do well, and I did reflect on the people that helped me along the way.

I went in with Bob Lemon, who I had known, and Freddie Lindstrom. I think the old umpire, I forget his name, God, I'm getting old, it was 1976. The ceremony was the first time it was ever rained out, so it was forced inside. It made it inconvenient for a lot of friends that came up, because it was hard to get into this one area. Now they have a gymnasium and everything at Cooperstown. That happened again when Palmer went in. I think it's only happened twice, but now they're more prepared for that, they have a better facility for it.

I was excited when I broke in. I reported to the ballpark at 6 o'clock at night. I had come up from Wilmington. I'd gone to the Bellevue Hotel in Philadelphia at about 4:30. I checked in, I reported to Shibe Park at 6 o'clock, and I knew the manager, Ben Chapman, because I'd been in spring training. And I walked into his office, and he said, "How you doin', Robin?" and I said, "Fine," and he said, "Can you pitch tonight?" and I said "Sure," and I pitched.

So I didn't really have much time to think much about that. I do remember that the first batter was a guy named Stan Rojek, who was a shortstop for the Pirates, who were on top of the league at the time. And I walked him on four of the wildest pitches you ever saw. I was very nervous, and the next batter was Frankie Gustine, and he swung and missed at a 3–2 fastball, and from that moment on I was alright. It was amazing how just that one out got me to relax, and the only other time I was excited like that for one batter was in 1955 when I had a no hitter into the ninth inning of Opening Day of the 1955 season against the Giants.

I got one out in the ninth, and the next batter hit a ground ball to short, and Ham threw it away, he threw it in the dirt, so now there's one out and a man on first and Alvin Dark fouled off about five pitches and then he singled to right field. I ended up winning the game, but they ended up getting a couple of runs. It was a battle to get 'em out in the ninth inning, but I remember being nervous like I was pitching to Rojek, and those are the only two times I remember being in a situation where my nerves were almost getting the best of me.

I lost the debut, 2–0, a guy named Elmer Riddle pitched for the Pirates, and they were on top of the league at the time, they had Westlake and Kiner and Rojek and Frankie Gustine and Danny Murtaugh. They were an older club, and they didn't win the pennant that year. Boston came through and won it, but the Pirates in June, I think it was June 17th, they were on top of the league the night I pitched against them. I pitched the whole ball game, I lost 2–0, I think I pitched a complete game, maybe they pinch hit and somebody else pitched the last inning.

After the Rojek thing I settled down, I felt like I could pitch up there. I felt disappointed that I lost, but I really was a confident pitcher as far as I threw strikes and I had good stuff, and that's a big part of it. I was excited at the start and then after I settled down I felt kind of relieved that I could get 'em out, and I felt like I belonged.

[For box score, please see interview with Richie Ashburn.]

BROOKS ROBINSON

© CHARLES SEGAR

There have been many fabulous defensive third basemen in the history of the game, but few would argue that Brooks Robinson was the best of the bunch. As is often the case, however, with great defensive players, many of the Hall of Famer's personal highlights are his best offensive days, along with his unforgettable performance against the Cincinnati Reds in 1970 when he was the World Series MVP.

I think that the two games I remember . . . The first was when I went five for five and became the first Oriole to hit for the cycle back in 1960. Actually I was dating my wife at that particular time in Chicago, she lived in Chicago and we were playing the White Sox, and I went five for five—home run, double, single, triple. I can remember going back and seeing her that night, and she said, "Well, how did things go?" And I said, "Well, not too good," and I didn't tell her anything. She saw the paper the next day and she said, "Well, now I know never to trust you again."

That was a big day for me. It was against the White Sox in Chicago. The other time, 1964, we were making a run for the pennant, and we ended up losing the pennant by two games. The White Sox lost it by one game to the Yankees, who won. We were playing the White Sox in a big game in Chicago, and I hit a three-run homer in the ninth inning off of Joel Horlen to win the game, and I always look at that particular hit as one of the . . . I think at that particular time it was really the first time that we had a chance to win, and I hit the home run in the ninth inning and we won the game. I always say that was one of my biggest games.

But those two come to mind more than anything else, although I hit a home run my first time up in a World Series game, that was exciting, against the Dodgers back in '66. So those three things more than anything else probably stand out as my happiest days.

Someone asked me, "What was the thing you cherished most?" I think being the Most Valuable Player in 1964, and that's for something you accomplish over 162 games. I always felt like that was the nicest thing that ever happened to me, and the thing I'm the most proud of, because we didn't win that year, but I still won the MVP award in the American League.

And the other one was just a specific game. I never had five straight hits, went five for five in a game, or hit for the cycle, so that was something . . . there's only been two guys in the history of the Orioles, that's Ripken and myself. Ripken did it a few years ago, and it just becomes obvious to me that hitting for the cycle is a lot tougher than people think it is.

It just doesn't happen a lot of times . . . you know, the Orioles have been around since '54, and you would think there would be a few people who have hit for the cycle, but there's only been two, and I was the first one, and that was a pretty happy day for me. I always think about what you say when you talk about hitting in the clutch, and that particular game it was such a big game and we had to win it, and I hit a three-run homer in the ninth inning to win it.

The last hit that I had to get was the double . . . I hit a home run off of . . . I remember Billy Pierce pitched, but I hit a double and that was the last one, I hit a home run off of Billy Pierce. I don't remember any of the other things, but I know I went five for five.

There really isn't one defensive highlight that stands out for me. I had a game against Cleveland, late in my career, where I just had a lot of chances to make a lot of great plays and made them. But I have no idea when that was or what it was, but people . . . Boog Powell, he was at first base, and I always say that was one of those days where everything was right.

In the World Series, we played the Cincinnati Reds five games in 1970 and I had a chance to do something spectacular in each of those games and make great plays, but I can't say one game was any better than the other. I just know that after about three games, I'm saying to myself, hey this is unbelievable, this can't go on, let's get this series over with, I can't keep doing this.

I've seen some films with Earl Weaver saying, "Well, Brooks Robinson does this every day of the season," something like that. Or Johnny Bench saying, "Hey, I've never seen anything like this," or Sparky Anderson on tape saying, "Hey, if we'd known he wanted a car that bad, we would have bought him one," you know, all kinds of little innuendoes like that.

July 15, 1960

BALTIMORE	AB	R	H	RBI	CHICAGO	AB	R	H	RBI
Brandt, rf	5	1	1	1	Aparicio, ss	4	0	1	1
Woodling, 3b	4	1	0	0	Fox, 2b	4	0	2	0
Robinson, 3b	5	1	5	3	Minoso, lf	4	0	0	0
Dropo, 1b	5	0	1	0	Sievers, 1b	2	1	1	1
Triandos, c	3	1	2	0	Lollar, c	3	0	0	0
Hansen, ss	4	0	0	0	Smith, rf	3	1	0	0
Busby, cf	4	0	2	0	Freese, 3b	4	0	0	0
Breeding, 2b	4	0	1	0	Landis, cf	4	0	0	0
Pappas, p	4	1	1	0	Pierce, p	1	0	1	0
					Torgeson, ph	1	0	0	0
					Lown, p	0	0	0	0
					Kluszewski, ph	1	0	0	0
Totals	38	5	13	4	Totals	31	2	5	2

Baltimore	002	001	002 — 5	
Chicago	010	000	010 — 2	

I tell people that I played almost twenty-three years professionally, and I cannot think of any five-game stretch where I had a chance
to make as many plays, plus I was hitting well. So that little five-
game stretch, I mean, as an infielder, you can play a week, two weeks
sometimes, and never get a chance to do anything spectacular, but in
this World Series . . . and people who are not even baseball fans kind
of tune in during the World Series, so they had a chance to see
Brooks Robinson play third base.

I tell people that the thing no one remembers is that in the first
game, in the first inning, the first ball that was hit that day probably
was hit to me, and I made an error. I made a high throw to Boog
Powell on about a 44-hopper. I think it was Woody Woodward who
hit it. And I'm saying to myself, "Oh man, here we go again, do you
believe this?" We played the Mets, and we lost to the Mets, and I
didn't distinguish myself in any way, and here the first ball is hit to
you in this series, and you blow it . . . and I was talkin' to myself.

But everything else was pretty upbeat.

As a youngster, when you were fourteen or fifteen years old,
you're pretty presumptuous. . . . I can remember saying, hey, "I'm
gonna make the big leagues," just matter of fact. But I don't think
anyone ever says, "I'm gonna make the Hall of Fame," that is so far
out in left field you never even think about it.

I played ten years, really, before I started thinking about the Hall
of Fame. But it was the fans, more than anyone else, who let me know
that you have a chance to attain the Hall of Fame. And after we were
in three straight World Series, I can remember they said, "Hey
Brooks, you've got a chance to be in the Hall of Fame," and I started
thinking about it then. But that was about ten years into my career.

It was wonderful. If you stop to think about all the years that
baseball's been played, there are 150, 160, 170 players there . . . it
kind of puts you on a little higher plateau. It's been wonderful.

I kind of was in a daze for about three days when the ceremony came, I really was. It's one of those things where when you get
there, they get you by the hand and you go from here to here to here,
and I just know it was a happy day for me with the family, and the
Baltimore fans turned out.

Two things made it real special. George Kell grew up about
sixty miles from me in Arkansas. He ended his career in Baltimore,
Opening Day of '57. I played third and George played first against
the Washington Senators. And he had kind of been an idol to me. He
had taken me under his wing that year, and we were together on the

field and off the field, and he was just the greatest guy and still is, one of my true heroes of the game.

We finished our career together, and in '83, George goes in the Hall of Fame through the Old Timers committee, and I go in through the regular phase, and we're on the podium together being inducted into the Hall of Fame.

The other thing was that on July 24th, in 1961, the Orioles were making their first appearance in Cooperstown, and I'm actually on the field, and I get a call. And they said, "Hey, Brooks, your first son was just born in Detroit." My wife went home to have our first child, and we named him Brooks David. I was actually on the field at Cooperstown when he was born, and then twenty-seven years later he comes back to see me inducted into Cooperstown.

So those two things made it special, plus the whole city of Baltimore, they just turned out. Cooperstown had never seen such a Hall of Fame induction as when Brooks Robinson was inducted.

FRANK ROBINSON

In addition to being one of the game's all-time greats, Frank Robinson was a pioneer in the game of baseball as well. As a player, Robinson won the Triple Crown, and he was also the only player to win the MVP Award in both leagues, for the Baltimore Orioles and the Cincinnati Reds. Known for his unbelievable clutch performances and for being an incredibly tough competitor, the savvy Robinson was also the first African-American to manage in the major leagues for the Cleveland Indians, and he was also one of the game's first black executives as GM for the Orioles.

I don't know what my greatest day was . . . it's hard to pick out of twenty-one years. I guess the first one is always the first game you play in the major leagues. That's one of my greatest days. I guess one of the other ones was when we won the World Series in Baltimore, the day we clinched the series against the Dodgers. And the other one was when I was notified that I'd been elected to the Baseball Hall of Fame.

What stands out about the first one is the day, when you first put on that uniform in the major leagues for the first time. It's a tremendous thrill, and an honor, really it is, and it's a lifelong dream that I had had, to play in the major leagues. And I had realized it, finally, and I knew that the battle had just begun, because the idea is to stay in the major leagues also. You know, it's very difficult to get there, but it's much more difficult to stay for any length of time.

I remember we opened against the Cardinals, playing against Stan Musial, that was in Cincinnati, Cincinnati always opened up at home, that was a tradition. Full house, you know, out at Crosley Field, people out behind me in left field and the terrace, you know there's the terrace out there and then that little hill. They put people out behind me on Opening Day, and they rope 'em off and put chairs out there.

I remember the fans being behind me in left field and facing Vinegar Bend Mizell at the time, a big left-hander. I was hitting down in the order, seventh at the time, and Ray Jablonski hit a home run, and I was the next hitter, and I hit a ball to center field and it just missed being a home by about a foot or so.

I got a double, and the next time up I got a single, and the third time up I got something that I considered quite an honor at the time, an intentional walk. Here's a rookie intentionally walked, but we lost the game when Stan Musial hit a home run in the eighth or ninth inning.

That was really a thrill, not only playing in my first major league game, but getting a couple of hits. I wasn't nervous; I'm not the type who gets what I call nervous, where I feel anxiety, but Opening Day is just a special time. You get those little butterflies in your stomach, that type of thing. But it wasn't in the days where they gave the scouting reports, where they gave you all this information about pitchers and whatever, it was just, you went up and you hit. So that first at-bat I just went up to hit, and I got a fastball and hit it, and each at-bat, I just approached it as just going up to hit.

I guess the point where I knew I was going to stay came after I went zero for twenty-two. After that, after the ball game, the reporters came around, saying, "What's the difference between the major leagues and the minor leagues?" and I said, I wasn't being cocky, I wasn't being overconfident, but what I said was that there was really no difference.

And what I meant by that was that the pitcher throws the ball over the plate, but what I proceeded to say was that the pitchers up here are much better because they can locate their pitches much better. But the thing that really made the news was that I said that the pitching was no different.

And I proceeded to go zero for twenty-two after that. Birdie Tebbetts called me back into the office after a road trip where I was like 0 for the road trip. He called me in, we were facing the Dodgers first game back, Don Newcombe was gonna pitch, and he said, "Hey, look I've seen a lot of careers ruined with young kids getting in over their heads too soon." He said, "I'm gonna sit you down tonight, and I want you to watch the game from the dugout and look at it." And he said, "Tomorrow or the next day you'll be back in there."

I sat and watched, and I was glad I didn't have to face Newcombe. I was back in the next day, and got going, and went on from there. I made the All-Star team. I guess at the end of the season is when you really feel relief and you say, "Hey, I did it." I guess when I really felt that I had a good chance of staying and having a good year was when I was voted into the All-Star game. I knew the fans did the voting, but I did have the numbers at the All-Star game.

I went and played in the All-Star game and that was when I really felt that I'd accomplished what I wanted to accomplish and I was accepted by my teammates, and you know, I felt very comfortable. Not to the point where I settled in, but I felt comfortable and I felt that I could play in the major leagues.

Well, I was embarrassed in the game. I had two at-bats, and I struck out both times on a total of six pitches, and the second time I got up there and I said to myself, "You know, this guy evidently didn't read my press clippings, he didn't understand, he didn't even waste a pitch." I said that's embarrassing, he didn't even waste a pitch, I said, "Jeez, he had no respect at all." So that's what I did in my first All-Star game.

The World Series was very special for Baltimore. Number one, I had played in the World Series in '61 with Cincinnati, and we were beat four games to one by the Yankees when Maris and Mantle had their big year. So my thought was, I want to get back again, and I want to be on the winning side.

We had a terrific year, the year that I was traded to Baltimore, in '66, winning the American League championship. We were gonna face the Dodgers, and all the headlines and all the news said that we had no chance against the Dodgers, with their pitching and whatever.

And I said we'd caught a break, because Koufax had to pitch

the last game of the season to get the Dodgers into the World Series, and they won it, but he couldn't start the first game of the Series. And I told the other players, and I told people, that's a break, really, because now we don't have to face him the first game. We were facing Drysdale, and that was no . . . you know I'm not knocking him and his skills and abilities, but still, you know . . .

So anyhow, the headline was that we didn't have a chance against this superior pitching, and I told the press when they asked me, I said, "I think we can beat the Dodgers, because our pitching is good enough to stop their hitters, and our hitters are good enough to score some runs off of their pitching, and I think we can win this thing." Nobody thought about a sweep.

We got out of the gate in the series in the first inning, I think Russ Snyder got either a hit or a walk, I can't remember, he was hitting second, and then I followed with the home run off Drysdale in the first inning. And then Brooks followed me with a home run and we were off to a 3–0 start in the first inning. It was a big help to us, because it took the pressure off of us and showed that we could score runs, and it also put the pressure on the Dodgers and took them out of their game.

Dave McNally struggled, and Moe Drabowsky came in and had a terrific outing as a relief pitcher; he struck out eleven in five or

April 17, 1956

ST. LOUIS	AB	R	H	PO	A	CINCINNATI	AB	R	H	PO	A
Moon, 1b	4	1	2	9	3	Temple, 2b	4	0	1	1	4
Schoendienst, 2b	5	1	2	1	1	Burgess, c	5	0	1	4	1
Musial, rf	5	1	1	2	0	Harmon, pr	0	0	0	0	0
Sauer, lf	4	0	0	0	0	Kluszewski, 1b	5	0	1	12	0
Boyer, 3b	3	0	2	0	0	Post, rf	5	0	1	3	0
Virdon, cf	4	0	1	3	0	Bell, cf	4	0	1	0	0
Sarni, c	4	1	3	7	0	Jablonski, 3b	4	2	3	0	0
Grammas, ss	4	0	0	2	3	Robinson, lf	3	0	2	3	0
Mizell, p	4	0	1	3	3	McMillan, ss	4	0	2	4	5
Kinder, p	0	0	0	0	0	Nuxhall, p	3	0	0	0	2
						Crowe, ph	1	0	0	0	0
Totals	37	4	12	27	10	Totals	38	2	12	27	12

St. Louis	100	100	002 — 4
Cincinnati	010	100	000 — 2

seven innings, and we went on to win the ball game 5–3. And after that we won the next one, that was the one with the three errors on Willie Davis in center field, he didn't have his great stuff.

Then we were saying among ourselves, "Hey, we're going home for two now. We win two at home we don't have to come back here." It wasn't, "No way, let's sweep," but we didn't have to come back if we won two at home. And we got terrific pitching from Wally Bunker in the third game, and Paul Blair hit a home run, and we won that one, 1–0.

And then we faced Drysdale again, and about the fourth or fifth inning I came up, and the first two hitters in the inning had hit the first pitches and made outs. And I'm walking up from the on-deck circle, and the old saying was, you don't let a pitcher have a chance of getting out of an inning with only three pitches, because your pitcher's going right back out to the mound.

So I said to myself, "I'd better take a pitch." Then, before I got in the batter's box, I said, "Wait a minute, this score's 0–0; if he just lays a fastball in here and it's a good pitch, I've got to swing at it." So I talked myself into it, and I said, "Make him get the ball up." I got a pitch about belt high, and boy, I hit it good. . . . I knew it was gone as soon as I hit it.

And we won that ball game, and we went on and swept the series, it was just a terrific conclusion to a terrific year. And then being voted the Most Valuable Player, the Triple Crown winner, and all that it was just . . . too good to be true. It was like a fairy-tale type story. If you went to Hollywood and saw that on the screen, nobody would believe you'd had that type of year. That was just a terrific year.

I would have to pick the first game as the greatest day, because I think it set the tone. I think that if they had jumped out on top of us, we'd have started having doubts, and their confidence would have gone sky-high. I think the first game really set the tone.

Going into the Hall of Fame, that's the hardest thing to describe, because each individual that's been inducted into the Hall of Fame has their own personal feelings about it. There're no two people who have the same feelings. I don't think anyone can prepare you for the actual induction ceremonies. People will talk to you, and they'll tell you this, and they'll tell you that, but let me tell you one thing: there's no feeling like it; once you stand up there on the podium and accept the plaque from whoever gives the speech or introduces you.

I went in with Hank Aaron, believe it or not. We had been rivals for ten years over in the National League, with Cincinnati and the Braves. It was just amazing. I went in with him, and I went in with Happy Chandler, and there was one other guy, an old-timer, his name just jumped right out of my head. The four of us went in.

It was just a terrific thing, and what I wanted to do was . . . I was given three speeches by different people that I respected, and I looked at all of 'em, and the morning of the induction I took the speeches and . . . not out of disrespect, but I just took 'em and I tore it up, just threw 'em in the trash. And I said, I'm just gonna wing it.

I said, "I have a lot of people to thank for me being here, on this day and having this honor bestowed on me, but I'm only getting this one shot at this time." I wanted to try and thank many people, so I just got up there and just, off the top of my head, talked until I felt like I had said what I wanted to say and thanked the people that I wanted to thank.

And I closed . . . it was just a terrific thing; there's just nothing to compare to it. I've never been through anything like that, I've never faced anything like that. I was in the World Series facing pitchers with three-and-two counts with the bases loaded, the bottom of the ninth, whatever . . . but there was no feeling like it; it was just a terrific day for me and the icing on the cake to a career that I'd never dreamed I would have when I was dreaming about playing in the major leagues.

The thing that stands out the most for me among the awards was that winning the MVP in the National League was the first step. But when I won the award in the American League and became the first and still the only player to achieve that, that is what I look upon as my greatest achievement as far as awards are concerned in baseball.

When I was announced officially as being the manager of the Indians at the news conference, that was a great day for me, because it had broken a barrier that had stood for a lot . . . for too many years it had been that way. And I had cracked the door open and walked through it, and hopefully it would allow others to achieve their goals in the major leagues one day.

That was a terrific day . . . I didn't want to throw that one aside, but that would be the fourth terrific day, because Rachel Robinson was there, and there was a huge media audience, and the commissioner was there, and it was just a terrific day to realize that it wasn't a dream of mine to be the first. . . . I wanted to manage in the major leagues. I just happened to be the first and it happened to make it even more special.

In a way I was realizing something, a dream that Jackie had dreamed, of one day having a minority managing a major league team. My thoughts were with him, for him, and silently I just said, and publicly I just said, "I'd like to thank him for what he had endured and for what he had to go through." And I thought, "[He] is the only reason I'm standing here now—the way he conducted himself and the way he carried himself on and off the field." I just wish that he could have been there to see that day. That would probably be the fourth day, and one of the most terrific days in my career.

My thoughts haven't changed as far as the trade was concerned. I wanted to be a Cincinnati Red for my entire career, because that was the organization I signed with, I chose to sign with that organization rather than another organization. I put my entire career in with that organization, I had good times, I had some bad times, I had great years, and I had some bad years.

And after ten years, I just felt . . . I said, "Hey, I've got ten. I'd just love to stay here with Cincinnati." When that call came on an evening in December, I was stunned. Anger entered into it, because it was like something was taken away from me, and it was also like a statement being made that I wasn't good enough anymore, they didn't want me, I'd been rejected . . . that type of thing. The first time all those feelings went through, and it took me about two or three days to kind of start to recoup from it, to start thinking straight.

After I started thinking straight about it, I said, "Well, at least Baltimore, the organization at Baltimore is saying to me that they want me. So there's somebody that wants me, and I'm going to a new city, and a new team, and a team that has been close the last couple of years. If I go over there and have the type of year that I'm capable of having, I may help them win the championship."

And I said, "This may be the best thing for me, because, you know, sometimes when you're in one place for a long time, you feel like they know you and you've given it all you have, and sometimes you need a change of scenery to really bring out the little extra in you." I thought I'd always given my best at Cincinnati, and I still do to this day. But maybe some days I didn't, I don't know . . . subconsciously, maybe I wasn't.

When I went to Baltimore, it was like a new life, a fresh start, new teammates, and whatever. And a terrific team, terrific ownership, it was "go" from day one. It was a good feeling, a good mix, and I really enjoyed the time, as brief as it was. You know, a lot of people think that I've been there longer than I was, because some people don't even remember that I played with Cincinnati, and some people don't remember that I only played six years with Baltimore. They say, "You only played six years?"

We won four times in six years, and this is what people remember. They remember winning teams, and I played on a winner, and basically people identify me now as an Oriole, and that's the way I look at it too. People sometimes are shocked, they say, "You played ten years in Cincinnati?" and I said, "Yes, I did."

But that was probably the best thing that could have happened to me, at that stage in my career.

I guess it was a motivator through spring training, maybe the first couple of months of the season. You know, everybody . . . even at the end of the year . . . and boy, you had that going for you, you wanted to show Billy DeWitt, but I said, "No . . . after a while you have to let go of those things, because those things only go for so long." I think that after the first couple of months, you turn your attention to other things and what's at hand, and that was helping the team win ball games. You can only carry that type of feeling for so long. You can't carry it all year, because if you do it's not gonna work for you.

When you do something for the first time, it has a special feeling and a special meaning and it always is there. You never forget that. Yeah, we had some terrific years, in '70 we weren't supposed to beat the Big Red Machine, either. It was special, but it wasn't as special as the first one. The trade . . . the first year with a new team that had never won before, we were going up against the mighty Dodgers, we weren't supposed to win and we wind up sweeping them and everything fell into place, it was just a fairy-tale type year for me.

ALEX RODRIGUEZ

Imagine being twenty years old, and being a rookie in the major leagues. Imagine being on the way to a Triple Crown-level season in which you bat .358, hit thirty-six home runs, and drive home 123 runs. Then imagine that in the middle of that season, you sign a big contract that virtually guarantees you financial security for

*the rest of your life, as everyone who watches you play declares you
to be one of the "shortstops of the future." With the stage set, we
bring you the story of Alex Rodriguez of the Seattle Mariners.*

My greatest day, let's see . . . it would have to be . . . actually,
it was my birthday. My birthday's July 27th. My coach was in town,
Rich Hoffman, my high school coach at Westminster Christian, in
Miami, Florida. It was my birthday, I signed a new four-year contract
that day, and I got three hits and a home run that day against the
Detroit Tigers.

I had a press conference, because I signed that day, and the
whole day was just like a magical day, everything was perfect, both

July 27, 1996

DETROIT	AB	R	H	RBI	BB	SO
Higginson, lf–cf	5	2	4	2	0	0
Curtis, cf	2	1	0	0	2	1
Pride, ph–lf	1	0	0	0	0	1
Fryman, 3b	4	0	1	0	1	1
E. Williams, 3b	0	0	0	0	0	0
Fielder, 1b	4	1	2	2	1	0
T. Clark, dh	5	1	1	2	0	2
Nieves, rf	3	0	0	0	2	1
M. Lewis, 2b	2	0	0	0	2	0
Parent, c	4	1	1	1	0	1
A. Cedeno, ss	4	1	1	0	0	1
Totals	34	7	10	7	8	3
SEATTLE	AB	R	H	RBI	BB	SO
Cora, 2b	5	2	2	1	0	0
A. Rodriguez, ss	6	2	2	2	0	1
Griffey Jr., cf	4	3	3	4	1	0
Buhner, dh	5	0	0	0	0	2
Sorrento, 1b	5	1	2	3	0	1
D. Wilson, c	5	2	3	0	0	1
Strange, 3b	5	1	1	0	0	1
Bragg, rf	4	1	2	2	1	0
Amaral, lf	3	1	2	1	2	0
Totals	42	13	17	13	4	6

Detroit	022	300	000 — 7
Seattle	525	001	00X — 13

before and after the game. We didn't talk much, because obviously I had to go to the ballpark. We just talked about how thankful we were and how gracious we really were, and how fortunate I really was. I thanked the Lord. We also spoke after the game, we went out to dinner, and we confirmed everything we had talked about earlier, just how fortunate we really were.

The game . . . I felt like I was flying, I couldn't do anything wrong. I hit a home run, got a couple of hits, made a couple of nice plays. We won the game, it was a great day . . . I don't even remember who I got the hits off of.

The reason that that's my greatest day is because I was out there playing, and that's what I like to do the most. That's what the man upstairs has blessed me with a lot of talent for, and that's what I love to do, and that's what my greatest day was.

My main focus is on winning the World Series, to go out and win as much as possible and put up great numbers every year. You've got to take it one year at a time, you've got to take it one day at a time, and I've done a lot more for my age, but there's a lot more that I need to do.

PETE ROSE

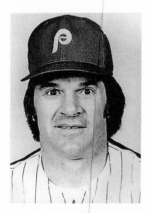

Pete Rose will be remembered for many things: his "Charlie Hustle" reputation, breaking Ty Cobb's all-time career record for major league hits, his relentless drive to win that helped produce titles for both the Cincinnati Reds and the Philadelphia Phillies, and the gambling controversy that tarnished his reputation after his playing days ended. Rose touched on many of those issues as he discussed his greatest days in the game.

I would say most guys' greatest days, I mean the type of guys you're gonna interview, are always gonna have monumental achievements, All-Star games or World Series or things like that. But for almost everybody their greatest day will be their first day in the big leagues.

Mine was probably more special than most, because it was like a boyhood dream come true, playing for the Cincinnati Reds in

Cincinnati. Being from Cincinnati, that was awfully important because of all the tradition Cincinnati has. I remember I was not nervous until right before game time, when a guy from the morning paper came down and asked to take my picture with my family. And that kind of woke me up to the fact that, man, I'm playing in Cincinnati and it's Opening Day.

Then you have the days where you get your first hit, everybody remembers that. It took me a couple of games to get that first hit, a triple off of Bob Friend, in Pittsburgh. And then I don't think you remember your 1,000th hit, or your 1,500th hit, in my case the 3,000th hit, the 4,000th hit, 4,192, and then of course your last hit.

And some of the things I remember off the field, because those are milestones. A lot of guys didn't really go through what I went through as far as the fans kind of being in your corner, the fans liking you, and stuff like that.

In fact, I can sit here and talk all night about 4,192, because until you're involved in a nine-minute standing ovation, you really don't know how to describe it.

It's tough to rate 'em, but obviously the biggest thing that ever happened to me individually was breaking Ty Cobb's record. I knew nothing about how that was gonna feel, because the whole situation was predicated on how the fans were gonna react. I didn't know what kind of a hit it would be, where it would happen, if it would be meaningful to the game, and those different things.

When I got 4,192, it was in the first inning, and I scored a run. I got another hit in that game, a triple, and we won the game, 2–0. I scored both runs. So that was a night you kind of remember for a long time. Plus you throw in the standing ovation; it was just overwhelming. There cannot be anything bigger than that that can happen to you in a baseball uniform. It was probably similar to someone getting sixty-two home runs, or something like that.

I kind of knew . . . I kind of had a good feeling about it, because I had a real good batting practice that night. I remember the night before, and this was the way it was when I was going for the record, I had gone zero for four the night before, I think. I always had a postgame interview, and one writer stood up and said, "You know, I got family I gotta see, and I got some dirty clothes I've gotta put in the laundry. When you gonna get this hit so I can go home?"

He was halfway kidding, but he kind of made me feel bad, and I went out and had a real good batting practice, and it kind of relaxed me. I had had some success against Eric Show in the past, so I knew I was gonna get a base hit. I was seeing the ball real good that night.

I looked for a fastball every pitch. I don't sit on a pitch; I look for a guy's hardest stuff every time he throws the ball, and for ninety-nine out of 100 guys that's a fastball. He threw it down and in, and I hit one of those typical line drives to left-center.

What happened in the middle of that ovation that people didn't understand was really in the course of nine minutes three generations of Pete Rose flashed in front of your eyes: me getting the hit, my son embracing me, and of course me kind of remembering my father, who had passed away in 1970.

And all that happened just because of the ovation. I mean, they come out and they take the base. Then they take the Corvette Marge gave me. That was the only time in my career I was on a baseball diamond and didn't know what to do. It really felt strange.

I was the type . . . it was just like my hitting streak, I was the type of player that relished the limelight, relished the cooperation with the press. I was always the first guy to give an interview if they wanted it. And I was real good at that. I'm the perfect type of guy to pursue records because I'm not gonna be bothered by the press and things like that; it doesn't bother me.

The greatest moment from the hitting streak was when it ended. I enjoyed that a lot, because to be honest with you, that was good for baseball. I made a lot of people a lot of money during that hitting streak, especially in Atlanta, because I remember one time on the next to last day, they had 29,000 people the day of the game walk up and buy tickets. That was a lot.

The World Series highlight would obviously have to be Game 6 from the '75 World Series. Maybe the most exciting game in the history of World Series competition. It was fun to play in, although we lost the game. I usually don't elaborate for any long period of time on games I lost, but that series and that game did a lot for the game of baseball.

Winning the first time, in 1975, sweeping the Yankees in '76 and winning for the second time, those are some things you remember, because no one's ever swept a playoffs and a World Series, and we did it in '76. I don't know if that's good for baseball, sweeping something like that, but it was good for us individually. And '75, after we won for the first time, and I was lucky enough to be the MVP, that was kind of rewarding.

I'll tell you, the most awesome sight I've ever seen in sports was

September 11, 1985

SAN DIEGO	AB	R	H	RBI	CINCINNATI	AB	R	H	RBI
Templeton, ss	4	0	0	0	Milner, cf	5	0	0	0
Royster, 2b	4	0	1	0	Rose, 1b	3	2	2	0
Gwynn, rf	4	0	1	0	Parker, rf	1	0	1	0
Garvey, 1b	4	0	0	0	Esasky, lf	3	0	0	2
Martinez, lf	3	0	0	0	Venable, lf	0	0	0	0
McReynolds, cf	3	0	1	0	Bell, 3b	4	0	1	0
Bochy, c	3	0	1	0	Concepcion, ss	4	0	1	0
Bevacqua, 3b	3	0	1	0	B. Diaz, c	3	0	1	0
Show, p	2	0	0	0	Redus, pr	0	0	0	0
JeDavs, ph	1	0	0	0	VanGorder, c	0	0	0	0
R. L. Jackson, p	0	0	0	0	Oester, 2b	3	0	1	0
Walter, p	0	0	0	0	Browning, p	4	0	1	0
					Franco, p	0	0	0	0
					Power, p	0	0	0	0
Totals	31	0	5	0	Totals	30	2	8	2

San Diego	000	000	000 — 0
Cincinnati	001	000	10X — 2

the post-World Series parade in Philadelphia. I just . . . it was overwhelming, with a million people in the middle of Broad Street, and the parade went out Broad Street to JFK Stadium, and they had 130,000 people waiting out there for us.

Just the enthusiasm of the people. I remember going back there periodically in the winter time to do different events, and the people all had the same expression and the same smile of contentment on their face. They'd just stick their hand out and say, thank you.

It was always going to be different from Cincinnati because that was my home town. It was kind of different in Philadelphia, because they waited ninety-seven years. There were some great players in Philadelphia, but they just didn't have the leadership or the togetherness.

Probably the most important thing was that I always had great support, I had great teammates. I've been very fortunate to play most of my career with the greatest catcher we'll ever see, Johnny Bench. I played with the greatest third baseman, I think, Mike Schmidt, and I played with the greatest second baseman, Joe Morgan.

And then you throw in guys like Tony Perez and Steve Carlton, who's one of the top two or three left-handers in the history of baseball . . . Tom Seaver, I played with him. So I've been around some really select people, and obviously the skipper of my career was a Hall of Fame manager, Sparky Anderson. Those guys made baseball fun for me, so I was always around a fun atmosphere. I've had too many days to really categorize one.

They don't have an award for the biggest accomplishments that I have. That would be the guy who played in more winning games than anybody in the history of baseball, 1,972, that's how many winning games I played in. Because based on 162 games a year, and based on my playing longer than anyone else, I think that probably puts me in the category of the biggest winner in the history of sports. And that's all you try to do is win.

RYNE SANDBERG

Early in the 1997 season, Ryne Sandberg broke the all-time record for career home runs for a second baseman, and the Cubs infielder was a perennial All-Star and Gold Glove winner for much of his career. But Sandberg's greatest day took him back to his salad days, when winning the MVP award led to one of the Cubs' rare postseason appearances.

I think my biggest day in baseball would have to be the night the Cubs clinched the National League Eastern Division flag after not doing so for so many years. It was a night in Pittsburgh, late September, this was '84. It was my first experience going through that. There was such a buildup for months and months, just to get to that . . . the guys that we had on that team . . . I just remember the ball game; the last pitch was from Rick Sutcliffe, and he got Joe Orsulak.

We were competing against the Mets. We had some real good series against them a few weeks before, and the Cardinals, actually, we were trying to fight them off as well, and we were hearing a lot of the talk about how the Mets came back and beat the Cubs in '69. We were talking about that; we heard that type of talk for at least a month before that night, so we were kind of fighting off that.

I think a lot of what had to do with it being so special was just the personalities that we had on the team. Bob Dernier and myself were called the "daily double," hitting one-two. Keith Moreland, Jody Davis, Leon Durham, Sutcliffe and Ron Cey, Bowa, a lot of personalities, and I think a lot of people were watching us, not only Cubs fans, but I think baseball fans were watching us.

That was my third year in the major leagues, and it was really a year where I kind of stepped it up a notch. I was named MVP that year, and I had a big game late June against the Cardinals where I hit two home runs off of Bruce Sutter, that was on national TV. That was a game that a lot of players and a lot of people said really got us momentum and got us heading to what we ended up winning. That game was involved in putting us into first place, and I think we held it from then on, which was a rarity at that time for the Chicago Cubs.

I think we had a six-game lead with about nine games to go, and this was really my first time going through magic numbers, and "Can we do this?" and "Do we have what it takes to do this?" and all this stuff. It was all kind of new to me, and I believe we lost the game the night before. I was a little bit worried, and I said to Rick Sutcliffe, "How we doin' here, do we have a chance to win this?" and he said, "Well, the numbers are in our favor. And by the way, I'm pitching tomorrow night, so we'll do it tomorrow night."

He was very confident, he won the Cy Young that year, going

September 24, 1984

CHICAGO	AB	R	H	RBI	PITTSBURGH	AB	R	H	RBI
Dernier, cf	5	0	0	0	Orsulak, cf	4	1	2	0
Sandberg, 2b	5	2	2	0	Lacy, lf	3	0	0	0
Matthews, lf	2	1	1	1	Ray, 2b	3	0	0	1
Cotto, lf	0	0	0	0	Thompson, 1b	3	0	0	0
Moreland, rf	4	0	2	0	Pena, c	2	0	0	0
Cey, 3b	4	0	2	0	May, c	1	0	0	0
Davis, c	4	0	0	0	Morrison, 3b	3	0	0	0
Durham, 1b	3	0	0	0	Frobel, rf	3	0	0	0
Bowa, ss	4	1	2	0	Wofus, ss	3	0	0	0
Sutcliffe, p	3	0	1	1	McWilliams, p	1	0	0	0
					Page, ph	1	0	0	0
					Tekulve, p	0	0	0	0
					Mazzilli, ph	1	0	0	0
Totals	34	4	10	2	Totals	28	1	2	1

Chicago	111	010	000 — 4
Pittsburgh	000	100	000 — 1

16–1 since coming over from Cleveland. When he said that, I just felt like we were gonna do it tomorrow. So that was the buildup going into the game. There was just a lot of anticipation, a lot of excitement during the game. We got off to a lead. I had a couple of hits and I scored a couple of runs.

I got hits off of Larry McWilliams, a lefty with the Pirates, two doubles. One other thing that came into play was that I was shooting for . . . I needed one more home run and one more triple to join a club of guys who had hit twenty or more in those categories. One of those doubles I might have been able to stretch it into a triple, but there would have been a play at third. With nobody out, however, I decided to settle for a double and think about winning the game . . . that's another thing that kind of stands out in my mind.

All the fans in Three Rivers were for the Cubs, cheering for us, maybe about 8,000, all Cubs fans, above our dugout. When the last out was made all the people came down on the field. That's what I mean. I think that season was wide-stretched across the country. All the Cub fans came out who lived outside of Chicago, and that was very evident there.

I just remember celebrating, and then going inside. Then we came back out, and up on the big screen in Three Rivers Stadium they had cameras outside of Wrigley Field, so we were able to stand outside and watch the streets full of people outside of Wrigley celebrating . . . that was kind of neat.

I don't know how I adjusted to the pressure, really. I think I just looked around and saw what the veterans were doing. We had a lot of veteran guys who had been there before. I was just a rookie, a young guy. I just kind of followed what they were doing. It was such a team effort and a group effort that there wasn't any pressure on any one player. We just went out and had fun and played. It was a great bunch of guys. The veteran players definitely had influence on me and made a difference going down the stretch.

I think that night was much more special because it took six months to get to that one night. It was my first experience with that, so when you work that hard and that long and that night comes and it's one game to clinch and go into the playoffs . . . it really took a lot off of all of our backs. All the history, all the things Cubs teams did years ago, which was all put on our shoulders during that season was just taken away. That was great.

RED SCHOENDIENST

As both a manager and Hall of Fame second baseman, Red Schoendienst has provided more than his share of baseball thrills to several generations of St. Louis Cardinal fans. Schoendienst's greatest day took him back to his first World Series appearance, a memorable showdown between the Cardinals and the Boston Red Sox in 1946.

World Series . . . the first one, always the first one. That was the biggest thing for me, anyway, and I was fortunate enough to be in nine of 'em. The first one's always the big one.

Well, we played the Boston Red Sox. They had the great team, you know, with Dom DiMaggio, Ted Williams, Pesky . . . they had a good ball club, an outstanding ball club. To win seven games, we finally came out on top, and it was a very good series. That was in 1946, so that's one you always remember, playing against guys like Williams.

I guess the last out, which was hit to me, would have to be the biggest moment, and I tossed it to Marion . . . it took a bad hop, and I blocked it with my left shoulder and caught it with my right hand and tossed it to Marion for the third out. The tying run was going across home plate, that was in the ninth inning, the top of the ninth, the tying run was going to second base, and we forced 'em, and the Series was over. That's one big memory I remember.

It was just a big thrill, everything is over and it relaxes you right after. We just had a good time, that's just about it, you know . . . I don't get too excited about anything.

In those days we only had eight clubs, so making the All-Star game, that was always a big thing. I hit a home run in the fourteenth inning of that All-Star game, the first extra inning ball game there was, that was in the old White Sox ballpark. I got in the ball game about the eighth inning or something like that. I was very happy, that was a big thrill. I think it was off of Ted Gray, he was a left-hander. I'm not sure what the pitch was . . . I think it was a cut fastball or a slider.

Again, as manager, it's the first pennant you win. We only had eight teams. It was in 1967, when I was managing the Cardinals. We won the World Series, the pennant and the World Series. I think that's always a big thrill. I could say that as a player I'd been in the World Series and won it, as a manager I'd been in the World Series and won it, and as a coach for the manager I'd won the World Series.

October 15, 1946

BOSTON	AB	R	H	PO	A	E
Moses, rf	4	1	1	1	0	0
Pesky, ss	4	0	1	2	1	0
DiMaggio, cf	3	0	1	0	0	0
Culberson, cf	0	0	0	0	0	0
Williams, lf	4	0	0	3	1	0
York, 1b	4	0	1	10	1	0
Campbell, pr	0	0	0	0	0	0
Doerr, 2b	4	0	2	3	7	0
Higgins, 3b	4	0	0	0	1	0
H. Wagner	2	0	0	4	0	0
Russell, ph	1	1	1	0	0	0
Partee, c	1	0	0	0	0	0
Ferriss, p	2	0	0	0	0	0
Dobson, p	0	0	0	0	1	0
Metkovich, ph	1	1	1	0	0	0
Klinger, p	0	0	0	1	0	0
Johnson, p	0	0	0	0	0	0
McBride, ph	1	0	0	0	0	0
Totals	35	3	8	24	12	0
ST. LOUIS	AB	R	H	PO	A	E
Schoendiest, 2b	4	0	2	2	3	0
Moore, cf	4	0	1	3	0	0
Musial, 1b	3	0	1	6	0	0
Slaughter, rf	3	1	1	4	0	0
Kurowski, 3b	4	1	1	3	1	1
Garagiola, c	3	0	0	4	0	0
Rice, c	1	0	0	0	0	0
Walker, lf	3	1	2	3	0	0
Marion, ss	2	0	0	2	1	0
Dickson, p	3	1	1	0	1	0
Brecheen, p	1	0	0	0	0	0
Totals	31	4	9	27	6	1

Boston	100	000	020 — 3	
St. Louis	010	020	01X — 4	

Other than that, what else can there be, unless you're a general manager and win it?

And you don't think about being in the Hall of Fame until the voting comes, but that was another big thrill . . . I've had about all the big thrills you'd want to have, including playing with Enos Slaughter, Marion, Mays, and all them guys, and playing against the great ballplayers way back, like DiMaggio, Ted Williams, Charlie Keller, some of the other great ones. It was always a thrill no matter what. It's a thrill here today, just to be here and around these young guys.

Going into the Hall of Fame is a big thrill. Once you're in the Hall I guess you can't do much more other than being around the young players today.

I go to the Hall of Fame every year; they let me go. I enjoy it no matter who gets in. I'm glad to see Nellie Fox in this year [1997], along with Tommy Lasorda. Tommy's been a great baseball man. He's been good for the game, and I'm happy that he got in.

Going in . . . it was hot that time, and of course I played with Spahn and Burdette, you know in my days in Milwaukee, and we won over there. The day I was inducted, we were in the building, which was air-conditioned, and the air conditioning broke down, and it was really hot, everybody was sweatin' pretty good.

We were sittin' there, about ready to be introduced, and Spahn was sittin' there and he says, "OK, Red, you've been a hell of a ballplayer, now don't mess up on this one." That was it . . . that's Warren Spahn all over.

OZZIE SMITH

PF SPORTS IMAGES

You could make a solid argument for shortstop Ozzie Smith as perhaps the greatest defensive player ever to take the field, for during his long career with the San Diego Padres and the St. Louis Cardinals, Smith made plays that were inconceivable to most people. But the switch-hitting shortstop's greatest day was also his most memorable offensive moment, when he hit his first major league home run from the left side to take out the Los Angeles Dodgers in Game 5 of the 1985 NLCS.

My greatest day in the game probably had to have been the home run in the playoff against the Dodgers. And I say that simply because at that point people started looking at me as much more than just a defensive player. Up until that point I was noted for my defensive prowess, and anything I did defensively overshadowed anything I did offensively.

So . . . not only in proving to myself, but to other people . . . I'd always felt like I was a much better offensive player than I'd been given credit for, but when you don't hit .300 and you don't hit home runs, people just assume that you can't hit.

I've always taken a lot of pride in all aspects of the game, and that particular day, I think, was my coming out. I think that, first of all, we were down. We had gone out to California, where we hadn't played well all year, and we had lost a couple of games out there. They were always very tough because of their pitching, so we knew that to give ourselves a chance we had to come back to St. Louis and play much better than we had played at any time during our life or that year.

My home run put us in the position of being able to win the pennant. Up until that point, I think everything that I had contributed was really from a defensive standpoint, and I think that everybody would like to be able to say that you contributed from all phases of the game. For me, to be able to help the club in a situation like that was great, and it was a lot of fun, and I think the excitement it created, not only for me but for the fans here in this town, you know, and the announcer I think became noted for the phrase, "Go crazy, folks." I mean, that was just one of the phrases that came out of it that became very popular.

It was a very tough game. I think that Fernando Valenzuela had started for Los Angeles, and I don't know exactly who we started that particular game. But with the score tied I was facing Niedenfeuer, and it was late in the ball game, and there was a lot of tension. So we didn't know exactly who was going to be the person to step up to help us get over the hump.

I guess in many instances what you do is you watch for situations like that when you're able to have a game on the line and you're able to respond. And in that particular instance what I was trying to do was no different than what I had done all year, which was just trying to get myself in scoring position. I'm not a home run hitter, therefore I wasn't swinging for the fence, and one of the things I accomplished that year was my consistency in executing the fundamentals and making sure my approach was consistent.

I was just trying to hit the ball down in the corner and get myself in scoring position. I think Niedenfeuer supplied all the power, and my technique and everything was there. I can remember fouling back a sequence of fastballs up and in, which was the way they tried to pitch me all the time.

So in my learning process and everything I felt like I had become a much better hitter at that time in my career as the year had gone, because that was one of my better offensive years when everything came together for me. I fouled a couple of fastballs straight back, and sure enough, he tried to get me out with a fastball up and in again, and he left it out over the plate, and my technique, it all worked. I applied it and the ball went out of the park.

It was kind of an unbelievable experience for me because it was the first time that I had hit a home run in the big leagues left-handed, and it wasn't something I was trying to do. So it came to me too as a total surprise, and here again it just came from trying to be consistent in my approach, and it worked.

That particular day I can remember everybody waiting at home base for me, and I had a chain around my neck that got broken off. I can remember going down to the press room, and the chanting, people wouldn't leave until I came back out on the field. So all of that excitement, and of course all of the trips going out to L.A., which gave us a chance.

We knew that now, realistically, we had a chance at winning the pennant. We had the only chance we were going to have, because we had to sweep, which we were able to do. We went out, and Jack landed the knockout punch in the sixth game.

I think that what it did is that it probably said to the Dodgers that destiny was on our side, because the blow came from one of the most unlikely sources. And when that happens, sometimes, you know, there are messages being sent. I think that it probably did have its effect, and it lifted us at the same time it dropped them an octave.

When you go to your opponents backyard and have to play, it's still not easy. We knew it wasn't going to be easy, because it was always so tough for us to win out there during the course of the season. But here again, now it all boiled down to one game, and we were ready for the challenge.

The offensive transition was really just a learning process. I had no formal teaching as far as offense was concerned. I could always run, but I said, wow, I can do it. For me, I had to learn to hit against the likes of the Nolan Ryans and the J. R. Richards and the Jerry Koosmans and the Steve Carltons and Tom Seavers. That's not an easy task for anyone. That's not an easy task for guys who come here and have great offensive ability.

When you don't possess a lot of power, you're a guy who is a singles hitter, that's not an easy thing to do. I couldn't come in the big leagues and stand it on its ear from an offensive standpoint as some guys have been able to do. I was here because of my defensive prowess, and that continued, but that did not stop my learning process or my willingness to continue to work to be the very best I could be from an offensive standpoint.

I knew that being as good as I was from a defensive standpoint there was no reason for me, if I achieved some kind of understanding of what I was trying to accomplish from an offensive standpoint there was no reason for me not to be able to do that. And that's exactly what I did. I just went to work at learning the art of hitting, which I had had no formal teaching for up until that point, and I just learned, that's all.

I think the one person who probably spent the most time with me was Dave Ricketts, who would go down to the cage with me. But here again, he allowed me the freedom to find myself, and I think that it's very important to be able to find yourself, because no matter who it is you work with they can't go to the plate with you.

He learned the things I was trying to do. We talked about it a lot, and I think that that was probably the most important thing, was the understanding of what it was you were trying to accomplish and what was meant by swinging down through the ball, and keeping the ball out of the air, and things like that. So I think the mental aspect of it was what was important, and once you understand it mentally, then the physical part becomes a little bit easier.

I don't know about my greatest day defensively. I did so many things defensively that it's very hard to pick a day. There are probably a lot of things that I have forgotten about that I was able to accomplish from a defensive standpoint, and I'd have to sit and go over tapes to see just what some of the things are that I have forgotten about.

For me, it really was, as I played, a situation where I really didn't appreciate my accomplishments while I played, and it wasn't until after I got done that I started appreciating what I was able to accomplish over nineteen years.

Theoretically, I guess going into the Hall of Fame could be my

October 14, 1985

LOS ANGELES	AB	R	H	RBI	ST. LOUIS	AB	R	H	RBI
Duncan, ss	3	0	0	0	McGee, cf	3	1	0	0
Landreaux, cf	4	1	2	0	O. Smith, ss	3	2	1	1
Guerrero, lf	4	0	0	0	Herr, 2b	4	0	1	2
Madlock, 3b	4	1	1	2	J. Clark, 1b	3	0	1	0
Marshall, rf	3	0	0	0	Cedeno, rf	3	0	0	0
Scioscia, c	2	0	1	0	Landrum, lf	3	0	0	0
Brock, 1b	1	0	0	0	Pendleton, 3b	4	0	1	0
Cabell, 1b	3	0	1	0	Porter, c	2	0	0	0
Niedenfuer, p	0	0	0	0	Forsch, p	0	0	0	0
Sax, 2b	3	0	0	0	Dayley, p	2	0	1	0
Valenzuela, p	3	0	0	0	Worrell, p	0	0	0	0
Matuszek, ph	0	0	0	0	B. Harper, ph	1	0	0	0
					Lahti, p	0	0	0	0
Totals	30	2	5	2	Totals	28	3	5	3

```
Los Angeles   000   200   000 — 2
St. Louis     200   000   001 — 1
```

greatest day or my greatest accomplishment. But right now, people talk about the Hall a lot, and they ask me what I think about it. Basically, I try not to give too much thought to it, but I think what happens is that a lot of people who do the voting for the Hall are people that may have forgotten what it was that you accomplished. And sometimes, without being able to see the person play every day, they lose some of the impact of what a person was able to achieve.

As I sit down and look at it now, I listen to games and I do some color for games, and I hear people talk about what a good play that was and so forth and so on, and the things that I see as great plays today were things that were very commonplace for me, each and every day out.

I think that as you go, if you don't have a chance to see a person . . . it takes a big impact to be able to make people remember that long. So I think that as I played, people really got a chance to see me do some fantastic things that, as we get closer to the Hall of Fame, I think some of those things may be forgotten unless those tapes are put in front of people.

It's just a natural thing . . . out of sight, out of mind.

I want to be remembered for the things that I was able to accomplish. I think it really doesn't matter to other people how well you did offensively, because I think my going in is going to be predicated on what a defensive player I was, or on how I changed the game from a defensive standpoint.

I want to be known as a well-rounded player. I think there's no player that wants to be noted as a one-dimensional player, and I'm no different as far as that's concerned. I'd like to think that I was much more that just a defensive player.

JOHN SMOLTZ

Before he won the Cy Young Award in 1996, Atlanta Braves pitcher John Smoltz put together one of the most unusual seasons in baseball history during the Braves drive to their first National League pennant and their memorable World Series battle against the Minnesota Twins in 1991. Smoltz talked about his comeback and turnaround in the context of his greatest day.

I would just say it's more like my greatest journey, the second half of '91, where I persevered by getting mentally back on track. I persevered from a 2–11 first half, where everyone was pretty much having me sent down, to going 12–2 and being virtually unbeatable in the second half, and pitching the three most important games in Atlanta Braves history at the time, the clincher, the season clincher, the seventh-game clincher, and then the seventh game of the World Series.

The way it worked out, ultimately it was the greatest ride that anyone could be given, from 2–11. . . . If somebody had told me I would have pitched those games, I would have said, "You're crazy, you need to be put in a home." So it was truly . . . it was almost like a mission. I was . . . I just felt like I was supposed to be there at the end, you know?

I think they will always be remembered as truly the three best games I ever pitched. There're games like this past year, Game 5, which we didn't win, but it was one of the best games given the situation and conditions. In time, I think, because we didn't win it, it takes a little bit of the glamor away from '91, but to go from last to first, to shock the world, as a player it'll never be duplicated.

I remember the first game after the All-Star break. I guess you could consider that the turning point, because that was gonna dictate whether or not I was gonna go down in the bullpen. . . . You know, I turned around some of the things, the misfortunes that I had in the first half. I turned them around into a positive in that game, and turned it all around, and I found the winning streak.

It was against the St. Louis Cardinals. I remember first and second, one out, three and one count in the very first inning. I'd been having a lot of trouble with getting out of jams. Gerald Perry hit a

October 17, 1991

ATLANTA	AB	R	H	RBI	PITTSBURGH	AB	R	H	RBI
Smith, lf	3	1	0	0	Merced, 1b	4	0	1	0
Mitchell, lf	1	0	0	0	Bell, ss	4	0	2	0
Pendleton, 3b	5	1	1	0	Van Slyke, cf	4	0	0	0
Gant, cf	3	1	1	1	Bonilla, rf	4	0	1	0
Justice, rf	3	0	0	0	Bonds, lf	4	0	1	0
Hunter, 1b	4	1	2	3	Buechele, 3b	4	0	0	0
Olson, c	3	0	1	0	LaValliere, c	3	0	1	0
Lemke, 2b	3	0	0	0	Lind, 2b	4	0	0	0
Belliard, ss	3	0	1	0	Smiley, p	0	0	0	0
Smoltz, p	2	0	0	0	Walk, p	1	0	0	0
					Espy, ph	1	0	0	0
					Mason, p	0	0	0	0
					Wilkerson, ph	1	0	0	0
					Belinda, p	0	0	0	0
Totals	30	4	6	4	Totals	34	0	6	0

Atlanta	300	010	000 — 4
Pittsburgh	000	000	000 — 0

ATLANTA	IP	H	R	ER	BB	SO
Smoltz, W	9	8	0	0	1	8

PITTSBURGH	IP	H	R	ER	BB	SO
Smiley, L	0.2	3	3	3	1	1
Walk	4.1	2	1	1	3	3
Mason	2	1	0	0	1	0
Belinda	2	0	0	0	2	2

fly ball out to center, and I got out of the inning, and I went on to win the game. It just really rejuvenated all my confidence.

As for the mechanical adjustments that I had to make, physically I was still pitching the same, there was absolutely nothing I did different. Mentally, I was able to make some adjustments, like I spoke of, get out of trouble, let that inning go, let some things go that were causing me a little trouble in those innings, 'cause I was in a lot of games, I just couldn't get out of a certain inning. The second half I was mentally tough; I felt like there was no one who was gonna beat me.

It's tough to pick out one of the postseason games: Any time you get to the World Series is probably the most memorable, so Game 7 of the NLCS when I shut out the Pirates was big. That's the time you feel the most pressure.

You know, we were given four runs or three runs early, and that was the most pressure I felt, because once you're given runs early, it's yours to protect. And I was able to pitch nine innings and a complete game. I think my most memorable game, though, would be pitching against Jack Morris in the seventh game of the 1991 World Series and not giving up a run and still not winning.

The awards are all nice, but the World Series rings are what we play for, and that's truly what I like. I'd almost rather not accomplish anything and be part of a world championship, if that makes sense, because that's pretty much what you're trying to do.

It was neat, because we [the pitchers] were the reason . . . well, I shouldn't say that, we started when we were terrible and we got to the point where we were pretty darned good. You know, the pitching has definitely been a big part of this organization, hopefully it will continue. It's been a great journey, one that didn't always start out good, and we went from worst to first, and we became the elite pitching staff, and it's nice to try to continue that.

It seems like just yesterday that we struggled so badly, and that keeps humility, it keeps you from ever thinking that . . . you know, we've been through the worst. It helps for when you're on top, because you never want to go back, and it means making a lot of adjustments, a lot of hard work. It's just that once you've been there and you appreciate it and you know how to handle it, you can overcome anything.

Once you've always had success and then failure comes after having a ton of success, it's hard to take.

TERRY STEINBACH

An excellent defensive catcher and a solid hitter with a knack for getting it done in the clutch, Terry Steinbach was one of the unsung heroes on the great Oakland A's clubs of the late 1980s who later went on to play for the Minnesota Twins. A perennial All Star early in his career, Steinbach's greatest day took him back to his first All-Star game, when he was a controversial choice to start for the American League.

The greatest day in baseball for me was the '88 All-Star game. It was filled with controversy—I was hitting .214 at the time. I'd like to think that I was elected by the fans for the previous year, '87, which was my rookie year. It was also McGwire's rookie year. I hit sixteen home runs as a rookie, Mac had forty-nine, so it kind of got overshadowed, but the A's were in the process of coming to a turning point. We were getting a lot of attention and we were getting more media coverage, the attendance in the Coliseum was starting to pick up.

It was a real positive note to take it into '88, but I got off to a slow start. I had an injury that sidelined me for a few weeks; I got hit with a ball in the eye, and I had to have surgery in the eye socket. They had to restructure it; I fractured the orbit. I picked it up from there, but I could never really get it going.

It was the sophomore jinx—you hear a lot of people talk about it. It was a classic sophomore streak that I had: you have a solid rookie year, you come back the next year and get off to a slow start, so I had to change something. Instead of just saying that you got off to a slow start and saying, "Stay with what you got, stay with what got you here," which is something I think you learn in games by experience, in looking back now, I thought I had to change something and I did.

At that time we had a veteran staff, and Tony [LaRussa] and the pitchers, they were tremendous, they drilled in me and stressed in me, being a converted third baseman, that now that I was a catcher my number one job was catching. They pretty much beat it into me, that if I had an 0-fer or if you take a bad at-bat, you pretty much have to leave it here in the dugout and go back out there; catching's gotta be your number one job.

Lachemann was in on that group, and over the course of time you find out that if you're not hitting you have to make sure you work with your pitcher, to make sure you give him every opportunity to succeed.

It wasn't until a week before the All-Star break, I'd been listening to a lot of people, friends, hitting coaches, and I just couldn't find it [my hitting stroke]. Finally I made my own decision, I just said, "Look, if I'm gonna go down in this game I'm gonna go down my way." I've always been a gap-to-gap kind of guy, and so I started doing some drills that I remembered doing in the minors.

I took it into Detroit and had a couple of home runs in that game, and then I really started to hit the ball. My attitude going in was to deal with the whole All-Star game controversy by asking myself, "Are the best players going?" I don't even remember who the other catcher was, for some reason I want to say it was Tim Laudner. He was the guy who wound up backing me up, maybe the other guy was Sandy Alomar. It wasn't so much that they were upset that it was me going in, they were upset that it was a person hitting .214 going in. It could have been at any position.

The controversy was around whether it was the best guy who was going, or whether it was a popularity contest. At that time we had big numbers in Oakland, attendance at the Coliseum was going up, we had big ballot pushing. Even watching it coming up through the minor leagues, you don't want to take it out of the people's hands, because the people say it's their game, and I believe that. But I also wish that it wasn't the case that the best players that particular year are not always going. That's a thing you can debate forever.

The attitude toward the media was that I was happy to be there, I'm gonna have a good time, say whatever you want about me, I don't have control of this. It was intimidating to a degree, but I also felt that based on '87, and even some of '88, that I was up-and-coming, and people were seeing me play because of the TV coverage that we were getting, and I felt that my peers knew. Your teammates and your opposition, they know what kind of player you are, and that you might be having a bad year, and I can live with that.

But more importantly, we went from Detroit into Cincinnati and I had a real good All-Star game. I hit a home run and a sac fly. The game itself was a lot of fun. I was very nervous, as you can imagine, and it was kind of intimidating walking around with the high-profile players, but once I got between the white lines it was kind of like you get in your own environment again.

The first at-bat I hit the home run. It was off Gooden, and I think I hit a high fastball and missed, I thought it was maybe 0–2 or 1–2 when I hit the home run. It was a fastball that was up, a high fastball, and as soon as I hit it I knew I hit it all right, but I'd never played in Cincinnati, and I didn't know if it had enough to get out, and it just made it.

I was just trying not to embarrass myself. I wasn't thinking about hitting a home run to get the MVP or anything like that. I was looking for a fastball, with Gooden by all means I was looking fastball. When you've never faced a guy you really don't know what kind of a pitch you can handle. I guess if anything you try not to chase the bad fastball that you can't handle. You try and lay off the high one and see if he'll give you something you can handle.

I had another at-bat where we had bases loaded, I don't know if it was tied 1–1 or if it was 1–0. At that point it was just concentrating on hitting the baseball, bases loaded, less than two out, make sure you get a ball up in the zone that you can get out into the outfield and get that sac fly. I got a real good pitch to hit, if I'd taken a more aggressive swing at it I maybe could have hit it better than I did. It was off of Nipper, and I went out and got the fly ball.

I know the one guy I caught was Viola, he had a real good year in '87. It was really nice, because he was very friendly, very easygoing, very nice to work with. He's the one that sticks out in my mind the most. I know the next year in '89 I caught Nolan, which was a lot of fun.

The reaction I got was very supportive. Mac was real supportive. I remember him coming up to me and I almost felt like he was more excited than I was. I had no idea of the whole process of All-Star MVP selection, and Mac came up to me and said, "Hey, you won the MVP," and I was like, "What do you mean?" And then once they announced it I remembered him. It was almost like a team, the tremendous amount of encouragement I got, guys you'd been with forever.

That carried through the whole time there, and these guys are your opposition ninety-nine percent of the time, and I wouldn't say you're expecting animosity, but I really didn't feel like there would be this huge sense of camaraderie in your first game. There were all these American League guys there, saying, "Hey, this is the National League, let's go out and beat 'em," and I was just trying to get through the game. Odd isn't quite the word, but it was a bit peculiar. I had the opportunity to be in a few more games, and that's just how it is. That was a nice eye-opener for me.

Having that World Series ring would definitely be more of an accomplishment, though. There's no doubt about it, that's 162 games with twenty-five guys of going through the battle, going through the war, going through the grind of the whole season. Where the All-Star game is "Let's show up, let's have a good time, thank you very much, you're gone," and it seems to be more of an individual thing. It's throwing a bunch of guys out there and you all show your individual talents.

Going to the World Series is "Let's show 'em what our team is." It's much more of a team concept. I would still tend to think that winning the World Series is better overall, but for that one particular moment, you could say that one game is it.

The more time that elapses the more it adds meaning to it. Your kids start getting older, and they start asking questions about the All-Star game, and you can say, "Well, I was in a few of those games," and they just say, "Really?" And then they just pull out the media guide for that game for that event and they see who the players were.

I got the ball and the bat . . . I think Cooperstown took it. It's kind of ironic because I think I used a bat in that game that had my name on it, but it was spelled with a "k" instead of a "ch." It kind of fit with the whole Cinderella story—this guy hitting .214, who the hell is he? And he's got a bat with his name spelled wrong.

It definitely ranks up there on the resume and has its special place, and a special feeling. But I still think I would put it second to the World Series. That's the ultimate feeling, the ultimate sigh of relief and accomplishment is the final out of a World Series game. It's like . . . you set a goal in spring training, you work toward that goal, you grind the 162 out to get to the playoffs, and then you get to the World Series, and then you win. That last out, it's like closure, it's like we're there. And you get an opportunity to look at other established players, Hall of Famers, that never had that chance, never had a World Series ring.

It's so hard to compare them because there's that team thing that you spend six months doing, and then there's that one day. When it takes six months to get something as opposed to one day, you've gotta work a lot harder for a lot longer. There's a lot more trials and tribulations that you go through. Whereas with that one particular day, it could almost be a fluke, any one particular player on that one particular day could almost accomplish that. Anybody could have that one day where they're just on top of the baseball.

DARRYL STRAWBERRY

Few players get to win a World Series twice in New York, playing for different teams each time, but home-run hitting outfielder Darryl Strawberry was an unusual player right from the get go. In 1986, "Straw" helped lead the Mets to victory over the Boston Red Sox in one of the game's great World Series. Ten years later, Strawberry played a pivotal role in the Yankees win over the Atlanta Braves in yet another memorable, dramatic climax to a great baseball season.

Well, yeah, of course, winning last year, you can't really compare that to too many things, you know? Winning another championship in New York, ten years . . . 1986 to 1996. To be able to accomplish that two times in one place is a memory that will stick with me for the rest of my life.

I think it probably was a little bit greater for me this time around . . . to be able to overcome all the odds, and to be able to get back out and be a part of another championship ball club when no one thought you could do it. That's probably going to turn out to be one of the greatest memories of all time.

You get a little older, and you get a little wiser about life, and you basically just take it one day at a time and you just learn that something is possible. By being young, you get excited by a lot of things, but as you get older you don't get so excited. You get to a point where you can accept it and deal with it and go about your business.

It was actually a fine time. It worked out extremely well, me being a role player. You realize when you're a team, everybody plays a big part. Everybody has to go out and do their part, and for me to be in that situation, I was truly thankful.

From the pennant drive we had last year, I think the greatest moment about that was that it was the whole team concept . . . we all stuck together. We lost the first two games, and everybody thought we were done, and we went down to Atlanta, and we played like we knew we were capable of playing.

To come back and win the whole thing, just the drive to make you believe in coming back and wanting to win again, no question about it. That's the approach that you have to have.

The greatest day was the parade . . . riding down Broadway, having three million fans in New York cheer for something you accomplished. It was just amazing, to see so many people out, and to see how the city embraced the ballplayers . . . that was a great feeling.

FRANK THOMAS

The confrontation between pitcher and hitter will always define the game, but it's the battle between sluggers that the fans come out to see. The day before the 1995 All-Star game at The Ballpark in Arlington in Texas, Frank Thomas and Albert Belle of the Cleveland Indians gave the fans a special treat, a see-saw battle in the pregame home run derby that Thomas finally won with a mammoth shot, foreshadowing the home run that Thomas would hit the next day to help lead the American League to victory.

Actually, I'd probably have to look at two days. First, there's the home run derby in the All-Star game in Texas. I remember the competition was really out there that day. We really wanted to win. It was very hot, and I barely edged out Albert Belle in the home run contest, so that was a good day. And then the following day, I hit a home run to give us the lead, I think it was off of John Smiley, and it gave us a 2–0 lead.

That's probably my best day, I think . . . I mean, I've had better days, but as far as the world watching and being part of an All-Star game, that would be my greatest day. It was just one of those days, everything clicked for those two days. The world was watching and I was winning a home run hitting contest and I hit a home run in the All-Star game. It was a beautiful thing, you couldn't ask for anything more out of an All-Star game or just out of any game.

July 11, 1995

NATIONAL LEAGUE	AB	R	H	RBI	AMERICAN LEAGUE	AB	R	H	RBI
Dykstra, cf	2	0	0	0	Lofton, cf	3	0	0	0
Sosa, cf	1	0	0	0	Edmonds, ph–cf	1	0	0	0
Gwynn, rf	2	0	0	0	Baerga, 2b	3	1	3	0
Sanders, rf	1	0	0	0	Alomar, pr–2b	1	0	0	0
Mondesi, rf	1	0	0	0	E. Martinez, dh	3	0	0	0
Bonds, lf	3	0	0	0	T. Martinez, ph	1	0	1	0
Bichette, lf	1	0	0	0	Thomas, 1b	2	1	1	2
Piazza, c	3	1	1	1	Vaughn, 1b	2	0	0	0
Daulton, c	0	0	0	0	Belle, lf	3	0	0	0
McGriff, 1b	3	0	0	0	O'Neill, lf	1	0	0	0
Grace, 1b	0	0	0	0	Ripken, ss	3	0	2	0
Gant, dh	2	0	0	0	DiSarcina, pr–ss	1	0	0	0
Conine, ph	1	1	1	1	Boggs, 3b	2	0	1	0
Larkin, ss	3	0	0	0	Seitzer, ph–3b	2	0	0	0
Offerman, ss	0	0	0	0	Puckett, rf	2	0	0	0
Castilla, 3b	2	0	0	0	Ramirez, ph–rf	0	0	0	0
Bonilla, 3b	1	0	0	0	Rodriguez, c	3	0	0	0
Biggio, 2b	2	1	1	1	Stanley, c	1	0	0	0
Morandini, 2b	1	0	0	0	Johnson, p	0	0	0	0
Nomo, p	0	0	0	0	Appier, p	0	0	0	0
Smiley, p	0	0	0	0	D. Martinez, p	0	0	0	0
Green, p	0	0	0	0	Rogers, p	0	0	0	0
Neagle, p	0	0	0	0	Ontiveros, p	0	0	0	0
Perez, p	0	0	0	0	Wells, p	0	0	0	0
Slocumb, p	0	0	0	0	Mesa, p	0	0	0	0
Henke, p	0	0	0	0					
Myers, p	0	0	0	0					
Totals	29	3	3	3	Totals	34	2	8	2

```
National League   000   001   110 — 3
American League   000   200   000 — 2
```

As a kid you always dream of playing in an All-Star game, and then to win the home run hitting contest and then hit a home run in the game when the world was watching, I think that that was my greatest day.

At first everyone was just having fun, hittin' the ball pretty far and everything, but as we made it into the second round it began to get a little more serious. Everyone wanted that nice trophy, so once everybody went around, I won. But as an individual day, that was my day, everything was up.

I think those things happen when you don't try. You know, in a home run hitting contest you try to hit, and in the All-Star game you're definitely not trying to hit a home run and you're on national TV and everything like that. I just wanted to hit the ball hard, and it seemed to work out, and that's when those things happen for you.

It was fun . . . you've got the best players there, or the majority of the best players there, and they all crowded around to hear what was going on. They were raggin' me and giving me a hard time, trying to make me lose my focus a little bit, but it wasn't happening. Guys were really locked in.

Albert didn't say much, we were just competing. I barely beat him. I beat him by one home run, so . . . those things happen.

The awards are great, but I really don't look back at 'em. I just try to keep on developing that focus, because if you start looking back at what you've done, that's when you're gonna start to be in trouble. I just try and stay focused and get the most out of my ability that I possibly can, to keep driving forward and build what I've done day-to-day up until that moment.

I look back at the end of the season and say, well, this is what I did in an individual year, and that's over. Nothing you can do, because that's over, you've gotta come back and help the team next year. Once you set high standards, you've gotta continue to do it, because there's a bit of a letdown if you don't. So with me, staying focused and not worrying about what happened is up my alley, because I have no choice.

Individually, 1993 was the biggest team accomplishment because we just played well the entire season, and a lot of people didn't pick us that year, but we showed the kind of talent we had, and we made everything happen and we won the division. We made it to the playoffs, and we were disappointed because we lost to Toronto, but those things happen. We gave it our best, but unfortunately we lost Game 6. I think that if we had won that game we would have got there.

I remember Kansas City was a game-and-a-half ahead of us, and I hit a two-run home run in the ninth inning off of Jeff Montgomery to hold those guys off, bumping the lead back to two-and-a-half games. That was a big point in the season for us, because we went on a seven-game winning streak right after that to eliminate those guys. It was in Chicago, it was one of those things that happened, and we were happy.

I think the first game really hurt us in the playoffs. We left twelve runners on base in scoring position, and we didn't score but three runs. That really hurt us, because we had a chance to put up a big lead in the first game, but we missed out on our opportunities. We had a strikeout with the bases loaded with one out and another double play with one out and men at first and third. We had second and third with no outs and didn't score.

Those things add up. We just didn't accomplish anything in the playoffs. There was a lot of pressure, and I think a lot of guys let themselves down, not as a team, but they let themselves down. The focus was on us, and I think if we'd won that first game we had a chance to win the series.

I don't have much time to think back on what happened, because I just try to go out and do my best every day. I just don't think that way. People say to me, "Well, how do you keep your focus?" That's how I do it. I put all that stuff behind me. If I go deep or hit a double, all those other things that are supposed to happen, it's because I worked so hard for it.

But once it's over it's over. I don't sit there and gloat over a home run for four or five innings. Once I hit one it's over.

I think the five category thing I've been working on for the last five or six years or so is the only record I think about—over twenty home runs, over .300, over 100 RBIs, over 100 walks, over 100 runs scored. It's very important because it's never been done before, and I'm closing in on it again this year, and I take pride in that. That's an accomplishment, it's tough to do that every year. I'm closing in on my sixth straight season of it, so I take a lot of pride in that.

LUIS TIANT

One of the great showmen ever to take the mound, Luis Tiant broke into the major leagues in the mid '60s with the Cleveland Indians, and he will forever be remembered for his great years with the Boston Red Sox in the 1970s and his unforgettable performance in the 1975 World Series against the Cincinnati Reds. But Tiant's other greatest day was a memorable family moment when his parents finally made it to the United States seventeen years after Tiant left Cuba to seek a major league career.

I think my greatest day in baseball was . . . the first was my debut in the big leagues in 1964. I came up from Portland, then I opened the season. My first game was my debut against the Yankees. I shut 'em out 3–0, striking out eleven guys. I tied a record for a rookie in my first start in the big leagues. I think that's my top one.

Then it would be coming to the World Series, bringing my father and mother here. I had not seen my father for seventeen years. I think it was my biggest feeling in that particular way, you know, you're missing your parents, you don't know if you're gonna see them again, and then they come, and that was the greatest thing that happened for me, my family, we were all together. And they lived to see me pitch in the major leagues.

In 1964, when I came into the big leagues, my debut was during a doubleheader at Yankee Stadium. Sam McDowell pitched the first game, and we lost. I started the second game, and Yogi Berra, he used to say, "I know him," he had seen my father pitch, too.

And then, by the sixth inning it was a tie ball game, and in the dugout they were saying, "Keep it close, we'll get it, we'll get it." I was pitching against Whitey Ford. And then in the fifth inning, I went in to change my shirt, and then I came back and I finished the game. Like I said, it was the highest point in my career, because when you're starting for the first time, and you do good, that's great, that's a push, a big push.

If you do bad, then maybe that's the last game you pitch. You may lose confidence, and say, "What happened, what'd I do here," things like that. I won that game, and I think that was the biggest push I could have had, especially pitching against Whitey Ford. That was the last year the Yankees won after so many years in a row. They had the catcher, Elston Howard, Tommy Tresh, Tony Kubek, Richardson, and Mickey was there, but he didn't play that game. He had played the first game. Maris was there, he played . . . they had a great team.

Plus I was pitching against Whitey, I think that was one of his last years in the big leagues. He won fourteen or fifteen games that year, so he was still throwing the ball good. That was a good feeling, being a youngster and making my debut against the Yankees. You're kind of nervous in the beginning, in that first inning. They had a big crowd that day, a lot of people from my country, a lot of Cuban people were in the ballpark, people I knew from my childhood. All around it was a great evening for me. Winning boosted my confidence.

I think my greatest day in the World Series was in the first game when I pitched against Cincinnati in 1975, and I shut 'em out. Everybody knows the kind of team they used to have, from the first to the last hitter they were good, that's why they were called the Big Red Machine. They hit home runs, and their pitching was pretty decent. I was facing the left-hander they used to have as the pitching coach over there, Gullett. I beat him both times. He was having a good year that year; I think he won 18 games, something like that.

All around, that's what everybody was talking about . . . they were the best team. But I know from what I'd seen that we had a good team, too. We had Carl Yazstremski, Carlton Fisk, Denny Doyle, Rico Petrocelli, Freddie Lynn, a good team. I had seen them all year, but everybody was talking about the Red Machine, and we were the underdogs.

I didn't feel that way when I was facing them. I said, "Hey, they've got to hit it, we've got to hit it, it's going to be between the pitchers, our pitchers against their pitchers." If you don't make mistakes then you've got a chance to get them out, and that's what I did. I was lucky. I had pretty good control and they didn't know me that well because I'd never pitched over there—they'd never seen me. I think I had a chance to do my thing. I got a big hit and got lucky and beat them.

Bench, Pete Rose, Griffey, Concepcion, Tony Perez . . . forget about it, they really had a good team. You look at the way they played. They were a more mature team. Our guys were younger, Freddie Lynn, Jim Rice, Cooper . . . young kids who had just come into the league. I didn't know if they were as good as the Cincinnati players, but they were good.

We played good games . . . they scored, we scored, and that's why to me it was the greatest World Series. They'd score four, we'd come back and score five, we'd score three, they'd come back and score four. Everybody came in every inning, it was very emotional, wondering what was gonna happen, they're gonna score, we're gonna score . . . the whole game, every game we played was like that. It was really exciting.

But to me, bringing my parents over, that was everything, after seventeen years without seeing my parents. The situation was that we had a chance to get them out, but there were papers. They were in Cuba, and they weren't letting Cubans come over here. And then you have to come over in the boats, and they were too old for that.

Then the senator from Massachusetts did the paperwork and he talked to a general about the possibility of going to Cuba and talking to Castro. He sent a letter to the general for Castro to see asking if they could bring my parents out. And he said, "Yeah, they can go if they want to go, and they can stay if they want to stay."

It was during the season. I was in California when they come here. They arrived in Mexico City . . . I couldn't wait. Three days after they came back, they arrived in Massachusetts. I went to the airport, I picked them up . . . I cried. My mother, she was happy. My mother was a strong woman, and she said, "You should be happy," and I said, "That's why I cry."

I didn't want to see . . . it surprised me, because I thought they'd be in worse condition, but they were in pretty good shape, both of them. We hugged, and I walked them through the airport—all the stamina they had, and they cried.

The first game they saw was against the California Angels. I didn't do too good. I lost that game. My father was mad at me. I threw a home run ball. He was really mad. He said, "You say you're a pitcher, you're not a pitcher. You can't pitch, the guy hit a home run." I said, "Hey, that's only one game." You know how the old guys are.

The next time I pitched he saw me win. I beat Cleveland, back at home. I pitched a good game, went nine innings, and won 3–1. After a while, we sat down and we talked, and he used to tell me how good the people treated him in Boston. He couldn't believe it. People were nice to him. They even brought bats for him to autograph, and I said, "Well, that's how you see that people love you." He was really happy.

My parents, they came over in '75 . . . and in '76, they died. They saw the World Series game in '75. At their funeral I saw a lot of my friends, the people that I had known as kids, and they told me what a great guy he was. They both died, but there might be a reason . . . there was one day difference. We had to bury them the same day. They're in Massachusetts, in a cemetery in Milton. I go there three times a year to see the grave site, clean it up, bring them flowers.

JOE TORRE

Few players or managers have ever had a more memorable World Series than Joe Torre did in 1996. With his brother Frank, a former major league player himself, in a Manhattan hospital awaiting a heart transplant, the Yankee manager led his underdog club into the 1996 World Series against the Atlanta Braves. After losing the first two games in New York, the Yankees went to Atlanta and won three straight, setting the stage for Game 6 in New York. The following spring the for-mer Brave and St. Louis Cardinal great talked about that game, and also about his most memorable games as a player.

It had to be Game 6 in 1996 . . . it had to be. I mean, I started the day, all during the postseason games Reggie Jackson was pretty much with me every day, and he said, "You're surprisingly calm." And I was calm during the whole postseason.

Game 6 came, and I was a nervous wreck. I said, "Reggie, you finally got your wish . . . I'm scared to death." You're at a point now where you can't do anything anymore. You write the line-up down, but it's a very helpless feeling to sit there. You've got Jimmy Key going; you feel good about that. If you need it, you have Game 7 with David Cone going; you feel good about that. You don't want Game 7, you want Game 6.

It was as exciting as it gets. The next most exciting, probably the one closest to that, was Game 5 when we clinched it against Baltimore in the playoffs.

My perspective on it hasn't changed since it happened . . . it's every bit as emotional right now as it was last October. I don't know how many things came to mind when Charlie Hayes squeezed that last pop-up . . . my brother getting a new heart the day before, why is this all happening? Why all of a sudden should it be this good?

You never look back . . . although I did say to myself when you watch other guys celebrate, other people win big games, "Why not me once in a while?" Although you never verbalize that, there are so many people, so many bad things happened in my life in com-parison. But when everything happened last year the way it hap-pened, it was so emotional. I'll watch and listen to a replay, call the

Yankee offices and hear the broadcast, and I'll get choked up listening to that stuff.

I made appearances all winter, and when I watch Charlie Hayes or Girardi's triple, I start welling up in the eyes. It was pretty impressive, and it always will be. It's something that can never be taken away from me.

From the seventh inning on you start counting outs . . . nine outs to go. And it really made that very easy. You've got it down to three, and John Wetteland came in, and I knew it wasn't going to be . . . we had a two-run lead, but I knew they were gonna have men on base by the time this thing got through, because John did that all year.

But I trusted John. He made a quality pitch to Lemke, after making a quality pitch right before that on the 3–2 count. And getting the pop-up . . . from my vantage point on the bench, I knew it was in play. That was pretty incredible.

I think back to John Wetteland . . . I think back to Game 5 against Baltimore, and it looked like he stumbled on the mound in the ninth inning. And I asked the umpire, I said, "Let's go out and talk to him. I think he may have hurt himself." I went out there, and I said, "John, are you all right?" And he looked at me right in the eye and he said, "I'm just not letting the ball go."

So honest . . . I think that's what the signature of our team was last year. He was so open and honest. And I couldn't obviously say, "Well, let it go," because that would mean I would be charged with a trip at that point in time, so I said, "John, if you're foot's alright, you'll be fine." And I walked away.

I have a special warmth for John Wetteland, and I called him on Christmas day just to tell him, again and again, that he renewed my faith in the ballplayer. Because in spite of not being happy for a time last year, he was very professional, and I always appreciate that.

My greatest day as a player . . . well, you know when I led the league in hitting in '71, that was a start to finish thing. There was no one day where you could say it got me over the hump. I won the thing by twenty points or whatever it was.

As a player, the one at-bat . . . well, there were two at-bats. The one I think was in '71 against the Braves, my old team that I really didn't do well against. We were losing by two runs on Bat Night in St. Louis, and Cecil Upshaw was the pitcher. With nobody out, bases loaded, Ted Simmons was on first base, and I'm trying to hit the ball to the right side of the diamond so that I can get one run in and one run over and maybe tie the game up.

I wind up hitting the ball in the gap in right-center field, 2–0 pitch, and as I'm getting into second base I'm watching the runner, Ted Simmons, rounding third and going home, and I said, "I'm going to third, because they can only tag one of us out." And he scored the winning run, and the game was over, and that was a very memorable at-bat for me, it really was.

The other one was when we were in the pennant race, it was either in '73 or '74 with the Cardinals. And I was struggling. It was against Philadelphia, the game was tied in about the tenth inning, or the eleventh inning or the ninth inning, whatever it was it was the bottom half of one of those innings.

The bases were loaded with one out, and I must have fouled off about six or seven pitches off of Gene Garber before lifting a ball that I thought was going out of the ballpark, but I just had to hit a fly ball. It went off the fence in left field. It didn't win a ball game, but it was a very big ball game, because I wasn't doing too well at the time, and I felt that I was able to lock in in a very important game in a very important at-bat.

After winning the whole thing last year, you sort of become a winner. That was special for me, especially going to St. Louis in '69, when they had just won the World Series in '67 and '68, and hearing all the war stories about winning, and you couldn't really make a contribution. And I think maybe I'm the only one that looks at it that way, that you become a winner all of a sudden after all these years of being an also-ran and one of the masses, to sort of "get your degree" and make your accomplishment.

MO VAUGHN

The Boston Red Sox club that copped the Eastern Division title in 1995 was an unlikely winner, predicted to finish third or fourth. A major-league record fifty-three players passed through the club-house doors during that season before the Sox went down to defeat in the first round of the playoffs against the Cleveland Indians in three straight games. Through all the injuries and line-up changes, the one constant was the slugging of first baseman Mo Vaughn, who also won the MVP that year.

For me it would have to be clinching the division. We'd been coming in third and fourth in the standings, and a bunch of people just came up with some great years, and it was unbelievable. I was coming off a pretty good year last year and the year before, but you really don't know what's gonna happen the next year. You don't know how you're gonna feel, you don't know how you're gonna approach it, but you always think that if you've worked harder, you can do it again.

Jose Canseco gets hurt, and you just fall into a situation where you're just driving in runs and slugging and doing everything you can do to win games for your team. You have those ups and downs, but it was probably the best time I've ever had, trying to keep myself together and trying to keep twenty-four guys together, to come together and win.

That was the thing, we had so many guys on the team, we had this formula that there was no "I" in "team," everybody had to follow through. We had guys come into this clubhouse that we didn't think were going to fit in and they did. It seemed like before every game somebody new would come in, and it would be like, "this is what you gotta do," being here, it was great.

It was nice because it was my time, and Timmy [Naehring] was playing well, and Val [John Valentin] was playing well, Greenie [Mike Greenwell] was playing well, and I was playing well, and Rocket was coming back. We had Mike Macfarlane, who had a great attitude. We had [Eric] Hanson, and Rick Aguilera came over in the bullpen in that second half. We had some veterans in there too, maybe it was a club that shouldn't have got broken up.

This team had a killer instinct to it. We were eight or ten games up, and I think we felt it right before the All-Star game. We were about four games ahead or something. All of a sudden everybody was making all these trades and we came back that second half and won something like ten out of thirteen and opened up a wide gap. I think that's what happened, we opened up this big enormous gap.

This team wasn't the kind of team that let things slip. We kept winning and kept winning and widened the gap but somebody else kept winning and all of a sudden it was back down to seven. It was like there was no light at the end of a tunnel. Every day it was like we were winning games where everybody was contributing, hitting home runs in the bottom of the ninth, making great plays, turning double plays. It was a great thing.

We came up to the last series where we clinched, and I don't even remember who we were playing [the Sox clinched against the Toronto Blue Jays]. I think the game we clinched was a 4–2 game, and it got down to the top of the ninth and Aggy was in the ball game, and I honestly couldn't believe we were finally there, we were winning and we were on the door, we were right there.

We got that one out and then we got the second out, and I think the count was 1–2, and he threw the fork ball, when he released it, it was like slow-motion and time had stopped. We saw him swing through it, and the place just erupted, and I just couldn't believe it was over. Roger just knocked me down on the ground during the celebration, 'cause we had done something that no one had thought we were gonna do.

I'll never ride a horse again. Everybody was saying, "You gotta ride the [police] horse, you gotta ride the horse. The horse is good luck." The horse is not good luck—I was zero for fourteen in the playoffs. I think you know before that, you're sitting up there, and you never know what's gonna happen. Let me tell you, no one ever knows what's gonna happen, no one can tell anybody what a situation is about until it's done.

When that last game was over, I was sitting here in front of my locker and everybody was throwing champagne around. I was tired, I knew I was drained, I knew I was pretty down, and I think that's what really hurt me in the playoffs. I had worked so hard to get us to the pennant, when I got to the playoffs I just couldn't get my brain going.

But I came back outside, and the whole crowd was chanting. It was an unbelievable experience. You never know what people expect; you never know what your contributions are. Everybody always thinks about doing things when people are gone, but I was able to live something right in the moment while I was here living, and I just have a great appreciation of the talent I have to be able to do that.

There were the games along the way. I hit a home run in Baltimore, off a left-hander who was throwing about ninety-five miles an hour, I think Embree was his name. I think I must have fouled off about five pitches, and he kept coming at me and coming at me. I think the score was 5–2 or 4–2, and I think we won 6–4 or something like that. I remember that game.

I don't remember one specific thing. It was just the overall mentality to drive in runs, to keep driving and pushing. I think the team brawls were more important. Those were the times when people came together, more and more. We fought with California three or four times. Macfarlane got into it with Tony Phillips, that's one of the things I remember.

I thought it was nice to be considered for the MVP, but you never really know about stuff like that. When I'm going through a season, my head is down, my head is never looking up at what's coming. It's always down in my business. All of a sudden, you look up and there it is. You're talking about most valuable players, but you never knew what was gonna happen.

I really didn't get excited about it until the season was over. It was Friday, and the day before the balloting came up everybody started hyping it up. That's when I knew I might feel a letdown if it didn't work out the right way. When I heard I was MVP I was playing a video game, and that ride from my house in Canton to the Red Sox offices, that was the best ride I ever had. That was my whole life of playing baseball wrapped up into a fifteen-minute period, one conversation. I couldn't believe it. I never would have thought it would happen.

I don't know how it compared with clinching, clinching was such a relief. It was like, God, I can't wait to get this done. MVP was like an individual thing, you can't explain that. It's something that's individual that you've worked hard for, especially since in the play-offs, I didn't play well. It made a lot of things good for me.

I think of my career goals, the first is to play a certain amount of years. If I can play those years, then I'll have some pretty good career goals because I'm gonna continue to get stronger and more knowledgeable and become better in the game. There's always work to be done. You have to work at it and get better at it.

But it's definitely great to attain this early in my career. I'm putting up similar numbers right now, but I feel that MVP really has to do with the team. The team has to win. There's player of the year, but for MVP your team's gotta win, that's how I look at it.

You sit down and think about it, Carl Yazstremski and Ted Williams won it in these uniforms. You look at that line-up and it makes you think. Ted Williams is probably the greatest ever. Roger Clemens is one of the greatest pitchers in Red Sox history, with three Cys. So to be put in that company was definitely nice because the Red Sox have tremendous history, so it would be nice to go out and get two and do it again.

EARL WEAVER

The roster of managers who led championship teams, spent their entire career with a single team, and won during virtually every year of their tenure is an extremely short list that starts in the modern era with Walter Alston and also prominently features Tommy Lasorda and Baltimore Hall of Famer Earl Weaver. Renowned primarily for his love of the three-run homer and his ongoing, entertaining feuds with various umpires, the feisty Weaver was also a great strategist and motivator whose Orioles clubs almost always featured great pitching and defense as a central part of their winning style.

Well, two things stand out for me. The first is when Baltimore gave me a day, when I was retiring in 1982. The other is the last day of that season in 1982. That was kind of a bittersweet day. We were playing the Milwaukee Brewers that day for the Eastern Division title. We lost that day, but I'll never forget it when the fans called us back onto the field after we lost to Milwaukee.

Another day that was big for me was the day that I found out that I'd been voted into the Hall of Fame. The Veteran's Committee voted me in, but I'd been on their final list for three years and I didn't think I was going to make it after the first couple of years . . . the first year they voted Leo [Durocher] in, and then the year after that it was some umpire that made it.

I remember I didn't want to stay home that day, so I went out onto the golf course. And my wife got the call and she came out and found me on the golf course and told me, and there was a lot of emotion to that. I remember it brought tears to my eyes. Then of course there's the buildup for the ceremony. You have to deliver a decent talk, and you have to remember to thank everybody. There's a lot of emotion when you actually get up and talk.

Of all the teams I managed, I'd have to say that that first group was the one that stands out, the '69, '70, '71 teams. That team won 109 games, and then 108, and then 100 games. We were only the second team in baseball history to win over 100 for three years in a row. That was the group with Frank [Robinson]

October 3, 1982

MILWAUKEE	AB	R	H	RBI	BALTIMORE	AB	R	H	RBI
Molitor, 3b	5	1	1	1	Bumbry, cf	3	0	1	0
Yount, ss	4	4	3	2	Shelby, ph	1	0	1	0
Cooper, 1b	5	2	2	1	Gulliver, 3b	4	1	2	1
Simmons, c	3	1	2	1	Ford, ph	1	0	0	0
Ogilvie, lf	5	0	1	1	Singleton, dh	3	0	0	0
G. Thomas, cf	4	1	0	0	Ayala, ph	1	0	0	0
Howell, dh	2	0	0	0	E. Murray, 1b	4	0	1	0
Money, dh	2	0	1	1	Lowenstein, lf	3	1	1	0
Edwards, pr	0	1	0	0	Roenicke, ph	1	0	0	0
Moore, rf	4	0	1	0	Dwyer, rf	3	0	1	0
Romero, 2b	4	0	0	0	Ripken, ss	4	0	0	0
					Dempsey, c	3	0	2	0
					Crowley, ph	1	0	1	1
					Young, pr	0	0	0	0
					Sakata, 2b	0	0	0	0
					Dauer, 2b	3	0	0	0
					Nolan, ph	1	0	0	0
Totals	38	10	11	7	Totals	36	2	10	2

Milwaukee	111	001	015 — 10	
Baltimore	001	000	010 — 2	

MILWAUKEE	IP	H	R	ER	BB	SO
Sutton, W	8	8	2	2	5	3
McClure	1	2	0	0	0	0
BALTIMORE	IP	H	R	ER	BB	SO
Palmer, L	5	4	4	3	3	0
T. Martinez	2.2	3	1	1	0	1
D. Martinez	1	2	3	3	0	1
Flanagan	0.1	2	2	2	0	1

and Brooks [Robinson] and Boog [Powell] and Belanger and Davey Johnson. We were able to stay together and accomplish a lot. Of course we averaged between ninety and ninety-five wins for the entire time I was there, and then there was that '79 club. Boy, that team had a lot of guts.

There were three guys that went into the Hall of Fame from that first group—Frank, Brooks and Palmer. Brooks and I were together for a long time, and of course Jimmy Palmer and I were together for seventeen years, so we had some fun together.

BERNIE WILLIAMS

Perhaps the ultimate hero in the New Yankees victory in the 1996 World Series was outfielder Bernie Williams, who got the winning hit in Game 6. It was a remarkable year for Williams, a season in which he solidified his position as one of the primary producers in the Yankee line-up and made one highlight film play after another in the outfield.

Game 6 in New York . . . it was just great. The last three games, the one prior to that, and then facing Maddux, pretty tough pitcher. I got a base hit that ended up being the winning run, and after the last out going through the experience was just, realizing that we were world champions . . . that's what you dream of when you're a little kid, playing in the sandlots, thinking about what would it feel like. It's very different, definitely one of my greatest days.

I don't remember too much about that at-bat now; it happened so quick, but I know it was an inside pitch. I kind of cut at it and I got jammed, but I was fortunate enough to get enough of the bat on it to get it through the middle. And I remember I was thinking that with Derek on we had a chance to score the run, and there was an overthrow and I ended up going to second base on the play.

That was the only thing . . . I was just pretty pumped about it. It was Maddux, and it was an important part of the game. Those were the only three runs we scored in the whole game, and it was just great to be a part of it.

You've just gotta hope that [Maddux] makes a mistake. He doesn't give you many. I was thinking during that at-bat . . . if you're fortunate he'll give you one pitch to hit. You've just gotta be lucky enough to put it in play somewhere, and I was lucky enough that day.

I remember trying not to think too much about it, trying not to get my expectations too high because it was so close. I was just trying to focus on getting it over, and concentrating on just not being caught off guard if a play happens, so I wasn't thinking too much about what it would feel like if we won. I was just thinking about getting it done. I think in that sense I didn't get to enjoy it enough, because I was too caught up in that and trying to finish the game.

I think everything in New York stopped during the celebration . . . literally, for the next day or two. It was amazing, every car, every house, every park . . . everywhere. We knew what they were watching . . . even if you weren't a Yankee fan, even if you weren't a baseball fan. I knew what they were watching.

We got a chance to go to some of the places in the city, and we were like famous rock stars. You'd step out of the taxi, or you'd step out of the car, and everybody would go, "Look, that's . . . ,"and everybody would try to touch you or something. It was amazing.

I think the parade stands out the most . . . definitely the parade. One of the most amazing days, period. I mean, not even baseball related. Just going through the experience of seeing a sea of people. They were just chanting . . . you and your peers . . . wow. It gives me the creeps when I think about it. My hands got tired of waving . . . it was one of the most amazing things that I've ever seen in my life.

I think the difference for me has been approach and attitude. You've gotta have enough confidence in your ability to be able to realize that no matter what you do, no matter what happens, you're here to be able to play the game. Play it according to your talent. You're the first one that has to tell that to yourself. The competition's gonna be hard, so that's gonna motivate you to work your hardest, day in and day out, because you can't play this game halfway. It's either all or nothing.

If you have that attitude, and you're lucky enough to get the talent, I think, it has the makings for you to be a consistent player, playing up to the level that you're capable of.

I think the one that happened in Texas would have to be the defensive highlight, off of Rusty Greer. He hit a ball back to the fence, and the ball was out of the field, and I was able to snatch it back. Because of the situation of the game, early in the game, I was able to take the crowd out of the game at that moment. And we were able to . . . it got easier, because the crowd wasn't really into it that much.

At the start there, they were tough, you know. It's tough to play under those conditions. Being able to do that, it kind of took the air out of them early in the game. We were just able to capitalize after that, so I think that's maybe one of the most memorable ones that I can remember.

[For box score, please see interview with Wade Boggs.]

BILLY WILLIAMS

Ernie Banks may have earned the moniker "Mr. Cub," but when it comes to being on the field, driving in runs, and hitting homers, there was no Cub who was more consistent than Billy Williams. This Hall of Famer's greatest day took him back to the 1969 campaign, before the Chicago Cubs and the "Miracle Mets" engaged in their memorable battle for first place.

If you're talking about one of the greatest days in baseball, it would have to be . . . as a matter of fact, it seemed like the whole year, 1969. But the definite date in that particular year was June 29th, 1969. Through everything that was happening we were in first place, and on June 29th, 1969, the Cubs had prepared a day for Billy Williams at Wrigley Field.

We were playing the Cardinals, we needed to beat the Cardinals to go into first place. And I didn't think the game was going to be played, because that morning it was raining pretty good, and I thought the game was gonna be canceled. Well, we played at 1:20. . . . It was a packed house, and there were about 10,000 more people who wanted to come in the ballpark that particular day, but they couldn't get in.

We faced Bob Gibson, who was a tough pitcher to face, in the first game. We had a doubleheader that particular day. In this first game, Fergie Jenkins and Bob Gibson were pitching, and you always knew when those two guys hooked up it was gonna be a duel. Quick game, too, real quick.

I remember about the seventh or eighth inning, I hit a double and I wind up on second base. . . . I don't think we got but four or five hits that first game. I think I got a double, and either Santo or Ernie drove me in, and we went ahead and beat Bob Gibson that first ball game, 3–1.

Now it's tied . . . the league is tied. The Mets were down, you're talking June 29th, they were about ten or twelve back, nobody was thinking about the Mets. Because we had some young players who were beginning to make their way in the major leagues, everybody was talking about the Cardinals, because the Cardinals were right there. You're talking '69 now.

We had a twenty-minute break, we go in the clubhouse after we beat the Cardinals in the first game. So the second game started, and I forget who was pitching, but we had to win that game to move into first place. Between games they showered me with a lot of gifts, stuff like that. They drove cars on the field, they drove boats on the field. You know, anybody who played the game of baseball at that time, thought they got a lot of money for playing the game. It was a lot of money at that time, but you really just enjoyed playing baseball.

And when the club you were playing with sets aside a big day for you, for playing in a certain number of games. So all these things were intertwined, a thousand ball games, moving into first place. So after the ceremony and everything, we started the second game. And normally, the player is so nervous, you get wrapped up in all of this, and baseball is secondary, but I kind of kept my focus going into the second ball game.

I think the first time up I had a single. The second time up . . . you know, I don't know who I got the hits off of, but the second time up I got a double. I also had a triple. I tried the next time and didn't do it. My last at-bat, I could have hit a home run, I could have hit for the cycle. And I came up to the plate in the last or eighth inning, it's like 10–2, we're rolling along, we were swinging the bats good. So the last at-bat, the only thing I needed was a home run, this would be the climax, this would be the icing on the cake for an enjoyable day. It was already enjoyable, but it would have been like a storybook finish at that time.

I got up to the plate, and I had one thing on my mind, and the pitcher knew that, too. So I wind up being a little bit more aggressive than I wanted to be, and I wind up striking out. And as I was walking back to the bench, I looked around in the stands, and everybody was standing up, and they were applauding, and I think it went on for about five or ten minutes.

The people in Chicago, they were joyous for the day that happened for me. They were joyous about the Cubs moving into first place, and of course they knew what I was trying to do, to get that ball out of the ballpark. Everybody in that ballpark stood up and gave me a standing ovation. So that was the one.

It was a special moment, and that year was a great year. That day, because the Cubs set aside a day, and showered me . . . you don't look for a day like that. You look for just playing baseball.

We moved into first place, of course, and playing in a thousand ball games that day, so that was just a special day for me, and I will always remember that particular day, because everything went well, nothing went wrong. We won a doubleheader, I was hitting the ball, I was instrumental in the first game, and of course I had all the hits in the second game, and we win the first place.

It was a special day with my family there, of course, with all the girls on the field. But I was extremely pleased, and it was special for me because my mother was also there. I remember talking to her, and she hadn't been in a crowd like that before. And I told her, "You're gonna come on the field," and she said, "I'm gonna faint," and I said, "No, you're not, don't do that to me."

But she wasn't used to it. She was used to just sitting in the stands and enjoying the game, and they ushered her out on the field. And of course she stood there, and I still have pictures of that today, and she was a little excited, but she got through it. She was just thrilled about what her son had accomplished, and just being there with me at that time, that joyous time.

And of course my wife, too, she was really happy, and the kids. I often let them see that picture now, they were small back then. It was just a joyous day, everything went right, that time is one I wish could have stood still. All the other stuff, I knew I had to move on, but that time was real pleasing to me, and I just enjoyed that day.

There's another incident . . . when you play baseball, you enjoy the game, you don't think about the Hall of Fame, being inducted into the baseball Hall of Fame. You know that you've been consistent, through being out there, playing in a thousand ball games, a lot of people said I wouldn't play in that many games, I wouldn't do that. But I was like a little squirrel, accumulating nuts, accumulating numbers.

And now when you get out of the game after eighteen, nineteen years you look around and you say, "Man, I've got so many home runs, I've got so many base hits." Now when you finally get that call from Jack Lang in New York, you get a call and he says, "They voted for you, you're in the Hall of Fame." You listen, but you don't grasp it.

I think you finally grasp it on that Saturday when they come to pick you up at Cooperstown that Saturday night when you go over to the museum. And as you're walking through there, walking through there and seeing these plaques . . . it's like a house where a guy is on the pedestal. Your picture's not there yet, but you know it's gonna be there. I went in with Catfish Hunter and Ray Dandridge.

That's when you finally realize that all you've done in baseball wasn't in vain . . . you enjoyed the game, and then you get up on stage with all those Hall of Fame players the next day, and that's a great thrill. And you're still getting thrills. It's a lasting thrill, because most of your Hall of Famers visit up there every year. They go back, so each year it's another burst of freshness, being with the guys who are being inducted.

A lot of guys you read about, you heard about, you played against 'em in All-Star games, some guys were your teammates . . . they're all there. When you go up there, there's so much respect for the other guy. It's just like you guys have been playing together for twenty years, because everybody knows what the other guy has accomplished, and you're a Hall of Fame player, and you know you've done a lot of things, and you deserve it, and you've played a lot of games, and you're there for a reason.

DICK WILLIAMS

Dick Williams managed many great clubs during his long career in baseball. He's perhaps best known for leading the Boston Red Sox to the World Series in 1967, but he also guided the Oakland A's to their memorable string of championships in the early '70s, and he also had some fine teams in the National League in the 1980s during his stints with the San Diego Padres and the Montreal Expos. Early in his career Williams had a reputation for being volatile and feisty, but his occasionally combative approach was especially effective in turning around losing and mediocre ball clubs.

Well, I've had a few of 'em. I've been in the game fifty years. As a manager, I'd have to say my first year managing in the major leagues, with the Boston Red Sox. We were 100–1 longshots, and we did what they call in Boston "The Impossible Dream," 1967, that would certainly have to be a thrill . . . it was a big one. It got me started in my career.

But we lost to the Cardinals in seven games, and I'd have to say my bigger thrill was in '72 and '73 with the Oakland ball club. Had a pretty good array of talent, two of 'em ended up with the Yankees here, Reggie Jackson and Catfish Hunter. I'd have to say '72 and '73 were huge.

Of course I also won at San Diego in '84; we lost to Sparky Anderson's Tigers in five games. They annihilated everybody in their league including us. I took over a club, I think one of the greatest things I've ever been associated with was when I took over the Montreal club in 1977, when they had lost 107 games the year before.

And inside of three years, we won ninety-five . . . it wasn't good enough to win, we finished second, and the next year we won ninety-two, ninety-three, somewhere around there, and we finished second again. So we turned the franchise around, but they didn't have the money to keep all those players, and they've been leaving ever since. But it was a great place; I enjoyed Montreal.

I played on some great Dodger teams, too . . . the Yankees always beat 'em in the World Series, but I was on the club in '51, when Bobby Thomson hit the home run to beat us, that was a big thrill for baseball, even though it wasn't for the Dodgers. In '52, I was on that club, and '53, I was on that club, the Yankees beat us both times there.

But I'd have to say that my managerial career certainly outweighed my playing career in the major leagues, although I played thirteen years.

Oakland had never won, and it had been twenty-one years since the Red Sox had won. San Diego had never won, and they haven't won since, so during the course of the year you have so many peaks and valleys, whether you're winners or also-rans or what have you. So it's really hard to decipher what is the biggest thrill.

I do recall a player having . . . I've never watched a player have the kind of year he had, and that was in 1967 with Carl Yazstremski [the year he won the Triple Crown]. This was unbelievable. I played with some good players on that Brooklyn club, Jackie Robinson and Pee Wee and Hodges and Campanella and all those guys, Snider . . . but I've never watched a player have one complete year like Yazstremski had. I don't expect to see it again, either. It was just phenomenal, in all phases—running, throwing, fielding, hitting, hitting with power. He was the ultimate team leader . . . he wasn't the captain, because I stripped him of his captaincy at the beginning, but he was still the leader on the ball club.

I'm taking over a club that finished either a game or a half a game ahead of the Yankees in a one division, ten-team league. They had finished ninth, the Yankees had finished tenth. It was twenty-five cabs for twenty-five guys, and I said, "We don't need a captain, we need a leader, and I have a one-year contract so I'm gonna be that leader, and sink or swim, I'm gonna do it my way." Yaz understood, and Yaz gave me a supreme effort all year long. That to me . . . he's a Hall of Famer, and well he should be. He was one of my first of a few Hall of Famers that I've been able to manage.

In '72 we went seven games to win it against Cincinnati. Six of the games were decided by one run. They blew us out in the sixth game of the series, and I got to use all my other pitchers, but I went mainly with my four guys and Fingers. Fingers just did a tremendous job, that's when you had a four-man rotation, you didn't have five. So that was a big, big thing as far as our ball club.

The following year in the playoffs against the Mets, we're down three games to two going back to Oakland. And there's an off day there, and they're set up to pitch Seaver on that final day with the proper rest. For some reason they pitched him the day before. I guess they wanted to finish us off, and we beat 'em. Now we had Matlack going, and he has to go a day early, and we beat him.

To me that was a big highlight, because we played that whole series with just twenty-four men to their twenty-five, because Charlie Finley had sold Jose Morales to Montreal after the first of September, and we could not . . . the Mets would not let us use another player in his place. And also Charlie fired Mike Andrews, and he missed one game, so at one time we had twenty-three men to their twenty-five. So that was a thing we really enjoyed, beating the Mets the way we did, and I disagreed with a lot of their moves, and it was in our favor, so that was good.

And then I can recall we won 101 ball games in 1971, and I think we set a record for most wins on the road that year. We played Baltimore, and they beat us three straight in the playoffs, and the first game was Blue against . . . I think it was Palmer. We lost that ball game in the eighth inning and Paul Blair hit a double inside the third base bag, it was a 1–1 score, he hit a double and we got beat I think 3–1, something like that.

I think we won fifty-five ball games on the road, I'm not positive, but at the time I remember it was a record, whether it's still the same or not I don't know. Maybe the Chicago Bulls have beaten it. [Laughs.]

I can't pick one managerial achievement . . . I'll just let my record speak for itself. I've been with six different ball clubs, and they say, "Well, that's a lot of ball clubs," but I've won three places, and only two of us have ever won with three clubs, and that was Bill McKechnie, who's in the Hall of Fame, and myself.

When Sparky and I played, Detroit against San Diego, whoever won that World Series, and Sparky won it, would be the first manager to win the World Series in both leagues. As far as managing goes, I had twenty-one years with six different ball clubs . . . had to turn a lot of 'em around, because they hadn't won in a while, or had never won.

October 21, 1973

NEW YORK (N.)	AB	R	H	RBI	OAKLAND	AB	R	H	RBI
Garrett, 3b	5	0	0	0	Campaneris, ss	4	2	3	2
Millan, 2b	4	1	1	0	Rudi, lf	3	1	2	1
Staub, rf	4	0	2	1	Bando, 3b	4	0	0	0
Jones, lf	3	0	0	0	Jackson, rf	4	1	1	2
Milner, 1b	3	1	0	0	Tenace, 1b	3	0	0	0
Grote, c	4	0	1	0	Alou, rf	1	0	0	0
Hahn, cf	4	0	3	0	Davalillo, cf	3	0	0	0
Harrelson, ss	4	0	0	0	Johnson, 1b	3	0	0	0
Matlack, p	1	0	0	0	Fosse, c	1	0	1	0
Parker, p	0	0	0	0	Green, 2b	4	0	0	0
Beauchamp, ph	1	0	0	0	Holtzman, p	2	1	1	0
Sadecki, p	0	0	0	0	Fingers, p	1	0	1	0
Boswell, ph	1	0	1	0	Knowles, p	0	0	0	0
Stone, p	0	0	0	0					
Kranepool, ph	1	0	0	0					
Martinez, pr	0	0	0	0					
Totals	35	2	8	1	Totals	33	5	9	5

New York	000	001	001 — 2
Oakland	004	010	00X — 5

NEW YORK	IP	H	R	ER	BB	SO
Matlack, L	2.2	4	4	4	1	3
Parker	1.1	0	0	0	1	1
Sadecki	2	2	1	1	0	1
Stone	2	3	0	0	0	3
OAKLAND	IP	H	R	ER	BB	SO
Holtzman, W	5.1	5	1	1	1	4
Fingers	3.1	3	1	0	1	2
Knowles, S	0.1	0	0	0	0	0

The Montreal ball club I was let go with the . . . that was when we had the strike year, when . . . '81, when they had the first half and a second half. Well, we were a game-and-a-half behind St. Louis, and we had just beaten Philadelphia when I was let go. I thought it was very unfair, but I'm not the general manager, and he made a change.

They went on to beat the Cardinals and win their division in the second half, beat Philadelphia for the outright Eastern Division championship, and then the Dodgers beat 'em on Rick Monday's home run off of Steve Rogers and then they went on to play in the World Series. So I could count that too, and that would have been four different clubs.

My philosophy was to play as a unit, give a hundred percent of what you have on the field, and don't make mental mistakes. I believed in execution . . . the little things . . . a man on second, nobody out, and you advance that runner, you give yourself up to hit to the right side.

Defense . . . you had to have defense. Pitching and defense wins ball games. The three-run home run, as Earl Weaver does, that's good if you've got the guy, the Boog Powell or Frank Robinson, to do that.

But in Oakland, we had Reggie Jackson, and he was our home run hitter. But we didn't have one guy other than Reggie the three years I was there who ever hit .300 . . . .275, .280, .285, but they played together as a unit. They say we fought a lot, but we didn't fight any more than anybody else, except we got notoriety with our funny-looking uniforms, and our moustaches, and Charlie Finley, our owner. We got the job done . . . it's a funny thing, when you win, they really can't say much.

If we'd have lost against Cincinnati . . . I made 'em change a rule, because I kept going out to the mound—it's two trips now, either the manager's gone or the pitcher's gone. But while the rule was in effect, a lot of people were upset with me. We got results, and as long as the rule was out there we utilized it. I wasn't out there to win friends, I was out there to try and win ball games.

DAVE WINFIELD

In a way it seems fitting that future Hall of Famer Dave Winfield got the hit that brought baseball it's first international champion when he doubled in the eleventh inning of the sixth game against the Atlanta Braves in the 1992 World Series to win it for the Toronto

© JOHN CORDES

Blue Jays. Winfield's great career was something of a journey in its own right, from his early days of excellence in relative obscurity with the San Diego Padres to his controversial stint with the Yankees in which George Steinbrenner derisively labeled him "Mr. May." But Winfield will probably be best remembered for his years with the Blue Jays, when he shed the stigma of his New York days and emerged as a leader in Toronto.

I played the game for twenty years, and I was forty years old . . . to be able to get the hit that drove in the winning runs, and to be able to celebrate with my teammates after that, it was a thrill. I think I was so emotionally and physically drained, more emotionally drained than physically drained.

It was just the greatest feeling, because when I was eight, ten years old, practicing and playing ball with friends, my brother and everything, you always finish up the day . . . up to bat . . . I'm up, men on base, bases loaded, bottom of the ninth, that type of thing, and then here's the pitch . . . and bang, you get that hit and you win.

That's what it was all about. It was the culmination of probably a vision that I had for many, many years. In baseball you realize that you're very fortunate if you play for a good team. You play with good players, you can have good years. . . . I had all those things. But until that point, until you've won it all, that's when you realize what it's all about.

I just thought that from the beginning of that year . . . I was a free agent, I left the California Angels . . . I had the chance to go to a couple of teams. I went to Toronto, and it was a city that always liked me, where people were always kind to me, a world-class city. I was going to play with a manager, a guy who helped me when I first started playing, Cito Gaston, so I felt really comfortable going there.

The first day I went to spring training I knew that we had the best team in all of baseball. That's a great feeling. It was just a matter of executing and doing it all. We had a fellow Minnesotan there, Jack Morris, there, I was playing for Toronto, a team that was always close but had never been there before.

I just think that playing for a team that didn't quite ever feel like they were the best, and then again they weren't even an American team. Just to help try to instill that confidence and belief, all the things we did all year long, shaking guys up in the clubhouse, team meetings, players-only meetings to get 'em back and never let 'em get off track. And then we just had fantastic years, fantastic players. When you have that chemistry . . . it's not overrated. I just thought we could win it all . . . and we did, just fulfilling that dream.

I remember getting the hit, and the only thing better is a home run where you can be greeted by your teammates—at home. But we were on the road, and there were over 50,000 people in Atlanta, and they were speechless. You get the hit, and they can tell, it's like the dagger into their heart. You're in the middle of the stadium, the run's scored, and it's virtually silent except for a couple of small enclaves of Toronto fans, cheering. That's a unique sensation.

I think I prided myself in my career on driving in runs and kind of a being a nemesis to people, particularly on the road. I felt if they boo you, it was because they feared you. When you're the opposition, and you're playing against the home team, they're gonna boo you when you come up, even though you're a good player. You know, they booed, but I give the Atlanta fans credit, they were very cordial, very nice. It was a good civil series.

I was coming up, and they debated whether to bring Jeff Reardon, a right-hander, in against me, but they kept Charlie Leibrandt, a left-hander, in against me. A lot of people questioned it. It surprised me. I don't know the statistics, one way or the other, how I hit against Leibrandt or anything like that, but I remember Kirby Puckett got him the year before. So I just thought, fine, he was either gonna turn it over, you know, give me a change-up away, or try to bust me in or something.

I was actually looking for the change-up away, and was prepared to react to the fastball. Yeah, just because we're talking about it . . . I think he threw the change-up. It was one or the other as far as I was concerned, one pitch or the other, and after all these years, you're prepared, you can't be single-minded or be on one path, you have to be able to make a quick adjustment. It was one of those two pitches, and I was able to handle it. It seemed like I hit it hard, down the third-base line, and when I saw Terry Pendleton couldn't reach it, I just knew those runs were gonna score.

It was just a thrill. It was like icing on the cake . . . I had baked a pretty good cake throughout my career, and that was the best. Around the fourth inning, they thought about taking me out for defense. I was playing the outfield, and I had only played the outfield maybe twenty-seven times that year. I said, "No, that's why I practiced out there all year long, because I knew we'd be in the World Series and I'd have to play out there."

I remember, that inning I went out and made a diving backhand catch in the outfield. I threw it in, and then I came up and got another chance to hit, and I got a hit. So that was great.

The only thing that you get mad about is that they do so many interviews that you can't celebrate at the precise moment with your teammates. Jumping on the field was the best . . . and then I couldn't get off the field fast enough to celebrate the moments with my teammates. You can be high so long, and then they kind of come down. I mean, I got a chance to celebrate with them, but that's the only thing where you don't get that celebration precisely at that time. Basketball is a little different, but that was the only thing.

I remember that celebration was great, and the locker room, but also when we got back to Toronto, the parade was tremendous. A ticker-tape parade, it was unbelievable, because it wasn't like we won for a city, or a state, or a region. We had a whole country . . . and I think my relationship with Canada was solidified. I had a very good relationship with the people there.

I've had excellent days at the plate, days that I hit the ball, to hit for a cycle is fantastic, to hit three home runs in a game . . . I think I had fifteen or sixteen total bases . . . three homers . . . a double . . . a single . . . fifteen total bases, to do that and win a game was great.

I remember once in Detroit, this was after I hit the seagull up in Toronto and went to jail and stuff like that. I think the next series we went to Detroit, and it seemed like there were a lot of people there, and they were taunting me. They were all flapping their arms, doing this [flaps his arms], like the seagull incident. I hit the ball harder that day. It seemed like I had five at-bats or something like that, and I hit the ball so hard . . . it almost amazed me. I hit a line-drive over the third baseman's head, just over his head, and then it was . . . out of the park, over the top of the fence. I've had some individual great days, like getting five hits in a game three times in a month . . . you know, things like that, and good individual years.

Individual things don't add up . . . I think that you invest so much time, with so many people, and there are so many variables, for everything just to click into place. I think there are just more odds against you, and there are so many variables to fall into place, and have a really good time for the seven months you're together, almost eight months from spring training to the end. I think that is just the height of ecstasy in this game.

I have four years to think about going into the Hall, so it's still a ways off. When I finished my career, I mean, I look back at the beginning . . . I came out of college, drafted in three sports, could have played any one of three sports. I chose baseball. I could have been a pitcher or an outfielder. I chose to be an outfielder. All of the things that you go through, I could have been a pitcher, all of a sudden I'm an outfielder . . . and then to do well.

You never know what you're going to do in this game. I never thought it was easy, I never took it for granted, and I never knew what I'd accomplished until it was over. I'm just pleased that I was able to do so much . . . that's all I can say.

You never know what's going to happen. I was just very happy things did turn around, because there were a lot of years where I can say, although I did my job in a professional way, it wasn't always easy, and it wasn't always nice, it wasn't always pleasant.

To overcome a lot of adversity and things like that, I was just very pleased the way people viewed me during the latter part of my career, as a player, as a person, and when I exited the game. There are certain things that are just indelible, they can't take them away. I think they have the correct perception of me, and that's what I'm very happy about.

JIM WYNN

During the 1960s, the expansion Houston Astros were led by one of the most unusual home run hitters in the game, a center fielder whose nickname was "The Toy Cannon." Jimmy Wynn may have been relatively diminutive in stature for a power hitter, but he was a feared hitter throughout the National League who finally appeared in a World Series with the Los Angeles Dodgers near the end of his career.

My greatest day in baseball was the day that I signed my first major league contract. The second greatest day was when I was play-

October 12, 1974

OAKLAND	AB	R	H	RBI	LOS ANGELES	AB	R	H	RBI
Campaneris, ss	2	I	I	I	Lopes, 2b	5	I	0	0
North, cf	2	0	0	0	Buckner, lf	5	0	2	0
Bando, 3b	4	0	0	0	Wynn, cf	4	I	I	I
Jackson, rf	3	I	I	I	Garvey, 1b	5	0	2	0
C. Washington, rf	0	0	0	0	Paciorek, pr	0	0	0	0
Rudi, lf	4	0	2	0	Ferguson, rf–c	3	0	0	0
Tenace, 1b	3	0	I	0	Cey, 3b	3	0	I	0
Fosse, c	3	0	0	0	Russell, ss	4	0	I	0
Green, 2b	3	0	0	0	Yeager, c	3	0	I	0
Holt, ph	I	0	0	0	Crawford, rf	I	0	I	0
Maxvill, 2b	0	0	0	0	Messersmith, p	3	0	2	0
Holtzman, p	I	I	I	0	Joshua, ph	I	0	0	0
Fingers, p	2	0	0	0	Marshall, p	0	0	0	0
Hunter, p	0	0	0	0					
	—	—	—	—		—	—	—	—
Totals	28	3	6	2	Totals	37	2	11	I

```
Oakland       010   010   010 — 3
Los Angeles   000   010   001 — 2
```

ing in the World Series in '74 with the Dodgers and my father came to see me play. The third is being blessed by the good Lord in giving me this great talent that I have.

The thing that stands out when I signed my first contract was seeing my father, the expression on his face, tears coming from his eyes, knowing that if he had a chance he could have been in the place where I was supposed to be. My father was a great ballplayer, as a matter of fact he taught me everything I knew. He played semi-pro in Cincinnati.

The second thing was to bring him down into the clubhouse in Dodger Stadium to say hello to Sandy Koufax, Roy Campanella, Junior Gilliam and Tommy Davis. That made him very happy. The third . . . every day that I wake up I bless the Lord for the things that he's given me.

The World Series . . . we were a young ball club in 1974. We played against a very, very hot ball club in the Oakland Athletics. Those are the things that stood out in my mind, just seeing a great ball club playing against a team that hasn't been there in a while.

Just being there was the highlight. . . . I predicted in '74 in spring training that we were gonna win the National League pennant. We won it, and just being there and being part of the 1974 Dodgers, going to the World Series, that was a thrill.

The personal highlight would have to be the home run I hit in Dodger Stadium against Rollie Fingers. I hit a very good slider that he threw, and every time I see him, he says "How did you hit that pitch out of the ballpark?" I think it was two balls and one strike. It didn't have any impact. . . . We still lost the game 3–2 . . . but it kept it close.